ANIMAL HABITATS

DISCOVERING HOW ANIMALS LIVE IN THE WILD

Dr. Tony Hare

Checkmark Books™

An imprint of Facts On File, Inc.

Animal Habitats
© Times Media Private Limited

Published 2001 for Facts On File
for sale in North America only
by Marshall Cavendish Books
An imprint of Times Media Private Limited
A member of the Times Publishing Group
Times Centre, 1 New Industrial Road
Singapore 536196

For information contact:

Checkmark Books
An imprint of
Facts On File, Inc.
11 Penn Plaza
New York NY 10001

Library of Congress Cataloging-in-Publication Data
Hare, Tony
    Animal habitats : discovering how animals live in the wild / Tony Hare.
    p. cm.
    ISBN 0-8160-4593-3 (hardcover) — ISBN 0-8160-4594-1 (pbk.)
    1. Mammals—Habitat. 2. Mammals—Adaptation. I. Title.

QL739.8.H37   2001
599.156'4—dc21

                                                    00-068132

Checkmark Books are available at special discounts when purchased in bulk
quantities for businesses, associations, institutions or sales promotions. Please call
our Special Sales Department in New York at (212) 967-8800 or (800) 322-8755.

You can find Facts On File on the World Wide Web at http://www.factsonfile.com

Printed and bound in Singapore

CONTENTS

INTRODUCTION

An animal's habitat can be described as the area in which it is born, lives, eats, sleeps and dies. The form and size of its home depends on many factors. Apart from accommodating weather conditions and changing seasons, the animal's ability to survive in a given environment is also determined by the amount of food available and by the number of predators or rivals in an area. Lack of food, overcrowding, scarcity of good sites for nests or dens and the presence of predators are common causes that press a species to evolve, die out or move on to more suitable surroundings. Home territories for different species of animals may also overlap. For example, hippopotamuses share their territory with Nile crocodiles, Thomson's gazelles, African wild dogs, oxpeckers and carps.

Bearing these factors in mind, it seems amazing that animals have adapted to every imaginable environment on Earth, from the freezing cold of the Arctic to the tropical rain forests, from the ocean depths to high up in the treetops, from the countryside to the middle of towns and cities.

Animal Habitats has taken a representative cross section of mammals from the animal kingdom to show how the requirements of varying habitats have led to the evolution of very different forms of animal behavior. The selected profiles feature animals that are perfectly suited to their environment and generally have the ability to adapt to continual, and often unpredictable, natural changes in their surroundings.

Dr. Tony Hare

AARDVARKS

Because the aardvark is so dependent on termites for its food, it is limited to those places where termites can survive. Fortunately for the aardvark, termites are found in a wide range of habitats; this mammal is therefore found throughout Africa south of the Sahara.

The aardvark is a fairly common animal, but, being nocturnal and secretive, it is seldom seen in the wild. Often the only indications of the presence of aardvarks in an area are their burrows, scrape marks on termite hills, and the distinctive trails left by their tails as they drag along the ground. For a long time naturalists believed that they inhabited only savanna regions, but in 1906 aardvarks were discovered in the rain forests of Cameroon and Zaire. Because they dig burrows, they avoid swampy areas and very hard, stony places. Aardvarks can swim well, and one was seen swimming across 65 ft (20 m) of fast-flowing water.

Unlike other burrowing animals, aardvarks travel long distances in search of food. As a result, there are three types of burrows. The simplest burrows are just temporary holes dug while searching for food or escaping from predators. Only a little more complex are the semipermanent resting burrows, which are scattered several miles apart throughout an aardvark's home territory. This type of burrow is normally about 10–13 ft (3–4 m) long, and at the far end is a sleeping chamber just large enough for the animal to turn around in.

The most complex burrow systems are the permanent refuge burrows, which are excavated and maintained with some care and used, among other purposes, for raising the young. Such a burrow system may be up to 43 ft (13 m) long; and, although there is commonly only one entrance, there may be two, three, or occasionally four or five openings. The tunnels are about 16 in (40 cm) in diameter, and those leading away from the entrances slope down steeply at an angle of about 45 degrees. The tunnels follow a zigzag course, and at each bend there is a short blind tunnel, the

E. & D. Hosking/NHPA

This young aardvark (above) may seem defenseless, but looks are very deceiving. It can burrow into the ground with astonishing speed and, if need be, can fend off attackers with an armory of eighteen claws.

Anthony Bannister/NHPA

The rocky outcrops of the African plains provide all a hyrax's daily needs: food and water in the form of plants; shade and sun; and escape tunnels that it can use in times of need (left).

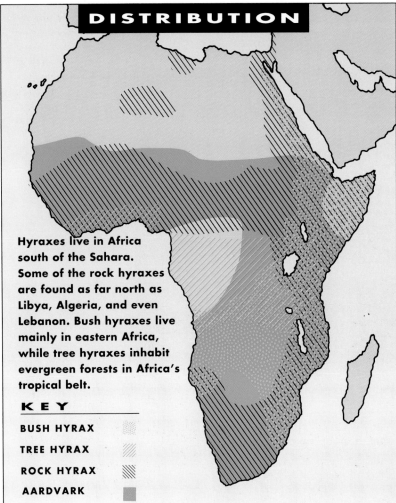

DISTRIBUTION

Hyraxes live in Africa south of the Sahara. Some of the rock hyraxes are found as far north as Libya, Algeria, and even Lebanon. Bush hyraxes live mainly in eastern Africa, while tree hyraxes inhabit evergreen forests in Africa's tropical belt.

KEY

BUSH HYRAX

TREE HYRAX

ROCK HYRAX

AARDVARK

purpose of which is not known. They may be used for storing soil from other tunnels, or they may be where soil is collected to block off existing tunnels. There is usually one nesting chamber, which contains no nesting material apart from loose soil.

When an aardvark is digging, it rests on its hind legs and tail and scrapes at the soil using its strong, sharp claws. As it digs, it pushes the soil under its body with its powerful forelegs and disperses the heap with its hind legs and muscular tail. As digging progresses, the earth collects in a hemispherical mound around the entrance to the burrow. How the animal breathes underground, during this very strenuous activity, is not clear. An aardvark digs at a prodigious speed. It can dig a yard of tunnel in anything from five to twenty minutes, depending on the soil type, and it is said that it can dig faster than a team of men with shovels—although the theory that aardvarks are impossible to dig out of their burrows has been disproved.

A PLACE OF REFUGE

Abandoned burrows are often taken over by other creatures. Warthogs, sometimes with their entire litters, often take over aardvark burrows, and it is thought that warthogs take up residence in some regions only if there are enough abandoned aardvark holes in existence. Other animals that have been found in aardvark burrows include porcupines, hedgehogs, jackals, hyenas, mongooses, rodents, snakes, and birds. A species of bat roosts in aardvark burrows during the day. In emergencies, such as during a bush fire, aardvark burrows can offer shelter to an even wider range of animals.

The aardvark's burrow is its refuge. Its main enemies, apart from humans, are hunting dogs, hyenas, pythons, leopards, and lions. Even

in SIGHT

SAVING WATER

Like many animals that live in dry conditions and consequently need to conserve water, hyraxes have kidneys that reabsorb the maximum possible amount of water from their urine, which thereby becomes extremely concentrated.

The urine also contains a high proportion of calcium carbonate, and as hyraxes are in the habit of urinating always in the same places, large, white deposits of the chemical often build up. Europeans as well as Africans have used these deposits for a variety of medicinal purposes.

warthogs prey on young aardvarks. Running off and digging itself into the ground is the aardvark's first line of defense, but if cornered it will lash out with its heavy tail and forefeet, or lie on its back and slash with its claws. Sometimes the entrances of burrows are stopped up with earth, possibly to keep predators out. If an aardvark is threatened inside its burrow, it tries to dig deeper at first, but eventually turns back toward the surface.

CONEY ISLANDS

In contrast to the specialized aardvark, hyraxes are highly adaptable creatures. Their geographical range covers most of Africa and parts of the Middle East and includes habitats ranging from forests and plains to mountains at altitudes of more than 10,000 ft (3,000 m). Tree hyraxes are confined to the forests of central and southern Africa, including the islands of Fernando Po and Pemba. They reach altitudes of up to 15,000 ft (4,500 m).

Rock hyraxes are best adapted to dry regions and are thus the most widespread. They are the "coneys" referred to in the Bible and are found in Syria, Sinai, and Israel, as well as in much of

Geoff du Feu/Planet Earth Pictures

FOCUS ON

THE SERENGETI KOPJES

At the end of the rainy season the Serengeti is a sea of waving green grass. Dotted around this sea are small islands of stone, called kopjes. This word means "peaks" in Afrikaans, and this is exactly what they are—peaks of granite sticking up from the basement rock that underlies the sediments that form the Serengeti plains. Slow erosion of the hard granite over millions of years has smoothed and shaped these peaks.

The environmental conditions that these kopjes generate, and hence the fauna and flora they support, are completely different from the surrounding grassland. Because rainwater collects in the rock fissures and heavy dew forms on the rocks and plants each night, water is more plentiful than in the surroundings and the vegetation is thick and luxuriant. This itself helps to keep the atmosphere around the kopje humid and provides a barrier to the fires that sweep through the surrounding dry grass. When the rains come and the plains are flooded, the kopjes become islands in an even truer sense, because they remain unaffected.

TEMPERATURE AND RAINFALL

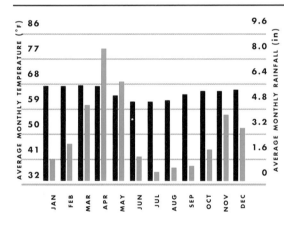

■ TEMPERATURE

■ RAINFALL

Lying so close to the equator, Tanzania experiences warmth all year round. The close passage of the sun in March causes a pressure drop, which results in heavy monsoon rains in April. There is a similar effect six months later.

Africa, particularly eastern Africa. They inhabit any rocky, scrubby area, in vegetation zones from arid to alpine where there is rocky shelter, or where they can dig burrows of their own. Bush hyraxes are restricted to northeastern and southern Africa. They, too, prefer to live among boulders and on rocky outcrops, but they are less well adapted for living in dry regions. In Africa the rocky outcrops that are found on the plains are called kopjes. They are like islands in a sea of grass, and they are usually inhabited by bush and rock hyraxes, which coexist happily because their food needs are quite different. The special "sticky" pads on the soles of their feet allow them to climb nimbly up the steepest and smoothest rock faces. ■

NEIGHBORS

The shady kopje plants shelter many animals. Antelope leap among the rocks, and birds of prey nest in the peaks. Baboons hunt lizards, and mongooses prey on hyraxes, rodents, and reptiles.

OLIVE BABOON

The olive baboon is an adaptable animal that includes both plant and animal matter in its diet.

EPAULETTED BAT

This fruit bat is common in eastern Africa, where it feeds on the fruits of savanna trees.

Illustrations Elisabeth Smith, Elizabeth Gray, and Edwina Goldstone

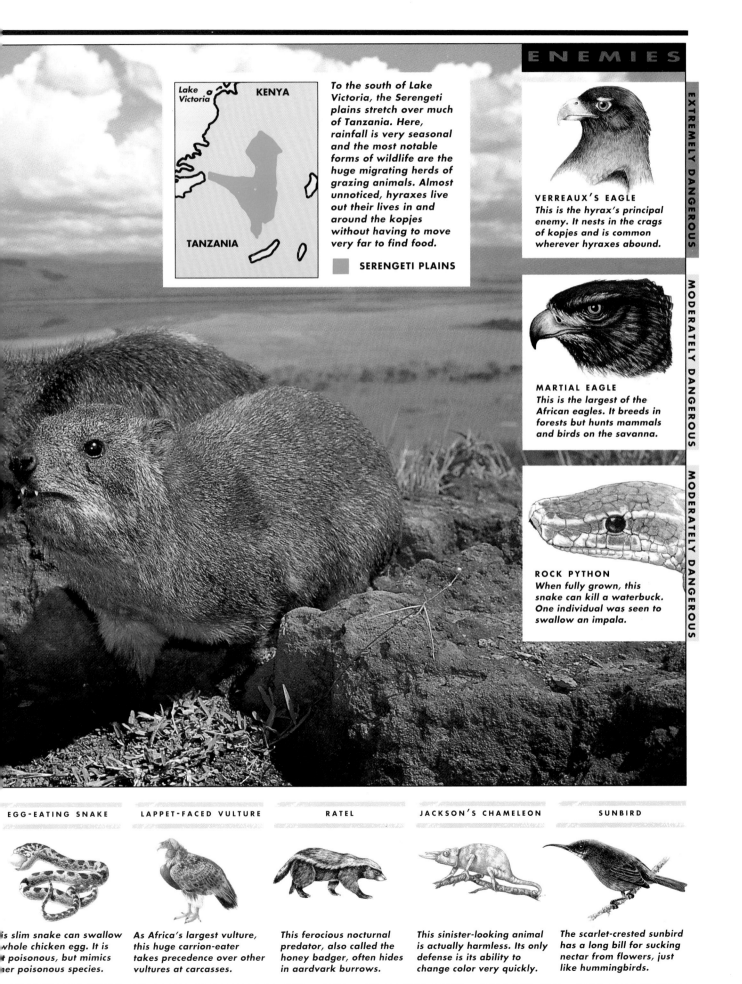

To the south of Lake Victoria, the Serengeti plains stretch over much of Tanzania. Here, rainfall is very seasonal and the most notable forms of wildlife are the huge migrating herds of grazing animals. Almost unnoticed, hyraxes live out their lives in and around the kopjes without having to move very far to find food.

Lake Victoria

KENYA

TANZANIA

SERENGETI PLAINS

ENEMIES

EXTREMELY DANGEROUS

VERREAUX'S EAGLE
This is the hyrax's principal enemy. It nests in the crags of kopjes and is common wherever hyraxes abound.

MODERATELY DANGEROUS

MARTIAL EAGLE
This is the largest of the African eagles. It breeds in forests but hunts mammals and birds on the savanna.

MODERATELY DANGEROUS

ROCK PYTHON
When fully grown, this snake can kill a waterbuck. One individual was seen to swallow an impala.

EGG-EATING SNAKE

is slim snake can swallow whole chicken egg. It is poisonous, but mimics er poisonous species.

LAPPET-FACED VULTURE

As Africa's largest vulture, this huge carrion-eater takes precedence over other vultures at carcasses.

RATEL

This ferocious nocturnal predator, also called the honey badger, often hides in aardvark burrows.

JACKSON'S CHAMELEON

This sinister-looking animal is actually harmless. Its only defense is its ability to change color very quickly.

SUNBIRD

The scarlet-crested sunbird has a long bill for sucking nectar from flowers, just like hummingbirds.

ANTEATERS

The true anteaters are restricted to tropical Central and South America, from southern Mexico to northern Argentina. This area encompasses a wide variety of habitats, from steamy rain forest to semiarid grassland, and the four anteater species have evolved to exploit them all.

OPEN-COUNTRY SPECIALIST

The giant anteater is an open-country specialist. Too heavy and clumsy to feed in the trees, it raids the earthen fortresses of large ground-nesting ants, such as the carpenter ants of the Venezuelan llanos, striding purposefully through the stiff grass with its long snout held just above the ground to detect the slightest trace of prey. When it is not foraging it curls up in a hollow in the ground, relying on the long grass for cover. Even where there is dense vegetation nearby, it rarely takes advantage of the security it might offer.

THE ANTEATER'S SIZE, POWER, AND CAN-OPENER CLAWS GIVE IT THE CONFIDENCE TO FACE ANY PREDATOR

The giant anteater's willingness to forage over large areas enables it to flourish in dry, virtually treeless regions where ant colonies are fairly thinly distributed, but it is most numerous in lush grassland and open tropical forest. In such areas it shares its habitat with the smaller, more arboreal tamandua.

BORDERLINE SPECIES

The two species of tamandua are found throughout the range of anteaters as a whole, with the northern tamandua occurring from Mexico to western Colombia and the southern tamandua from this point south throughout the Amazon Basin. The boundary between their distributions is sharply defined along a line west of the Andes, and the two are rarely found together. In the area near the boundary, the southern tamandua is distinguished from the northern by its lack of a black "vest" pattern; but farther south the pattern reappears on the southern, and individuals found in the far south look a lot like the northern species. For this reason the two were originally regarded as the same species with many local races; there are at least eighteen races recognized today.

Regardless of species or race, however, the habits of tamanduas are much the same from Mexico to Bolivia. Clumsy and awkward on the

Francois Gohier/Ardea

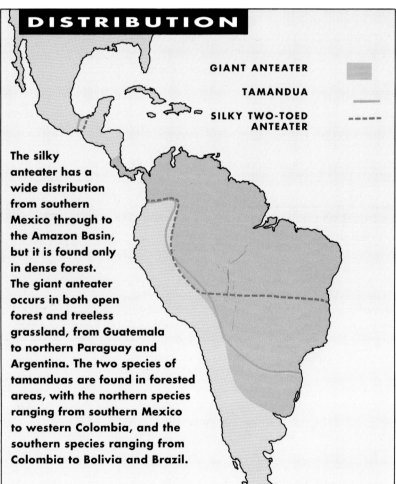

DISTRIBUTION

GIANT ANTEATER

TAMANDUA

SILKY TWO-TOED ANTEATER

The silky anteater has a wide distribution from southern Mexico through to the Amazon Basin, but it is found only in dense forest. The giant anteater occurs in both open forest and treeless grassland, from Guatemala to northern Paraguay and Argentina. The two species of tamanduas are found in forested areas, with the northern species ranging from southern Mexico to western Colombia, and the southern species ranging from Colombia to Bolivia and Brazil.

A giant anteater (left) testing the air. It has no teeth, but a long, narrow tongue, which it uses to extract vast amounts of ants and termites from their mounds.

ground, they often prefer to forage among trees and thorn scrub, where they can put their muscular prehensile tails to good use. Being lighter, less well armed, and slower than the giant anteater, they are also more vulnerable on the ground, so they normally sleep in trees where they are relatively safe from jaguars and pumas.

Provided there are some trees in the vicinity, however, tamanduas will readily feed on ground-dwelling ants and termites. In the tropical forests of Barro Colorado Island, Panama, the northern

> BOTH SPECIES OF TAMANDUAS ALTER THEIR HABITS TO SUIT THEIR HABITATS, AVAILABLE PREY, AND COMPETITION

tamandua spends roughly half its time feeding on the ground. In more open habitats it may spend longer, but nearly always retreats to the trees during the day. In densely forested regions of Venezuela, the southern tamandua may spend up to 70 percent of its time aloft, feeding mainly among the stronger lower branches of the forest trees. Competition can be a significant factor in open forest, where tamanduas and giant anteaters may forage on the ground for the same prey, but

The tamandua (right) spends most of its time in trees; it uses its prehensile tail to assist in climbing.

John Harris/Survival Anglia

in dense rain forest the competition between anteater species is reduced by the extra scope that the tree cover provides.

LAYERS OF LIFE

A tropical forest is a three-dimensional environment, like an ocean: Animals can live at all levels, spacing themselves vertically as well as horizontally, vastly increasing the potential number of animals per square mile. Because the nature of

---

> THE SILKY ANTEATER FALLS PREY TO OWLS AND EAGLES, WHICH PLUCK IT FROM THE BRANCHES LIKE RIPE FRUIT

---

the habitat changes at each level, however, the nature of the resident animals changes, too. The forest floor, the understory, the thicker branches, and the slender twigs of the canopy all tend to support different species, each constrained by their respective diets, climbing skills, and weight.

In the case of anteaters, the diets of the four species are very similar, but their climbing skills and weights cover a broad spectrum. The giant anteater is restricted to the forest floor, but the

tamanduas can feed at any level where the branches are strong enough to support them. The very highest levels, however, are the preserve of the silky anteater, a squirrel-sized acrobat capable of foraging for prey among twigs and vines barely thick enough to carry the weight of a bird.

The silky anteater occurs throughout the tropical forests of Central and South America. It is probably the most numerous of the anteaters, yet, owing to its nocturnal habits and reluctance to descend to ground level, it is rarely seen. ∎

FOCUS ON

AMAZON RAIN FOREST

South America is covered by Amazon rain forests, which are mostly situated to the north of the continent. The hot and damp conditions there have created a habitat for a wealth of animal and plant life.

Because the tall, evergreen trees cast deep shade, many of the animals are found living high up in the tree canopy, where there is more light. Even plants grow mainly high in the trees. The branches teem with birds, monkeys, and tree-dwelling snakes and amphibians.

On the forest floor are deer and antelope and tree-climbing cats, and the area is home to innumerable species of insects, many of them found in vast numbers. These include the ants and termites on which the anteater feeds.

TEMPERATURE AND RAINFALL

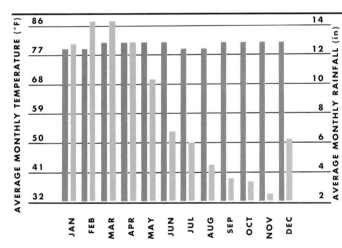

About one-third of South America is covered by warm and humid rain forests. Here, temperatures are always 65°F (18.5°C) or more and the annual rainfall is about 80 in (2,032 mm), with some rain falling daily.

NEIGHBORS

The rain forest is home to more wildlife per square mile than any other habitat. This rich diversity includes some awesome predators.

KING VULTURE

This large bird of prey, with a bald but brightly colored head, is found in all the anteaters' territory.

EMERALD TREE BOA

This bright green rain forest snake hangs in coils on tree branches, uncoiling to drop on its prey.

All illustrations Kim Thompson

THE AMAZON BASIN

The area around the mouth of the Amazon, which lies across the equator, consists of grassy marshland. Toward its mouth the river is 18 mi (30 km) wide and inland it is 2–4 mi (3–6.5 km) wide, with many tributaries. It is surrounded by rain forest, home to a diversity of life.

ATLANTIC OCEAN

BRAZIL

ENEMIES

JAGUAR
The only big cat of the Americas, the jaguar inhabits marshy grassland and wooded riverbanks.

GREAT HORNED OWL
This owl of the Americas hunts in mountains, swamps, and forests. Its head can rotate 180°.

HARPY EAGLE
This massive eagle of the Amazon can swoop at up to 50 mph (80 km/h). It nests in the tallest trees.

MODERATELY DANGEROUS

MODERATELY DANGEROUS

MODERATELY DANGEROUS

Jen and Des Bartlett/Bruce Coleman Ltd.

KINKAJOU

The monkeylike kinkajou has a long prehensile tail that it uses to climb trees and hang on branches.

PORCUPINE

The prehensile tail of the spiny South American porcupine has stiff bristles that help it grip trees.

CAPUCHIN

Central and South America are home to many species of the hairy-headed capuchin monkey.

TWO-TOED SLOTH

Smaller and slightly livelier than the three-toed sloth, it hangs faceup in the trees, hooked on with its claws.

PRAYING MANTIS

This tropical insect uses its hinged forelegs to grab its prey of insects and tiny vertebrates.

ARMADILLOS

Pangolins mainly inhabit the tropical and subtropical rain forests of Africa and Asia. Some species of armadillos live in the tropical forests of South and Central America and swampy forests of the southern United States, but they are not tied to forests in the same way as, for example, the African tree-pangolin is. Most armadillo species live in open grassland.

Tropical rain forests are characterized by tall trees, which spread their sun-seeking crown branches to form a canopy, like a vast green ceiling. There will also be some huge trees, projecting out of the canopy to heights of almost 200 ft (60 m) above ground; their supportive buttress roots may extend for 12 ft (4 m) up the trunk. Lianas (woody vines) commonly hang from these large trees, which may also have strangling figs and other tree-living plants, such as orchids, bromeliads, and pitcher plants, on their higher branches. The ground vegetation may be sparse: Little light penetrates to the forest floor, except where a giant tree has died and crashed to the ground, allowing light through and ground-living plant species to flourish before trees once again occupy this space. Annual rainfall may be in the region of 60–140 in (1,500–3,000 mm), leaving forest soils moist.

In the rain forests of tropical west Africa and southeast Asia, termites swarm along the branches in the thousands. Some species actually build their nests high in the trees, grazing on the

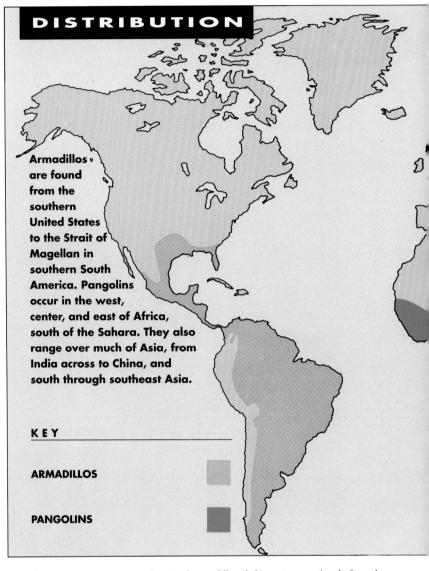

DISTRIBUTION

Armadillos are found from the southern United States to the Strait of Magellan in southern South America. Pangolins occur in the west, center, and east of Africa, south of the Sahara. They also range over much of Asia, from India across to China, and south through southeast Asia.

KEY

ARMADILLOS

PANGOLINS

A pair of armadillos (left) venture cautiously from the den — their only place of refuge against enemies.

lichens that sprout from the moist tree bark. The termites fall prey to tree pangolins, which patrol the branches by night.

SAVANNA DWELLERS
Many species of armadillos, and several of the pangolin species, live in savanna grassland habitats. Savannas are found around the world, mainly in Africa and South America, but there are also smaller areas in Australia and Madagascar.

These open, parklike, tropical and subtropical grasslands have scattered trees and shrubs, as well as a distinct dry season. Although many of the trees are deciduous, shedding their leaves during the dry season, the African savannas include numerous thorny acacias, whose very small leaves enable them to avoid losing too much water even though they remain on the trees all

(in)SIGHT

THE TERMITE MOUND

Termites are found throughout the tropics and also in the temperate zones of the world. There are more than 1,900 species of termites, which, although resembling ants, belong to a different order.

Termites live socially in mounds that they construct by chewing cellulose (a plant tissue). These mounds may be many decades old and grow taller than a human.

Each colony has three types of termites: workers to build and expand the mound, soldiers to protect the mound, and reproducers—a king and queen. The queen may live for 60 to 70 years and may produce up to 36,000 eggs per day over a 50-year period. Alates (winged termites) develop from some of these eggs when the colony is well established and on warm days take wing to establish new colonies.

Armadillos and pangolins have been known to be very choosy about which species of termites they will eat, actually steering clear of some termite mounds while actively seeking out their preferred species. The Cape pangolin, for example, which prefers juvenile ants and termites, is able to select the correct prey species simply by sniffing at the mounds.

Pangolins are superbly armored. They have little trouble devastating termite mounds (right).

year round. Other types of trees found in the African savanna include groups of date palms and the solitary baobab tree. This native African tree, with its swollen, barrel-like trunk, snaking branches, and gourdlike fruits, is a familiar sight in the African grasslands. The burning of these grasslands is a very common practice in Africa, so much so that only plant species that can withstand regular fires are able to survive there.

The Cape pangolin is one of the least well known of the larger African mammals; although occurring over most of southern and eastern Africa, it is generally uncommon throughout this range. It occurs in a range of savanna habitats, including both arid, scrubby areas and areas of higher rainfall in various types of savanna woodland. Cape pangolins do not occur in forest or desert areas. An important daily requirement for

this pangolin is shelter during the daylight hours when it is inactive—rock crevices, holes in the ground, or ground vegetation will be used.

PANGOLINS AT HOME

The giant pangolin lives in savanna and forested regions from west Africa east to the shores of Lake Victoria. Unlike the Cape pangolin, it cannot abide arid areas and depends on both a high rainfall and an abundance of termites for its survival. Within its home range, the giant pangolin often wears down tracks that lead to rivers and swamps, which suggests that it drinks regularly. In such habitats, termites are easily found—some species feed on the grasslands where livestock graze, while others prefer the forested valleys.

The giant pangolin's ground burrows vary greatly in their extent. In some cases, tunnels may be dug some 16 ft (5 m) below ground and up to a length of 130 ft (40 m), while other burrows are little more than scrapes, barely large enough to accommodate the animal's body. In the more extensive burrows, the giant pangolin enlarges a central chamber for its main refuge, from which several tunnels may radiate.

Tree pangolins are widespread throughout the lowland forests of Africa. Like its relatives, it

Jan & Des Bartlett/Survival Anglia

FOCUS ON

ETOSHA NATIONAL PARK

This prestigious national park in Namibia was named after Etosha Pan, "the great white place of dry water," which lies near the eastern end of the park. The pan is an extensive, flat depression, which is parched and barren during the dry months, but partially floods during the November–April rainy season. The brackish water that partly fills the pan is too salty for consumption; instead, it supports blooms of blue-green algae and provides an ideal breeding site for up to one million pairs of flamingoes.

The springs and rain-fed pools fringing the pan provide water for mammals, attracting them in hordes in the dry season. Plains zebra, wildebeest, hartebeest, gemsbok, kudu, springbok, giraffe, and many other species congregate there; in turn, these herds attract predators and scavengers such as leopards, lions, hyenas, and cheetahs.

The open savanna grasslands are dotted with wild fig trees, date palms, and tambouti, a deciduous hardwood tree. In more arid parts of the park, thorn-shrub savanna is more common.

TEMPERATURE AND RAINFALL

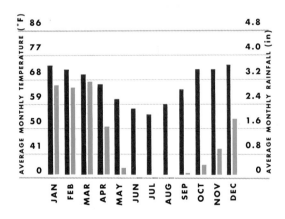

■ TEMPERATURE

■ RAINFALL

The figures given are for Windhoek, the capital city that lies in central Namibia. The north is moister, but this is due mainly to river drainage rather than to a higher rainfall. The average annual rainfall for the north is around 20 in (500 mm).

feeds on termites, but also on ants; these insects favor the type of forest that has been partially cleared by humans, then allowed to regenerate. The pangolin finds resting sites in hollow trees or in the sockets left in trunks by ripped-out branches. Often, such places of refuge are 50 ft (15 m) or more above ground.

In these forests, the tree pangolin is in its element. Aided by its prehensile tail, it clambers with care through the twisting lianas and branches and shuffles up broad trunks in search of prey. ■

NEIGHBORS

Lying next to South Africa, Namibia is probably most famous for the sweeping sand dunes of the dusty Namib desert; but in terms of plants and animals, it is a country of surprising richness.

MEERKAT

These sleek, burrowing carnivores are related to mongooses and live in close-knit colonies.

ELEPHANT

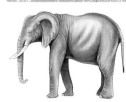

The African elephant is found in a range of African habitats, from semidesert high mountain forest.

Illustrations Kim Thompson & Craig Robson/Wildlife Art Agency

ETOSHA PAN

Etosha Pan lies in the north of Namibia, close to the Angola border. Namibia is dominated by the scrublands of the central plateau and the rolling, sandy wastes of the Namib and Kalahari. These deserts have a unique and special plant life.

ANGOLA

ETOSHA PAN

NAMIBIA

ATLANTIC OCEAN

BOTSWANA

LEOPARD

his solitary, nocturnal talker generally hunts mall and medium-sized ntelopes and deer.

OSTRICH

The largest living bird, the ostrich is also flightless. Adult males may stand nearly 8 ft (2.5 m) tall.

BLACK MAMBA

This venomous snake dens in open, rocky country. A relative of the cobras, it hunts small mammals.

PEL'S FISHING OWL

Rarely found in Namibia, this species shares its range with the Cape pangolin in Zambia and Tanzania.

NILE CROCODILE

One of the most dangerous of Africa's reptiles, this crocodile lies in wait for mammals at water holes.

BADGERS

The European badger has by far the greatest distribution of any badger species, extending throughout Europe—with the exception of northern Scandinavia—and also throughout temperate Asia. Although primarily a woodland animal, the European badger will take to many other habitats. Besides forest, wood, and scrubland, it may dig its sett in hedgerows, embankments, quarries, moorland, and open fields, and even in natural

---

BADGERS HAVE BEEN FOUND
DIGGING BENEATH IRON-AGE FORTS,
INTO COAL TIPS, AND EVEN IN
RUBBISH DUMPS

---

caves or coastal cliffs. Nearby pasture and crop fields are a bonus, although badger forays into these have never been popular with farmers. The protection given by deciduous woodland, however, is the favorite, and right across its range the European badger is mainly found in such areas.

The badger usually chooses a site with well-drained soil that is easy to dig and where there is a plentiful and varied food supply close by. It sets up runways through the undergrowth that it uses regularly—these soon become well-worn routes. A need to be near water is not urgent; if the European badger has plenty of its favorite food—earthworms—it rarely needs to drink as well.

*in*SIGHT

THE BADGER'S STINK

All mustelids have well-developed anal glands, and badgers are no exception. When threatened, the European, American, hog, and honey badgers exude a yellowish oily fluid with a pungent, skunklike musk. The honey badger's scent is particularly vile, while the other three are mild, but it is the stink badgers that really earn their name. These small creatures can, like the skunk, squirt the liquid with deadly aim into the face of an intruder.

Although repulsive in concentrated form, these anal secretions become comparatively sweet-smelling when diluted; stink badger scent was at one time used by Javanese sultans in the manufacture of perfume.

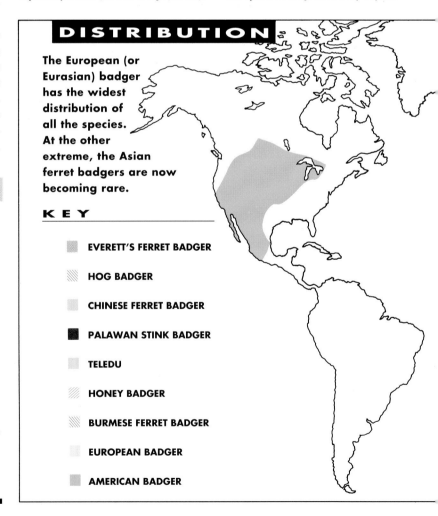

Woodlands are ideal for the badger, especially where the soil is soft (above).

The American badger (far right) is not afraid to confront a nosy coyote.

Tony Stone Worldwide

DISTRIBUTION

The European (or Eurasian) badger has the widest distribution of all the species. At the other extreme, the Asian ferret badgers are now becoming rare.

KEY

- EVERETT'S FERRET BADGER
- HOG BADGER
- CHINESE FERRET BADGER
- PALAWAN STINK BADGER
- TELEDU
- HONEY BADGER
- BURMESE FERRET BADGER
- EUROPEAN BADGER
- AMERICAN BADGER

Low-lying marshy areas are usually avoided, but, on the other hand, few European badgers live above the treeline on mountains anywhere across their range. In Britain they are found up to 1,935 ft (590 m). Woodland bordered by open pasture seems to be a particularly favored habitat. However, badgers are unlikely to choose a site that is regularly visited or intruded upon by humans.

The American badger seems more at home in open plains and farmland, only sometimes being

THE RATEL BURROWS LIKE OTHER BADGERS, BUT ALSO SHELTERS AMONG ROCKS AND IN HOLLOW LOGS AND TREES

found on the edge of woodland. It also favors relatively dry soils and countryside.

Across its range of southwestern Asia to Nepal, western India, and Africa, south of the Sahara, the honey badger may settle in most major habitats, although it is not a desert dweller. Again, it favors dry areas above others, but it is also found in forests and wet grasslands.

The hog badger is a native of the woodlands and forests of China, northeastern India, the

W. L. Miller/FLPA

Indochinese Peninsula, and Sumatra where it may venture up to elevations of 11,500 ft (3,500 m). Again, although it digs itself a burrow, it often spends the day sleeping in such natural shelters as among rocks and crevices.

The teledu is truly a badger of the mountains, only living above 6,890 ft (2,100 m). It spends the day resting in a simple, shallow sett that is seldom

KEY FACTS

● Badgers sometimes drag sticks down into a chamber to serve as a type of mattress between the grassy bedding material and the cold, damp soil.

● An indent in a wheat field, or a hollowed space in a hedge, may be a summer nest. Badgers occasionally use these surface stopovers in places where food is abundant, then return to the sett later in the season.

● Badgers favor chalky areas, as these drain extremely well and the rocky subsoil helps to reinforce the sett tunnels. Lumps of chalk gouged with claw marks are a fairly common sight.

more than 2 ft (61 cm) deep. It may excavate this itself or it may occupy one dug by a porcupine, in which this animal may still be resident. It makes its home in the mountainous areas of Borneo, Sumatra, Java, and North Natuna Islands; on Borneo, it is said to live in natural caves. The Palawan stink badger, an inhabitant of the Calamian Islands to the northeast of Borneo, favors grassland thickets and cultivated areas.

The Chinese, Burmese, and Everett's ferret badgers, found in China, India, Nepal, Burma, and other pockets of southeast Asia, are inhabitants of wooded country—forests or bushy, tree-covered steppes—and also grassland. These smaller relatives usually dig out a simple burrow, but occasionally sleep in hollow trees or even quite high up in the crook of a branch.

TAKING TO TREES AND RIVERS

The badgers' mustelid ancestors knew how to exploit land, water, and trees—habits borne out today by relatives such as the mink and otter. However, although woodland is the commonest home of badgers, few species make much use of the available space above them; only the south-east Asian ferret badgers climb trees regularly.

FOCUS ON
EUROPEAN FORESTS

Until about 5,000 years ago, woodlands and forests of various types thrived throughout Europe. Humans have exploited woodlands ever since, so that only a small fraction of the old forests remains. Replanting schemes in this century, however, have restored some of the losses. One of France's best surviving tracts of woodland is the forest of Fontainebleau, near Paris.

Woodlands of all types are home to an abundance of wildlife. Badgers are equally at home in oak woods or beech woods, the entrance to their setts usually sited on well-drained mounds in either environment.

Woodlands comprise various layers. The topmost branches form the canopy—where the high-nesting birds are found. Beneath this is the shrub layer, where smaller trees, such as hazel and hawthorn, grow. Blackbirds, jays, and garden warblers may be found here. This layer is often thinner in beech woods, where the canopy is so thick that light cannot penetrate to allow dense growth. Beneath the shrub layer is the field or herb layer where wildflowers grow. Again, woodlands vary greatly in the amount of growth at this level. It is here, however, that the badger will be found, making its nightly forays.

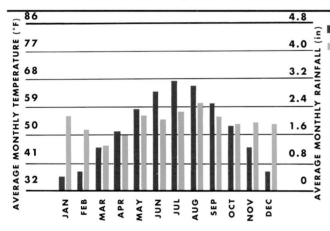

TEMPERATURE AND RAINFALL

■ TEMPERATURE
▨ RAINFALL

The figures given are for the Paris area, including the forest of Fontainebleau. On average, rainfall is greatest during the warm summer months, resulting in lush woodland growth. Badgers fare well in damp areas, where earthworms are plentiful.

The honey badger is a capable climber and does so particularly in the pursuit of a bees' nest—the site of one of its favorite foods. The European badger certainly can climb if it needs to, gripping the bark of the tree with its long, curved claws in the manner of a bear. More frequently it clambers over fallen tree trunks in its path, examining them for food. It can also swim quite adequately, if it has to. The American badger seems more at home in water, swimming and even diving on hot days, and sometimes squats down in shallow water if it needs to cool down. ■

NEIGHBORS

The badger shares its woodland home with a huge variety of other animals: an oak wood supports over 4,000 different species, as well as a rich diversity of plant life.

WOOD PIGEON

Woodlands provide a safe haven for this adaptable bird, which is also found in farming and urban areas.

TAWNY OWL

This nests large owl in tree holes. It swoops at night on mice, voles, and shrews.

P. A. Hinchliffe/ Bruce Coleman Ltd.

THE FOREST OF FONTAINEBLEAU

The small town of Fontainebleau is 40 miles (64 km) southeast of Paris. Some 600 years ago a royal hunting lodge occupied the site of the spectacular castle, built in the 16th century. The nearby forest is one of France's finest woodlands, covering 66 sq miles (171 sq km).

Melun

Fontainebleau

Forest of Fontainebleau

WOODPECKER

he greater spotted woodpecker sends out a accato drumming as it icks grubs from tree bark.

YELLOW LADYBUG

Ladybugs prey voraciously on tiny flies. They fend off attackers by exuding a foul scent from their leg joints.

RED DEER

This woodland deer has a massive distribution, from Europe through to Asia and Australasia.

RED SQUIRREL

Distinguished by its rufous coat and ear tufts, this woodland mammal builds a nest high in the canopy.

RED FOX

This little hunter is often found in badger country, enjoying the deep cover and abundance of prey.

BISON

The plains bison is a creature of the prairies, and proved itself capable of multiplying successfully within that environment even in the presence of humans. Yet most evidence suggests that the modern bison evolved in surroundings more like those in which the wood bison and the European bison now live: mixed forests with swamps and marshes.

The climatic changes that culminated in the series of ice ages called for special adaptations in animals. Greater bulk, providing nutritional fat reserves and increased insulating qualities, enabled certain bovids to thrive in the cold forest environment that developed. Representatives of the genus *Bison* were one such successful group, as were musk oxen, yaks, and aurochs.

Fossil evidence suggests that the bison fanned out from their origins in southern Asia near the end of the Pliocene era, about two million years ago. They swept into the forests of temperate Eurasia, establishing themselves across a wide band, from the Atlantic seaboard eastward to the Volga and the

Stirring scenes such as these (right) were once common across the entire prairie belt of North America.

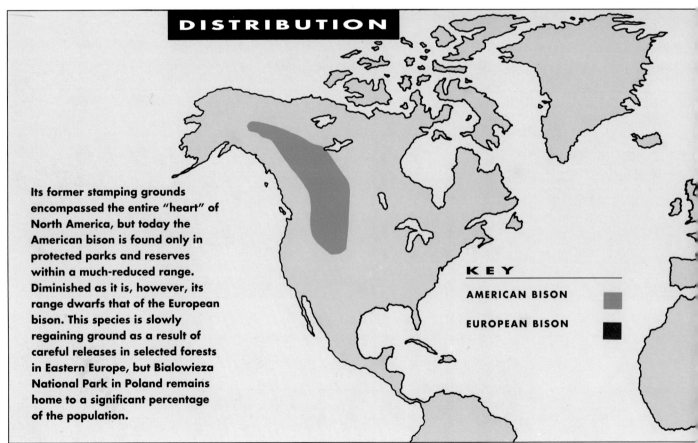

DISTRIBUTION

Its former stamping grounds encompassed the entire "heart" of North America, but today the American bison is found only in protected parks and reserves within a much-reduced range. Diminished as it is, however, its range dwarfs that of the European bison. This species is slowly regaining ground as a result of careful releases in selected forests in Eastern Europe, but Bialowieza National Park in Poland remains home to a significant percentage of the population.

KEY

AMERICAN BISON

EUROPEAN BISON

Franz Kamenzind/Planet Earth Pictures

Caucasus. The modern European bison developed in these surroundings, and, like today's American bison, it had two subspecies. The lowland, forest version still exists, but there seems to have been a separate mountain subspecies that lived on the forested slopes of the Caucasus and other ranges.

European bison had also thrived in the forests of northern Russia, with isolated pockets in the woods near the Urals and beyond. Some had been reported surviving into the 20th century in northeastern Siberia. These northern herds perhaps hark back to the time when bison crossed over the Bering Strait into North America during the Pleistocene ice ages. The terrain that they encountered would have been similar to the familiar Eurasian forest: The Canadian wood bison's similarity to the European bison indicates how little adaptation was needed to thrive in the new environment.

THE PRAIRIE BELT

The north-central region of North America retained its forest character in the period following the retreat of the glaciers, but further south there were great changes. Forests of spruce and other trees yielded to the march of grasslands across much of the Great Basin—the heart of the continent. Before white settlers arrived, the prairies formed a vast ocean of grass that extended to the low, distant horizons. This ocean extended from the deciduous forests of what are now Pennsylvania and Ohio to the Rockies in the west, and from the Mackenzie River in Canada south to the Gulf of Mexico. The vast valley of

California was once a sea of grass; drier grasslands extended through Arizona and southwestern Texas and into Mexico.

Within this huge region there is a great range of rainfall. Much of the western area is semiarid, as it is cut off from Pacific moisture by the Rockies, while in the much wetter east, humid air flows north from the Gulf of Mexico. Consequently, two types of prairie have developed. Shortgrass predominates in the west, on the high plains under the shadow of the Rockies, where blue grama and buffalo grass grow. Away to the east, from eastern Oklahoma to Ohio, the tall-grass prairie lies—before it was cleared for farmland. Here, bluestem, prairie cord grass, and Indian grass grew tall enough to hide a man upon a horse. An intermediate zone, between the tall and short grasses, is known as the mixed-grass prairie. This still survives in patches, where little bluestem, June grass, and western wheat grass grow. Bison country centered on the fertile swath of grassland from the Mississippi to the Rockies.

The prairies—such as they remain today—owe much of their fertility to the fact that, westward from the Mississippi, they slope up to altitudes of around 2,950 ft (900 m) at the point where they meet the Rockies. Rainfall washed sediments down from the mountains, providing a rich bed for the grasses. Sadly, this means that the prairies are now heavily farmed, and the nutrients are much depleted.

Yellowstone has long been a refuge for living symbols of the American wilderness (below).

David Schultz/Tony Stone Worldwide

The bison, an effective ruminant, was able to populate this terrain and extend its range despite the arrival of the first humans. Its dental and digestive adaptations enabled it to thrive on all species of grass, and its bulk and fur provided a bulwark against the cold winters. None of the mammals that once populated that region of North America—horses, mastodons, camels, llamas, elephants, and rhinos—survived into the post-Pleistocene period. Some died out as a result of climatic change; others were easy targets for early human hunters; still others could not survive on the narrower vegetable "menu" served up by the prairies. Pronghorn antelopes are the only other bovid to have survived on the prairies.

THE MARCH SOUTH

Bison moved steadily south and east from their origins in the northwest corner of the continent, first colonizing the shortgrass prairies but already established in the much richer tall-grass prairies well before the Europeans arrived in the 16th century. Making up for their poor eyesight with a well-developed herd instinct, bison were able to defend themselves, particularly their vulnerable calves, against prairie predators such as the wolf, coyote, and bear.

The natural size of a bison herd—then as now—was not much more than about 60, methodically

Darak Karp/NHPA

FOCUS ON

BIALOWIEZA FOREST

Bialowieza Forest in northeast Poland encompasses the last tract of primeval lowland forest in Europe. The forest covers more than 463 sq mi (1,200 sq km), straddling the border with Belarus about 124 mi (200 km) east of Warsaw. Some 13,300 acres (5,386 hectares) on the Polish side have national park status and are recognized as a United Nations Biosphere Reserve and a World Heritage site.

Pine, oak, and ash woodlands give way in places to peat bogs, marshes, and meadows. The forest is also the home of the largest herds of European bison. European conservationists joined forces in 1919 after the last wild bison in the forest was killed by poachers. They set up a breeding program with three captive Bialowieza bison—two cows and a bull—in 1929.

The bison population grew steadily and in 1952 the first animals were released into the wild. Then as now, they were kept under close observation, with every new bison given a name and listed in a pedigree book. The international rescue program is now acknowledged as a success story, and nearly 400 bison now browse in the equally preserved forest.

TEMPERATURE AND RAINFALL

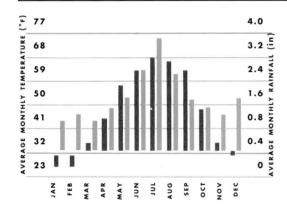

- ■ TEMPERATURE
- ▨ RAINFALL

Away from the bitter chill of the North Sea and Arctic, the land near Warsaw enjoys a climate bordering on the continental. Summers are wet and warm and the winters, though cold, are not so harsh as they would be further east.

grazing a range of about 11 square miles (28 square kilometers) in summer and 38 square miles (98 square kilometers) in winter. Numbers would be hugely swollen during seasonal migrations. Bison would undertake twice-yearly treks in huge aggregations numbering a million or more, searching for fresh grass or for milder weather conditions. Even today wood bison in northern Alberta can be observed migrating some 150 miles (241 kilometers) each November and May, between the forested hills and the Peace River Valley. ■

NEIGHBORS

Bialowieza is rich in oak, lime, hornbeam, and ash trees, and is a refuge for beavers. Woodpeckers and eagles find prey in and around the forest, parts of which have never been managed.

GRAY WOLF

Gray wolves are powerful, intelligent pack hunters that bring down prey as large as deer and horses.

LYNX

The lynx is a lone hunter, stalking its prey on the ground by night or lying in wait in low vegetation.

Illustrations Joanne Cowne

BIALOWIEZA

The National Park lies on the Poland–Belarus border. It occurs in Brest and Grodno provinces in Belarus and in Bialystok, Suwalki, and Lomza provinces in Poland. A former royal hunting ground, the forest is protected on both sides of the border.

█ **BIALOWIEZA NATIONAL PARK**

LITHUANIA

RUSSIA

POLAND

● WARSAW

BELARUS

WOODPECKER

he greater spotted
oodpecker drums loudly
pon tree trunks to find
sect larvae.

OTTER

The elusive otter lives along riverbanks and in wetlands. Its webbed feet and strong tail help it to swim well.

MOOSE

The moose is the largest of all deer species. It feeds alone on woody stems and aquatic plants.

EUROPEAN BEAVER

Unlike its American cousin, the European beaver usually burrows into a riverbank rather than building a lodge.

EAGLE OWL

With its tufted crown, the eagle owl is the largest European owl, killing prey as large as hares.

BROWN BEARS

In North America, brown bears occur from Alaska, south through most of British Columbia and western Alberta, to south-central Nevada. Even within these areas, they occupy a number of different types of environment, from thick woodland and forested areas to more open tundra and windswept coastlines. They are also found in and around meadows of subalpine areas.

At one stage, it seems, brown bears were common over the Great Plains to California and south into Mexico. Nowadays, their stronghold is Alaska and Canada; in the other states they exist in isolated populations, mostly in the protected national parks. More than 30 percent of brown bears found south of Canada and Alaska, for example, inhabit what is known as the Greater Yellowstone Ecosystem in Montana and Wyoming. This covers a 5.5-million-acre (2.2-million-hectare) area surrounding the Yellowstone National Park, as well as the 2.2 million acres (0.9 million hectares) of park itself. Within Montana, grizzlies are found in the Glacier National Park and Great Bear, Bob Marshall, Scapegoat, and Mission Mountains Wilderness areas. The Selkirk Mountains of Idaho and Washington also provide refuge to wild grizzlies.

The brown bears of northern British Columbia and Alaska, including the islands of Kodiak, Afognak, and Shuyak off Alaska's southern coast, are the largest in the world—even

E. & P. Bauer/ZEFA

AMAZING FACTS

● Polar bears and brown bears are so genetically similar that, in zoo experiments, they have been interbred and have produced fertile hybrids.

● It is often claimed that bears are highly intelligent animals. Although this is not conclusively proved, their brains possess several features that are similar to those found in the brains of primates. An American Indian myth relates how the grizzly was created as a more powerful and clever animal than any other.

● Brown bears have one of the lowest reproductive rates of any North American mammal.

DISTRIBUTION

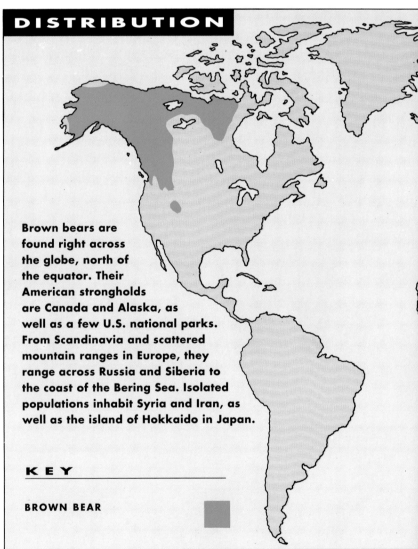

Brown bears are found right across the globe, north of the equator. Their American strongholds are Canada and Alaska, as well as a few U.S. national parks. From Scandinavia and scattered mountain ranges in Europe, they range across Russia and Siberia to the coast of the Bering Sea. Isolated populations inhabit Syria and Iran, as well as the island of Hokkaido in Japan.

KEY

BROWN BEAR

A grizzly bear looks out over its domain (left). Adult brown bears need a huge area in which to roam in search of food, shelter, and a mate.

A European brown bear lumbers through heavy snow looking for a meal (right). Bears sleep through much of the winter but will rouse themselves whenever hungry.

Reinhard Siegel/Aquila Photographics

outweighing all but the very largest polar bears. One reason for this is that their range is criss-crossed with salmon streams, full of this readily available food source that is rich in fat and protein. And there is plenty to go around. Not only can the bears gorge themselves on the salmon, but they need use little energy in catching them—both factors that help contribute to their bulk.

In Eurasia, where their range extends from Scandinavia to eastern Russia and south as far as Spain, Syria, and Iran, brown bears favor remote

> BEARS BASICALLY FAVOR THE SAME HABITATS THAT WE DO: FERTILE VALLEYS, WOODED SLOPES, AND LUSH MEADOWS

mountain woodland, where they can live undisturbed by humans. The Himalayas, Pyrenees, and Alps, and the Cantabrian, Carpathian, and Abruzzi Mountains, have all been home to the brown bear; it is possible that they survive today in the lower wooded slopes of these areas. They also inhabit Hokkaido, the northernmost island of Japan, in the wooded mountain areas.

Brown bears were once common in the formerly wooded areas of North Africa. Deforestation is not a new practice; the forests of northern Africa were largely felled by the Romans to support the needs of their great empire. As this happened, the brown bears withdrew into the partially wooded, mountainous regions of Morocco and Algeria, becoming extinct from there only at the end of the 19th century.

Across its current range, the brown bear will make seasonal migrations to visit rich food sources. Salmon streams are of interest when they are full of salmon traveling back to their spawning grounds; when berries are abundant in lightly wooded areas, bears will travel considerable distances to exploit them. At other times, they take to more open ground to dig out ground-dwelling, burrowing rodents and small mammals.

Just as the American black bear leaves evidence of its presence, so too does the grizzly. Overturned rocks—often of some size—fruit-bearing bushes pulled apart and pillaged, logs ripped into with deep claw marks, and similar scratches—often very high up—as well as tooth marks and stripped patches on tree trunks, all indicate that brown bears have passed by. Where they have dug for rodents, there may be large holes, surrounded by mounds of soil. Another clue is a carcass hidden in a shallow scrape and loosely covered with earth and vegetation. In this instance, the bear will not be far away, so trackers would do well to retreat to a safe distance!

Brown bears will often make a daytime bed, usually under cover of dense undergrowth. They either flatten the vegetation with their heavy bodies or hollow out an oval depression in the

FOCUS ON

THE CARPATHIANS

Forming a vast horseshoe of peaks and plateaus through eastern Europe, the Carpathian range is one of Europe's last mountain wildernesses. From the Czech Republic in the northwest, the Carp[...] arc south and east through Poland and Ukraine, finally twisting s[...] to the west in Romania to form the Transylvanian Alps.

Average altitudes are far lower than those of the European Alp[...] much of the Carpathian range is characterized by hilly plains cloth[...] undisturbed forests. The vegetation is, however, basically alpine [...] nature, varying with the altitude. The deciduous forests of the low[...] slopes, where brown bears roam, give way higher up to conifers [...] alpine meadows.

The Carpathians are home to one of Europe's few surviving wo[...] populations. In summer, the wolves follow the cattle, sheep, and [...] as they are herded up to the high meadows. Come the heavy win[...] snows, however, they descend the slopes and revert to their natu[...] prey of roe deer and wild boar. The lynx preys locally on the you[...] deer, as well as hares, susliks, and ground birds. One of the mos[...] majestic predators is the golden eagle, which nests in the rocky p[...] and swoops down to kill mammals and birds.

VEGETATION ZONES

- 9,020 ft (2,750 m)
  - **Alpine vegetation**
- 8,200 ft (2,500 m)
- 7,380 ft (2,250 m)
  - **Brush vegetation**
- 6,560 ft (2,000 m)
- 5,740 ft (1,750 m)
  - **Coniferous forest**
- 4,920 ft (1,500 m)
- 4,100 ft (1,250 m)
  - **Beechwood or mixed forest**
- 3,280 ft (1,000 m)

The graded altitudes of a mountain have a significant effect on the climate and plant life at its various levels. Forest predominates in the Carpathians, which enjoy a continental climate owing to their great distance from any oceans. On the highest ground, however, trees are small and scarce.

ground, some 1 ft (30 cm) wide and 4 ft (122 cm) long. This they may line with leaves or other soft vegetation. Routes that brown bears habitually take through undergrowth will show as trampled trails, and often their footprints are easily discernible in soft ground. The hind prints can be enormous—1 ft (30 cm) long and 8 in (20 cm) wide, with foreprints being as wide but only half as long, the long claws printing well ahead of the toe pads. The stride is about 2 ft (61 cm) at a walk—up to four times this if the bear is galloping. ∎

NEIGHBORS

Over much of their range, the Carpathians are barely inhabited by humans. Having largely escaped the effects of the last Ice Age, their wild woods have long been a refuge for wildlife.

SNOW FINCH

In winter, this high-mountain species generally moves to the lower forests where the bear lives.

CHAMOIS

The graceful chamois is a fairly common sight in the wooded slopes and high alpine pastures.

THE CARPATHIANS

This mountain range (shown left as dark green) arcs through some 800 miles (1,300 km) of eastern Europe. The bulk of the range lies within Romania. The western ranges drain away to the Baltic Sea, while the southern and eastern ranges drain into the Black Sea, via the Danube, Dniester, and other rivers.

POLAND

HUNGARY

ROMANIA

MOUNTAIN HARE

his inhabitant of higher elevations is similar to the rown hare but is a little maller and stockier.

GOLDEN EAGLE

Among the most beautiful of the birds of prey, this bird may be seen soaring over the highest peaks.

COMMON FROG

The common frog inhabits alpine areas as well as moorland and marshes, wherever there is water.

SWALLOWTAIL BUTTERFLY

The beautiful markings of this butterfly act as a defense, deflecting attack away from its body.

FIRE SALAMANDER

The range of this brightly patterned amphibian extends across Europe and into North Africa.

CAMELS

Despite originating on the rich and fertile grasslands of prehistoric North America, the ancestors of today's camels were successful in challenging new and unforgiving habitats. All the surviving camel and llama species now inhabit such environments.

THE BACTRIAN CAMEL'S NATURAL HOME IS THE GOBI DESERT—A WILD, DESOLATE LANDSCAPE WHERE ONLY THE HARDIEST OF CREATURES SURVIVE

The Bactrian camel is found throughout dry steppe and semidesert zones from central Asia to Mongolia, but its true home is the Gobi Desert, in the foothills of central Asia's Altai Mountains. In winter, when the ground is covered in snow, hordes of camels congregate along the rivers, but then move back to the deserts as the snow melts.

MADE FOR THE DESERT

The dromedary has been domesticated for too long for it to have a true native environment. However, its physical characteristics make it indisputably an animal of hot, arid lands. Indeed, for centuries it has lived in the desert regions of southwest Asia and North Africa.

The dromedary's supreme abilities as a desert

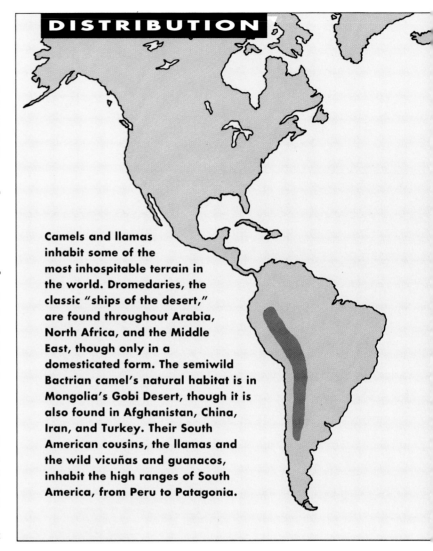

DISTRIBUTION

Camels and llamas inhabit some of the most inhospitable terrain in the world. Dromedaries, the classic "ships of the desert," are found throughout Arabia, North Africa, and the Middle East, though only in a domesticated form. The semiwild Bactrian camel's natural habitat is in Mongolia's Gobi Desert, though it is also found in Afghanistan, China, Iran, and Turkey. Their South American cousins, the llamas and the wild vicuñas and guanacos, inhabit the high ranges of South America, from Peru to Patagonia.

dweller and beast of burden led to its introduction into the remote arid areas of Australia and Central America, where it played an important role in the early exploration of those regions' interiors. In both places, camels soon escaped to begin a feral existence in the wild, and large herds of dromedaries are still found in parts of Australia.

HIGH UP IN THE ANDES

The South American lamoids have adapted to similar habitats—arid and mountainous—in the high plains of the Andes Mountains. Compared to Africa, the continent of South America has a remarkably small diversity of grazing animals—in fact, the guanaco is the dominant large South American herbivore.

J. Kugler/Telegraph Colour Library

Desert caravan: In a scene unchanged for thousands of years, dromedaries, supremely adapted to the hardships of the desert, make their way across the shifting sands of Arabia (left).

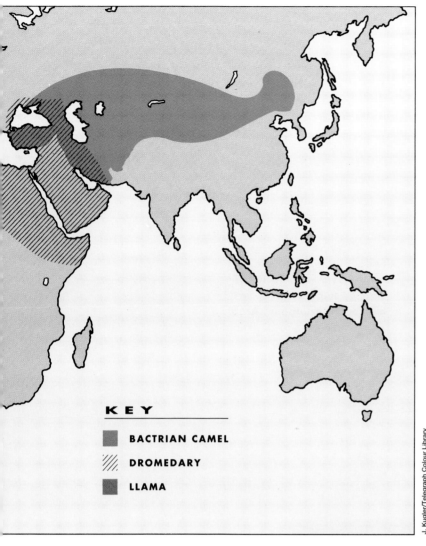

KEY

BACTRIAN CAMEL

DROMEDARY

LLAMA

● All camels are at home in water and are able to swim, although the Bactrian camel and the dromedary have rarely been observed doing so.

● Camels seem to have an innate ability to detect distant rainfall and green pastures and will often travel long distances to find them.

● The domestication of the Peruvian llama is thought to have taken place some 5,000 years ago in the area to the west of Lake Titicaca.

J. Kugler/Telegraph Colour Library

Today, the guanaco is the most widely distributed lamoid, found throughout the Andes from Peru to the southern tip of Patagonia, though its numbers have been greatly reduced.

It has shown itself to be capable of living in various habitats, from deserts and plains to forests (its padded feet can cope with soft sand, stony ground, or snow), and from sea level to altitudes of over 13,000 feet (3,962 meters).

ONE-TENTH OF THE WORLD'S WILD GUANACOS ARE FOUND ON AN ISLAND THE SIZE OF DENMARK, LOCATED AT THE TIP OF SOUTH AMERICA

One of its strongholds is the island of Isla Grande in Tierra del Fuego, at the southern tip of South America. It has been estimated that about one-tenth of all the world's wild guanacos are found here, in an area about the size of Denmark, with the greatest numbers on the west of the island, where

W. E. Townsend Jr./Bruce Coleman Ltd.

Dromedaries (above) were introduced to Australia in the 19th century as transport for the early settlers. The animals adapted well to their new habitat, and feral populations remain there today.

Llamas (left) congregate on a plateau in the Peruvian Andes. They are often found at altitudes exceeding 10,000 feet (3,048 meters).

huge ranches seem to offer protection from hunters.

Different populations of guanacos vary in their habitat requirements. Some family groups will occupy a specific area all year-round, while others migrate between winter and summer ranges to avoid snow or drought.

Guanacos are much more inquisitive than vicuñas, a characteristic that draws them to examine

> LARGE NUMBERS OF GUANACOS WENT TO THEIR DEATHS HUDDLED TOGETHER IN A VAIN ATTEMPT TO ESCAPE FROM THE EFFECTS OF THE BITING COLD

anything unusual, and they will run quickly over rough terrain to examine the source of their interest.

There is evidence that guanacos have long been at home in harsh conditions. In 1830, Charles Darwin found a number of guanaco bones in a low ravine and came to the conclusion that they shared communal cemeteries. This theory has now been discounted, as it is believed that the guanacos huddled together in large numbers in order to

escape the cold generated by the surrounding snow. Unfortunately, groups of them became trapped there and died in the ice.

The vicuña, a native of the central Andes, is generally found at even higher elevations than the guanaco—in its wild state, it is perfectly at home as high as 18,865 feet (5,750 meters). The environment at these heights consists of rough grasslands and plains, and the daily range in temperatures can vary by as much as 18°F (10°C).

A natural hazard for all the Andes lamoids is lightning, which strikes regularly at such high elevations. Each year it claims the lives of many hundreds of animals: sheep, cows, and goats as well as llamas, vicuñas, and guanacos. ∎

FOCUS ON
THE GOBI DESERT

Although the popular image of deserts is that of heat and sand, deserts are actually defined by their lack of rainfall—generally less than 10 inches (25 centimeters) a year. While it is true that most desert regions are found in the tropics, some are located in the world's colder regions. The Gobi Desert, which stretches from the mountains of southern Mongolia toward northern China, is one such region.

It is as bleak a place as any on earth: Small mountain ranges occur across its vast wastes, and the flatter areas are covered in tiny stones, known locally as *gobi*, from which it gets its name.

Temperatures in the Gobi Desert can vary from a summer midday heat of 110°F (43°C) to a winter cold of -40°F (-40°C), when the ground remains covered in snow for long periods. Always scarce, rainfall varies from year to year, so there is never a time when fresh plant growth can be assured.

For centuries, the Gobi has been home to one of the world's most primitive horses, the Mongolian wild horse, also known as Przhevalski's horse. Other large animals that were once common are the saiga herds and the gray wolf, the latter a predator on the more docile grazing animals and once the most widespread member of the dog family. Today its range is greatly restricted.

DESERT TEMPERATURES

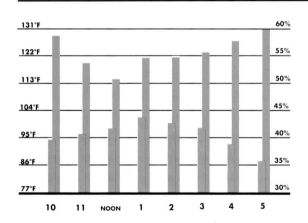

| | TEMPERATURE |
| | HUMIDITY |

Desert temperatures reach their peak at midday. Consequently, many desert animals are nocturnal, taking advantage of the relatively high humidity and very cool temperatures caused by the lack of cloud cover.

NEIGHBORS

Only the hardiest of creatures can survive the rigors of life in the Gobi Desert. Huge extremes in temperature and a critical lack of vegetation have led to a range of unusual adaptations.

LONG-EARED JERBOA

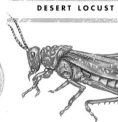

A nocturnal animal, the prolific jerboa moves swiftly through the desert propelled by its powerful back legs.

DESERT LOCUST

This insect migrates in huge flocks over vast distances. The male "sings" by rubbing its legs against its wings.

Illustrations Peter Bull

ENEMIES

WOLF
Packs of wolves, though rarer than they once were, may attack elderly or infirm camels.

THE GOBI DESERT

MONGOLIA

CHINA

Set in the middle of Asia, the world's largest continent, the Gobi Desert is simply too far from the sea for rain-bearing winds to reach it with any frequency.

What little moisture there is falls as rain when it reaches the Himalayas to the southwest or the Chinese ranges to the northeast. Because of this "rain shadow" caused by the tall mountains, there is little rain left by the time winds reach the desert.

Guido Alberto Rossi/The Image Bank

EAGLE OWL	LEBERTINE VIPER	DESERT HEDGEHOG	ONAGER	MONITOR LIZARD

he largest of all owls, the agle owl is distinguished y its brightly colored eyes. hunts small mammals.

This nocturnal viper lies in wait for rodents and lizards, which it bites with its poisonous, hollow teeth.

Lighter and faster than its European relative, the desert hedgehog moves swiftly in pursuit of insects.

Capable of speeds up to 40 mph (65 km/h), this wild ass can go for up to three days without drinking.

This large, aggressive lizard feeds on birds, rodents, and other lizards, which it swallows whole.

CHEETAHS

Until former times the cheetah lived across a very wide section of the Eurasian-African land mass, taking in a range of tropical and subtropical habitats. It once appeared in open terrain across most of Africa and southwest Asia, reaching as far east as central Asia and India, and shunning only the rain forest blocks of Central and West Africa and the deep interior of the Sahara Desert.

But the animal's range has been shrinking for several centuries at least, and that process has accelerated so much in recent decades that this species is now absent from vast areas and tends to have a fragmented distribution in regions where it does occur. It survives today in varied terrain, including clay deserts, semideserts, shortgrass steppes, park-like savanna, acacia scrubland, and light woodland such as the "miombo" woods that predominate across the middle southern zone of Africa.

The miombo, a characteristic especially of Tanzania, is dominated by the select few trees that have adapted well to a long dry season. The trees grow mainly during the November–May wet season, when some 32–47 in (813–1,193 mm) of rain may fall, but for much of the rest of the year the drought and daytime heat are intense. Local people manage the vegetation by means of controlled fires, and elephants cause significant habitat degradation as they forage, with the result that such ecosystems are highly fragile and can easily be upset.

It has been suggested that the color variant, the king cheetah, may be associated with the more well-wooded types of habitat. Individuals with this

Rocky outcrops and small hills known as "kopjes" pepper the flat East African plains; these are used by the cheetah as lookout posts (above).

KEY FACTS

• The East African equatorial plains are subject to a climatic phenomenon known as the Equatorial Trough. When the sun is directly overhead in September and March, the intense heat forms a low-pressure zone. This in turn causes airstreams to converge, rise, and form rain clouds. The maximum rainfall in such areas occurs in April and October.

• In East Africa, the equatorial regions alone experience two distinct rainy seasons. Toward the south—in southern Tanzania, for example—the December dry season contracts to such an extent that the rainy seasons more or less merge into one.

• In parts of East Africa, temperatures fall so suddenly at night that the emergence of nocturnal creatures, such as rodents, can be timed to within a couple of minutes' accuracy.

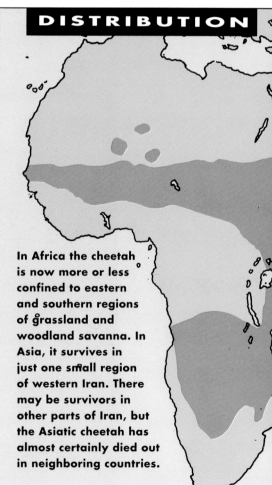

DISTRIBUTION

In Africa the cheetah is now more or less confined to eastern and southern regions of grassland and woodland savanna. In Asia, it survives in just one small region of western Iran. There may be survivors in other parts of Iran, but the Asiatic cheetah has almost certainly died out in neighboring countries.

overall darker and more strongly patterned coat may be more common in such terrain, where they would be better camouflaged against the dappled vegetation. Most king cheetahs have been reported from miombo habitats in Zimbabwe and Botswana.

A "JUST-SO" HABITAT

Essentially, the cheetah is an animal of fairly dry, open habitats. Humid areas tend to support too dense a growth of vegetation for an animal that lives by running down fleeing prey in a high-speed, horizontal chase. A cheetah would soon starve amid plenty in the rain forests of Central Africa. On the other hand, overly arid areas, such as the deep interior of the Sahara or Namib Deserts, are too extreme in the opposite sense to support the cheetah's needs for food, water, and shelter.

Ideal cheetah habitat appears to be level or gently sloping ground, with light cover in the form of bushy clumps, scattered trees, or medium-length grass. Grass predominates on the African plains, and it is a remarkable form of vegetation. Capable of withstanding fire, trampling, and grazing, it can grow afresh time and time again after its leaves have been damaged, because its growing points are at the base. This helps to explain why the plains can support such large herds of grazing animals.

Trees on the savanna provide the cheetah with shade, and also with "larders" for its kills (below).

The cover greatly helps the cat's hunting success since it enables it to approach close enough to prey, undetected, before rushing in to attack. On wide-open, shortgrass plains, intended victims frequently get too much of a head start to be caught before the cheetah is exhausted. Gazelles can spot predators at a distance of half a mile (800 m). But too much cover in the form of tall grass, thick bush, and uneven, broken ground can present a different kind of problem: all can impede the cheetah. There is a report of a sprinting cheetah rushing over the top of a hillock and then losing balance and skidding on its back as it tried to avoid an obstacle on the other side.

Good cheetah habitat on level plains will also include scattered vantage points from which the animal can scan the surroundings for food as well as keep watch for danger when it has cubs in tow. It is often easy to tell that such sites are favored—among them trees with low branches, stumps, hillocks, rocks, and termite mounds—because of the concentration of excreta deposited on them largely as a social signal to other cheetahs. Patches of dense vegetation are an extra habitat requirement for female cheetahs, since they need good protective cover for their lairs.

PREY AND PREDATORS

But the pattern of distribution of cheetahs is not just governed by the presence of suitable terrain and vegetation. For cheetahs to survive there must be an

K E Y

CHEETAH

adequate supply of favored prey, and, it seems, not too much threat from other carnivores. Depending on the region, cheetahs tend to rely heavily on one or two key species of hoofed mammals for their food, such as springbok and impala in southern Africa and Thomson's gazelles in East Africa. In areas where such animals are scant, cheetahs will be few and far between. Nowhere is this more evident than in Asia, where, for example, the disappearance of cheetahs from India largely followed the decline of blackbuck.

Recent studies have shown that some cheetah populations endure very high rates of cub mortality. Causes of death include exposure, disease, and fire, but cubs are killed mainly by predators, such as lions, hyenas, hunting dogs, and birds of prey. It appears that cheetahs coexist very uneasily with other big carnivores, and in some areas where these occur in high numbers cheetahs simply cannot sustain viable populations. Despite the presence of suitable habitat and plentiful game there, Ngorongoro Crater in Tanzania, for example, has almost no resident cheetahs. But it does have very high numbers of lion, and hyenas.

Altogether, the pressures of habitat and prey requirements, combined with susceptibility to predation, injury, and starvation, all seem to have made

Norbert Rosing/Oxford Scientific Films

FOCUS ON

EAST AFRICAN PLAINS

The grassy plains of East Africa are among the most spectacular of wildlife habitats in the world. Places like Amboseli and the Masai Mara in Kenya, and the Serengeti in Tanzania are renowned for the extraordinary richness of their mammal life. The plains vary considerably in character. Some are well wooded, some are patchworks of shrub, tree, and open ground, some have scattered, drought-resistant acacias and baobabs, others are wide open save for isolated rocky mounds or lines of trees following watercourses. But all provide a habitat for a diversity of hoofed mammals, among them giraffes, zebras, warthogs, buffalo, wildebeests, hartebeests, waterbuck, gazelles, and impala, the adults and young of which provide abundant food for predators. Each herbivore has its own habitat preference, and competition between these animals is reduced because they tend to feed at different levels. While giraffes, for example, browse the tree crowns, leaf-eating antelopes eat from lower branches or from shrubs. Similar differences appear between those animals that eat grass, which can grow tall on some plains. Zebras tend to eat the coarser, older grass tips, wildebeests graze the middle stalks, and gazelles move in to nibble the youngest, lowest shoots.

TEMPERATURE AND RAINFALL

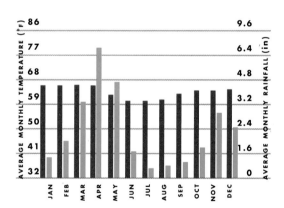

■ TEMPERATURE

■ RAINFALL

Conditions on these tropical plains are hot in the daytime, but often cool at night. During the dry season, which may last for several months of the year, the grasses wither, precious water holes shrink, and the grass is prone to fire.

the cheetah something of a victim of its own extreme specialization. It appears that, long before human influence on the species precipitated its decline, the cheetah was a rather naturally scarce, low-density animal, living quite close to the edge. Although exceptional concentrations of one cheetah in every two square miles (one in every five square kilometers) are presently found in some national parks, figures of one per forty square miles (one hundred square kilometers) are by no means unusual even in optimum habitat. ■

NEIGHBORS

The African plains are not merely a haven for hoofed grazers; they play host to hunters, scavengers, hares, rodents, lizards, birds, reptiles, and the hordes of termites and ants hidden from view.

TERMITES

Some termite species build large colonial mound nests that provide convenient lookout sites for cheetahs.

OSTRICH

This immense bird cannot fly, but it is a fast runner, and its powerful kick deter most would-be attackers.

Illustrations Joanne Cowne; Secretary bird, lion, and hyena Elisabeth Smith

EAST AFRICA

The best known of the broad, flat, grassy areas known as the East African plains lie in southern parts of Kenya and in northern Tanzania. In some cases, such as the Serengeti, the flatness of the terrain has resulted mainly from the ancient deposition and accretion of windblown ash from nearby volcanoes.

EAST AFRICAN NATIONAL PARKS

SUDAN

ETHIOPIA

ZAIRE

KENYA

TANZANIA

Indian Ocean

LIONS

Lions frequently harass or even kill adult cheetahs. They are a great threat to cheetah cubs.

SPOTTED HYENAS

Unlike lions, hyenas eat the cheetah cubs they kill. They are deadly when hunting in packs.

PEL'S FISHING OWL

om low perches around vers and pools, this owl woops over the water and eizes fish in its talons.

NILE CROCODILE

This reptile seizes plains grazers when they visit rivers. It pulls them into the water, where they drown.

BLACK MAMBA

The deadly black mamba is a hunter of rodents, birds, and lizards. Its bite is extremely poisonous.

SECRETARY BIRD

Even snakes have enemies, one of which is this bird. Its long legs protect its body while it kicks at its prey.

PYTHON

The rock python may grow over 17 ft (5 m) in length. Its crushing coils can kill small antelopes.

CHIMPANZEES

Steve Robinson/NHPA

Chimpanzees, like this juvenile (left), are basically arboreal, or tree-living, animals, though they can move across the ground on all fours equally well. Their preferred habitat is the rain forest, but they will also live in savanna and grasslands, providing there is some woodland cover.

Although the ideal habitat for chimpanzees is damp tropical forest, these highly adaptable creatures can also be found in deciduous woodland and in drier areas such as savanna and grassland.

In the past, chimpanzees were found in a broad swath from the Atlantic coast of central Africa almost to the western shore of Lake Victoria. The picture nowadays is one of declining numbers, where chimps persist only in separate pockets—mostly in central Africa, which contains about 80

IN THE IVORY COAST AND LIBERIA, CHIMPANZEES ARE LOSING THEIR FOREST HOMES TO OIL PALM AND RUBBER PLANTATIONS

---

percent of Africa's remaining tropical forest, particularly in Zaire, Gabon, and Cameroon. Pygmy chimpanzees, which have always had a much smaller range than common chimpanzees, favor the dense, rich rain forest of central Zaire.

RICH VARIETY
The climate in the tropical rain forest is constantly warm and wet. The Zaire rain forest, the largest in the whole of Africa, contains thousands of species of plants, the commonest of which belong to the pea and mahogany families. In fact, Zaire has more plant species than any other African country—over 11,000. The vast majority of these are to be found in the country's dense tropical rain forests, and a third of them cannot be found anywhere else in the

world. The forests also contain over 400 species of mammals, including gorillas, okapis, and elephants.

In the western part of the chimpanzee's range, especially in the Ivory Coast and Liberia, the forests have been much more affected by clearance and other disturbances. Large areas have been cut down for timber and used for agriculture. Land that once supported rich rain forest now has plantations of oil palm or rubber—and no place for chimps.

BEYOND THE RAIN FOREST
In the region's few remaining forests, rainfall varies over the year and there is a definite dry season. In the forests of Sierra Leone, for example, the rainfall may be as high as 131 inches (3,400 millimeters) a year, but this includes a dry period of three or four months. Here, the vegetation is known as tropical

FOCUS ON

THE ZAIRE RAIN FOREST

The rain forest of Zaire in central Africa is a constant, stable world of humid warmth, producing an abundance of fruit, insects, and vegetation. Annual rainfall can be as much as 120 inches (3,048 millimeters), spread evenly throughout the year, and the temperature varies between 68 and 86°F (20 and 30°C) during the course of a day. As most of the trees are evergreen, there is a permanent canopy over the forest with clearings only where trees have fallen.

It is ideal habitat for the chimpanzee—there are few predators and the trees provide safety at night when the chimps build their nests high in the branches. The trees also yield much of the food and moisture necessary to the chimp's diet.

Tim Laman/The Wildlife Collection

seasonal forest. If the dry period is longer than this, savanna replaces the forest.

Outside the main zone of the rain forests, both to the north and the south, the rains are too irregular to support closed forest and there is open woodland, savanna, or grassland, depending on the kind of soil and the rainfall pattern. The savanna usually receives only 40 to 59 inches (1,000 to 1,500 millimeters) of rain a year, with a dry season lasting anywhere between four and six months.

In these drier areas, chimpanzees seek out sites with clumps of trees, such as river valleys or gullies. In the driest parts, the trees thin out and gradually disappear, giving way to open, arid grassland. As chimps like to live within reach of good supplies of water, they usually avoid these areas.

In the savanna, chimps share their habitat with

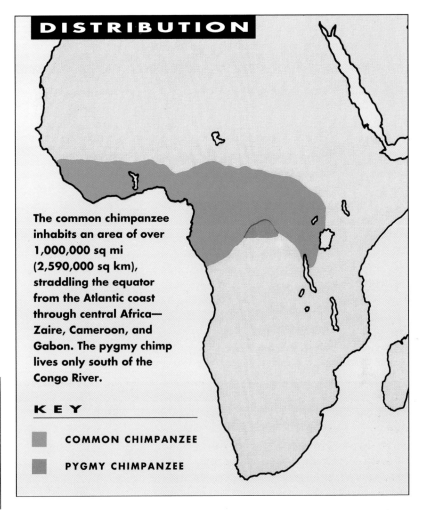

DISTRIBUTION

The common chimpanzee inhabits an area of over 1,000,000 sq mi (2,590,000 sq km), straddling the equator from the Atlantic coast through central Africa—Zaire, Cameroon, and Gabon. The pygmy chimp lives only south of the Congo River.

KEY

■ **COMMON CHIMPANZEE**

■ **PYGMY CHIMPANZEE**

large predators such as lions, leopards, and cheetahs, as well as jackals and hyenas, and vultures who feed on carrion. Herbivores include elephants, giraffe, bushbuck, buffalo, and warthogs. There are other primates in the savanna, too—olive and savanna baboons, patas monkeys, and vervet monkeys. ■

THE FOREST LAYERS

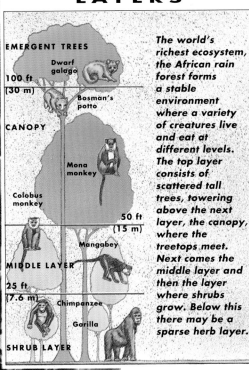

EMERGENT TREES
Dwarf galago
100 ft
(30 m)
Bosman's potto
CANOPY
Mona monkey
Colobus monkey
50 ft
(15 m)
Mangabey
MIDDLE LAYER
25 ft
(7.6 m)
Chimpanzee
Gorilla
SHRUB LAYER

Illustration Kou Kang Chen

The world's richest ecosystem, the African rain forest forms a stable environment where a variety of creatures live and eat at different levels. The top layer consists of scattered tall trees, towering above the next layer, the canopy, where the treetops meet. Next comes the middle layer and then the layer where shrubs grow. Below this there may be a sparse herb layer.

KEY FACTS

● It is estimated that there is now a population of up to 200,000 chimps and pygmy chimps in Africa, ranging over 15 countries.

● Chimps thrive in tropical rain forests, but they may also be found in drier conditions and higher, cooler altitudes of up to 6,560 ft (2,000 m).

● At night, chimps build nests 16–118 ft (5–36 m) high in the trees. In the rainy season, they also build day nests.

DEER

Members of the deer family are found in Europe, Asia, North Africa, North America, and South America, and they have also been introduced into Australia, New Zealand, and New Guinea. They are typically woodland animals and many prefer to browse in dense forest. However, some species feed in more open areas, and deer can be found in almost all habitats, including arctic tundra, mountains, and grassland.

Caribou are found in the northern regions of North America and Siberia. During April and May they migrate northward into the open tundra. There they remain until June and July, when there is a movement southward to the forests. In

---

THE WAPITI, OR ELK, IS THOUGHT BY SOME PEOPLE TO BE A SUBSPECIES OF THE EUROPEAN RED DEER

September there is a second movement northward into the tundra for the rut, but this time the caribou do not travel as far as they did earlier in the year. After the rut the herds migrate southward again to their winter feeding grounds in the forests, although a few small groups remain in the tundra all winter.

The moose, the largest living deer, is also found in the far north. It inhabits the wooded areas of Alaska and Canada and parts of the Rocky

DISTRIBUTION

Most deer live in northern temperate climates. Fallow deer are native to the Mediterranean region; mule deer inhabit western Canada and the United States. Chinese water deer are found in reed beds and grasslands in China.

KEY

▨ MULE DEER

▨ RED DEER

▨ MOOSE

▨ FALLOW DEER

▨ PERE DAVID'S DEER (reintroduced)

▨ CHINESE WATER DEER

Red deer (below) have increased dramatically in Scotland, and there is a danger of their damaging the forests.

William S. Paton/Planet Earth Pictures

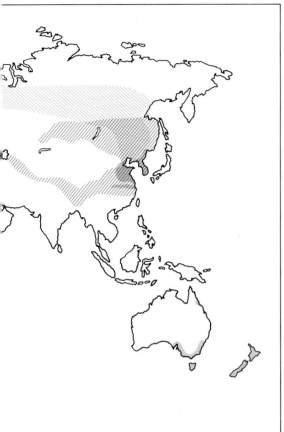

● **Where there is adequate shelter, mule deer are relatively sedentary animals, but in more open landscapes they may climb to altitudes of over 6,562 ft (2,000 m) in search of cool pastures, returning to lower levels during the winter. These movements amount to a form of migration.**

● **Reindeer are the equivalent of cattle to the Lapps and other northern tribes, but it is a moot point as to whether the Lapps domesticated the deer or vice versa. Like caribou, reindeer follow traditional migration routes, the only difference being that people travel with them. They are used as pack animals, for drawing sleighs, and, of course, to provide meat and hides.**

● **Moose are excellent swimmers and will not hesitate to cross rivers or sea inlets.**

Reindeer, or caribou, live in north Europe, Asia, and North America. Some races migrate to the Arctic in the summer.

Mountains in the northwest part of the United States. The species also lives in the Old World, where it is known as the elk. It can be found from Scandinavia eastward through Russia and Siberia to Mongolia and Manchuria in northern China. Moose are most at home in well-watered woods and forests consisting of willow and scrub with ponds, lakes, and swamps. During the summer, moose spend a great deal of their time wading through water, feeding on water plants. Wallowing in water has the added benefit of helping to keep off the hordes of flies and mosquitoes.

The red deer is considered to be a European species, although there are subspecies that live in

---

IN SPITE OF THE MOOSE'S HUGE SIZE, ITS LARGE, BROAD HOOVES ALLOW IT TO WALK ACROSS BOGGY GROUND WITHOUT DIFFICULTY

---

various parts of Asia, North America, and North Africa. It inhabits mature forest by preference, but in Britain, where most of the forest has been cut down, red deer have been forced to become moorland grazers. Except for the period of the rut, the females, or hinds, live in herds separate from the stags, which roam singly or in small groups.

Roe deer prefer to live in dense cover, where they are small enough to creep about largely unseen. They are found throughout Europe, and in Britain this species was formerly very widespread. But as human settlements increased in the south, it appears to have been driven northward, and by the late 18th century there were no roe deer in England. Since then, however, they have been

David Middleton/NHPA

reintroduced into woodlands in many areas and today this is once again a common species of deer.

Fallow deer, noted for their spotted summer coats, are thought to have originated in the Mediterranean region, perhaps as far east as Iran and Iraq. Their original range has been considerably altered due to both extermination and introduction into new areas. They are common in parks throughout Europe and have been introduced into the United States. They are grazing animals and feed in open areas, but they prefer to shelter in woodland.

FOCUS ON

NEW ENGLAND

New England is a group of six states—Connecticut, Maine, Massachusetts, New Hampshire, Rhode Island, and Vermont—in the northeastern United States. This picturesque and historic region contains rocky coasts, sprawling mixed forests, and low ranges—the northern parts of the Appalachian Mountains.

Summers are warm, with temperatures occasionally soaring to 105°F (40°C), but in winter and sometimes spring, severe cold spells send temperatures plummeting far below the freezing point. Heavy snowfalls give plenty of opportunities for winter sports.

New England is probably best known for its warm autumns, when the foliage of deciduous trees, including ash, beech, birch, maple, and oak, produces spectacular displays of color.

The deer that thrive in such a colorful terrain include the moose, the white-tailed deer, and the wapiti, or elk.

TEMPERATURE AND RAINFALL

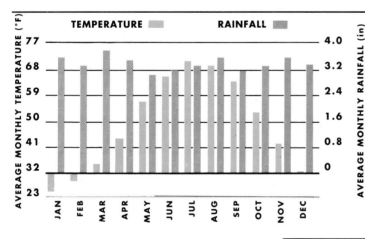

New England temperatures (represented here by Boston's statistics) peak at around 72°F (22°C) in July, and drop to 25°F (-4°C) in January. Rainfall is at its heaviest in March at 3.5 in (90 mm), but drops only to 3 in (76 mm) in May.

Related to both the fallow deer and the red deer is the sika of East Asia. This species lives in deciduous and mixed forests and has been introduced into many areas of Europe.

Similar in coloring to fallow deer are the beautiful and very common axis deer, or chital, of India, and the hog deer of India, which is found in herds in a variety of habitats, from lowland plains to the lower hills, among bushes, trees, or in bamboo thickets. Hog deer live generally alone or in small parties on grassy plains.

NEIGHBORS

The North American and Canadian terrain is rich and varied, comprising mountains, lakes, and forest. Deer share it with a wide variety of mammals, birds, fish, and insects.

SKUNK

Skunks are renowned for their unique defensive system—a vile-smelling, poison-gas-like spray.

DRAGONFLY

Dragonflies can travel at speeds of up to 60 mph (96 km/h), making them one of the fastest flying insects.

NEW ENGLAND RED DEER

The North American form of red deer is the wapiti, or elk. For much of the year the female and young live in herds, while the males form smaller, more loosely knit groups. The wapiti range extends east to west and north to south from Canada to Mexico.

NEW ENGLAND

ENEMIES

EXTREMELY DANGEROUS

COYOTES
The wolf's cousin has increased in range in North America, because it is cunning and adaptable.

MODERATELY DANGEROUS

BOBCAT
Lynx rufus preys on small deer and rodents.

MODERATELY DANGEROUS

BEARS
Heavily built and strong, bears have few enemies. The grizzly is reputed to be the most ferocious.

Gary Brettnacher/Tony Stone Worldwide

RACCOON

...he raccoon family, ...rocyonidae, contains 16 ...ecies and is found naturally ...nly in the Americas.

CARDINAL

This striking bird is found from the Colorado River through southern Arizona to California and Mexico.

GRASSHOPPER

Grasshoppers have special organs for receiving sound waves.

NORTH AMERICAN RED FOX

The red fox—Vulpes vulpes—is found throughout the Northern Hemisphere and is much valued for its fur.

ROBIN

The best known of all American birds, it is found in any wooded habitat, including parks and lawns.

DOLPHINS

Hans Reinhard/Bruce Coleman Ltd.

The bottle-nosed dolphin is found in all the warm and temperate waters of the world. Though the harbor porpoise has a more restricted distribution, it too is found in both the Pacific and Atlantic Oceans. The Indo-Pacific hump-backed dolphin inhabits the coastal waters, estuaries, and swamps of the Indian and Pacific Oceans, while the highly specialized boutu navigates the river systems of South America from the Atlantic to the Andes.

Tropic o

p

EQUATO

Tropic o

Dolphins and porpoises inhabit every ocean except the coldest waters of the Arctic and Antarctic, though most species prefer temperate or tropical seas, where there is plenty of food all year round.

Some species, like hump-backed dolphins, prefer to live near to the shore, though they do venture farther out into the ocean to hunt. Others—such as the spinner and bridled dolphins—are pelagic species, which means they inhabit the open seas.

Bottle-nosed dolphins are primarily a coastal species, although sightings are common in the open oceans (above).

BECAUSE MANY DOLPHIN SPECIES TRAVEL A GREAT DEAL, THEY CAN BECOME COMMON IN AN AREA ONE YEAR AND THEN DISAPPEAR THE NEXT

Because dolphins and porpoises spend most of their lives beneath the surface of the water, it is difficult to study every species in detail. Some, like the very rare Gulf of California porpoise (or cochito), are studied closely only when they are washed up on the shore or caught by fishermen.

ON THE SURFACE

Dolphins and porpoises live at the top of the food chain. This food chain originates in the sun-dappled waters at the surface, home to the tiny plants, or phytoplankton, with which the chain begins. These plants get their energy needs from the sunlight through a process called photosynthesis and are found in the top 320 feet (100 meters) of the ocean. They are a concentrated source of nutrients and make up what are aptly named the "pastures of the sea."

KEY

BOTTLE-NOSED DOLPHIN

HARBOR PORPOISE

INDO-PACIFIC
HUMP-BACKED DOLPHIN

AMAZON RIVER DOLPHIN
(BOUTU)

The strange, solitary Amazon dolphin, or boutu, navigates the slow-moving, silt-laden river basins that pass through the forests of South America (below).

Andrea Florence/Ardea

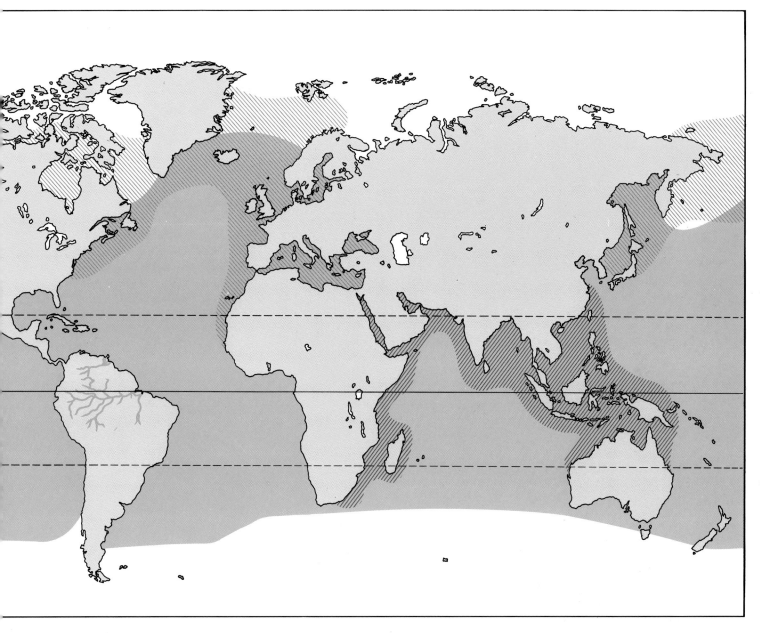

Tiny animals called zooplankton graze like cattle on the phytoplankton. These include the larvae of crustaceans, jellyfish, and bottom-living fish that start their life at the surface. They are eaten in turn by fish such as herring, which swim with their mouths open in order to gorge themselves on the plankton, and other species such as cod, mackerel, and anchovies, which form the dolphin's staple diet.

SEA OF PLENTY

Dolphins and porpoises are opportunists and often head for those areas affected by ocean currents such as the Humboldt Current. This flows off the west coast of South America and brings nutrient-rich cooler waters to the surface, which then sustain the food chain and provide ample feeding opportunities for the fish that prefer to live in warm

KEY FACTS

● The color and pattern of a dolphin's skin is a good guide to the kind of habitat that species prefers. Those that have dark skin prefer deeper waters, while those with black-and-white coloring blend well with the sun-dappled waters closer to the surface.

● No stranger to shallow coastal waters, the Indo-Pacific hump-backed dolphin uses its remarkably agile body to cross the mud banks that sometimes stand in the way of its journeys.

● Although harbor porpoises are most often found along the coasts and estuaries of the Northern Hemisphere, they occasionally make their way along major rivers. One once traveled over 200 miles (320 km) up Holland's Maas River.

waters. Dolphins and porpoises then proceed to feast on these incoming schools of fish.

Coastal waters also prove a happy hunting ground for dolphins. There the sea is enriched by sediments from the rivers that flow into it. In some parts of the world, especially northern Japan, West Africa, and Peru, the deposits from the ocean bed are moved by currents to the coast, and as a result they number among the world's finest fisheries.

COASTAL COMPANIONS

Along the coast, dolphins share their habitat with sponges, jellyfish, corals, and mollusks. There are also sea snakes, turtles, and many different seabirds, as well as other mammals like seals and otters.

Farther out to sea lie squid and octopus. The giant squid—which grows up to 65 feet (20 meters) long—is a ferocious creature when attacked. Even huge sperm whales have been found with scars on their skin made by the squid's tentacles.

A few dolphins live in a habitat very different from the open seas, such as the boutus of South

Bob Cranston/Jeff Rotman Photography

FOCUS ON
THE TROPICAL ATLANTIC

Bounded by Central and South America on the west and by West Africa on its eastern shores, the tropical Atlantic is a vast expanse of ocean that lies between the tropic of Cancer to the north and the tropic of Capricorn to the south.

The surface temperature of the tropical Atlantic is almost constant and is largely unaffected by any major currents. The surface waters, where most dolphins live, are uniformly warm.

Dolphins and porpoises thrive on the wide variety of fish that live there, such as tuna, hake, and herring. Other prey, which include octopuses, clams, lobsters, and crayfish, inhabit the coastal waters.

Apart from the dolphin fishing industry of the Azores and drift nets that may accidentally trap dolphins and porpoises, the greatest threats to dolphins in these waters are presented by predators like sharks and, in particular, the killer whale, ironically a close relation of dolphins and porpoises.

Two species particularly associated with this area are the spotted dolphin and the Atlantic hump-backed dolphin, but the tropical Atlantic is home to more than a dozen other species.

THE OCEAN LAYERS

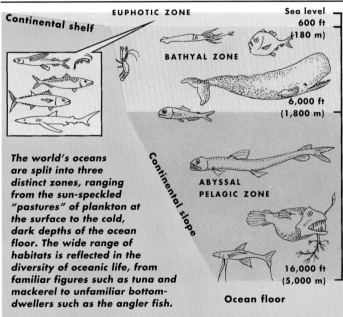

Douglas Ingram

EUPHOTIC ZONE

Continental shelf

Sea level
600 ft
(180 m)

BATHYAL ZONE

6,000 ft
(1,800 m)

Continental slope

ABYSSAL
PELAGIC ZONE

16,000 ft
(5,000 m)

Ocean floor

The world's oceans are split into three distinct zones, ranging from the sun-speckled "pastures" of plankton at the surface to the cold, dark depths of the ocean floor. The wide range of habitats is reflected in the diversity of oceanic life, from familiar figures such as tuna and mackerel to unfamiliar bottom-dwellers such as the angler fish.

America. Good eyesight is of little use in the river's murky waters, and these dolphins rely on their echolocation system to catch the fish and crustaceans that make up their diet.

The dry season, when river levels are low, presents special problems for the boutus–particularly the inexperienced young–because they can become trapped in stagnant ponds. However, as long as the ponds do not dry up completely, the dolphins usually survive. ■

NEIGHBORS

These animals coexist with dolphins and porpoises and reflect the extraordinary variety of life found in the tropical Atlantic: from slow-moving, passive reptiles to swift, vigorous hunters.

MANTA RAY

The manta is famed for its jumping ability—and the reverberating crash it makes when it falls back into the sea.

BARRACUDA

Known as "the tiger of the sea," this fast and fierce hunter changes color to blend in with its surroundings.

SEASONAL CHANGE IN THE TROPICS

The area of the tropical Atlantic is flexibly defined. When temperatures are at their warmest in the north (in August), the area defined as "tropical" reaches its northern limit. It reaches its southern limit in February, the south's warmest month.

☐ AUGUST ░ FEBRUARY

ENEMIES

EXTREMELY DANGEROUS

KILLER WHALE
Attacking in pods of five or six, killer whales will sometimes force other dolphins to stay underwater until they drown.

MODERATELY DANGEROUS

GREAT WHITE SHARK
This giant of the tropical seas will attack anything that moves, though dolphins rarely number among its victims.

MODERATELY DANGEROUS

TIGER SHARK
Dolphins usually outwit sharks, but this fearsome opportunist poses a threat to old or sick creatures.

MORAY EEL

The eel's snakelike body is perfectly suited to the nooks and crannies of tropical reefs where it searches for its prey.

SAILFISH

Capable of speeds reaching 70 mph (110 km/h), this superbly streamlined fish is a game angler's favorite.

PORTUGESE MAN-OF-WAR

This dangerous jellyfish stings indiscriminately, secreting poison powerful enough to do serious harm to humans.

BLUEFIN TUNA

Closely related to mackerel, this tuna ranks among the largest of fish, reaching up to 12 ft (3.5 m) in length.

GREEN TURTLE

This huge, edible reptile lays hundreds of eggs on the seashore, then abandons its nest and returns to the ocean.

ELEPHANTS

Once all elephants were probably forest-dwelling animals, but today they have adapted to many different habitats. Wild African elephants are distributed throughout sub-Saharan Africa, inhabiting woodland, savanna, and forest.

The two varieties of African elephants are classed according to where they live: The savanna elephant is found mainly on the African plains and in savanna woodland, and the smaller forest elephant lives in the forests of West Africa and the Congo basin.

The North African Atlas elephant, which was once tamed for domestic use, has now disappeared. This was a version of the African savanna elephant and, it is supposed, the elephant that Hannibal used to cross the Alps.

Asian elephants range from Bangladesh to Bhutan, Cambodia, China, and India, and through to

DISTRIBUTION

KEY

AFRICAN ELEPHANT

ASIAN ELEPHANT

The elephant is found throughout the Old World tropics, though its numbers are much reduced. The African elephant, now limited to land south of the Sahara, is most common in East and Central Africa, though colonies exist in Angola, Namibia, and South Africa.

The largest populations of Asian species can be found in predominantly rural Myanmar (formerly Burma) and Thailand. Smaller scattered populations are found in south and Southeast Asia.

Mary Tracy/Jacana Ltd.

On the march: Sunlight breaks through the dense forest canopy as these Asian elephants go in search of food (left).

Indonesia, Laos, West Malaysia, Myanmar, Sri Lanka, Thailand, and Vietnam. Most live in forests, but some also live on plains and in marshes.

There are about 40,000 wild Asian elephants, although some countries have fewer than a hundred. In addition, about 14,000 to 17,000 domesticated elephants work in Asia, mostly in logging, in places where machines cannot easily go.

> THE SIZE OF AN ELEPHANT'S EARS REFLECTS ITS HABITAT: THE HOTTER THE CLIMATE, THE BIGGER ITS EARS, WHICH ARE BETTER FOR COOLING

Elephants need lots of living space because they only eat plants. Plants do not give as much energy as meat, so elephants have to graze over wide areas to find enough food for their needs. This is especially true in desert areas, where food is scarce.

The elephant is well adapted to survive in tropical climates. Its big ears have very fine veins, or capillaries, lying near the surface of the skin. The

HERD SIZE AND HABITAT

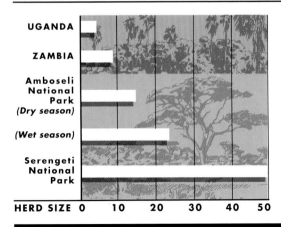

WOODLAND

SAVANNA

The size of an elephant herd is dependent on habitat. In general, the more fertile a habitat is, the larger the herd it can support. There are seasonal factors, too: Herds in Kenya's Amboseli National Park increase substantially in size during the more fruitful wet season.

HERD SIZE 0   10   20   30   40   50

UGANDA
ZAMBIA
Amboseli National Park (Dry season)
(Wet season)
Serengeti National Park

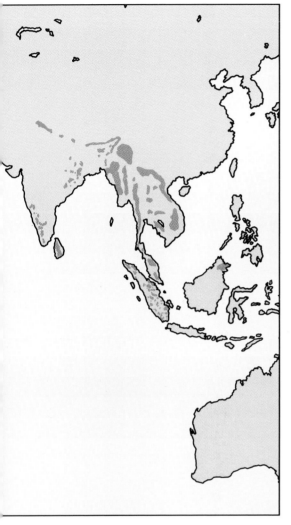

KEY FACTS

● In some areas of elephant habitat, the elephant's tree-destroying behavior allows sun-loving plants to flourish, thereby supporting a whole nonforest ecosystem.

● The baobab tree is richer in calcium and trace elements than any other tree. Only the elephant is capable of felling it.

● Elephants are found in climates with annual rainfalls ranging from 20–200 in (50 to 500 cm) and at altitudes ranging from 330 ft (100 m) to over 6,560 ft (2,000 m) above sea level.

all elephants carry seeds of their food plants to new places in their digestive systems. In fact, many tree seeds will not germinate, or begin to grow, unless an elephant has digested them first.

Elephants also improve their habitat for other creatures. Their trampling and rolling activities at water holes makes the holes stronger by compacting the walls, and the mud carried away on their bodies slowly enlarges the pools.

Where elephants have knocked down trees or dug to find minerals, the soil is loosened so that it can absorb the rain. In dry weather, elephants dig down to underground water supplies, which other animals can then use for drinking and bathing. ■

A herd of African elephants (below) passes through woodland savanna in front of the snow-capped peak of Tanzania's Mount Kilimanjaro.

blood passes through these capillaries and is cooled down as the elephant flaps its ears back and forth. This helps the animal regulate the temperature of its body. In general, the hotter the habitat, the bigger the elephant's ears—this is why the African elephant has larger ears than the Asian species. Elephants also cool down by splashing themselves with water and mud from water holes.

INTREPID TRAVELERS
Although they cannot jump or gallop, elephants are extremely agile and can travel across almost any terrain. These heavy animals can climb steep slopes and tackle mountainous areas with ease.

The elephant's walking pace is about the same as human's, but they can run at a speed of up to 30 mph (48 km/h) and, because of their great size, bushes and shrubs are no obstacle to them. Surprisingly good swimmers, elephants cross rivers and lakes using their trunks as snorkels.

Though they are insatiable foragers, elephants often improve their habitat and, through their everyday activities, aid plant growth. For example,

FRUIT BATS

Fruit bats are only found in the tropics of the Old World, from sub-Saharan Africa, through the Middle East, to the islands of the South Pacific, although the pollen- and nectar-eating species of bat are less widespread. However, within this area they are found in most habitats, including humid swamps, tropical islands, mountain slopes, and even in the homes of people. One of the reasons

---

AUSTRALIAN BIG-HEADED FLYING FOXES CAN MIGRATE UP TO 620 MILES (1,000 KM) IN SEARCH OF FOOD

---

for this is that fruit-bearing trees are common in tropical areas and rely on bats—along with other fruit-eating animals—to spread their seeds. And the lack of seasons in such areas means that there is a year-round food supply for the bats.

Another more obvious reason for their widespread distribution in the tropics is their ability to fly. Apart from birds, they are the only other vertebrates capable of sustained "true" flight. The earliest remains of fruit bats were, in fact, found in the southern parts of Europe. They then spread to Africa, Madagascar, the East Indies, and on through to the South Pacific. Their ability to fly

Straw-colored fruit bats, roosting in a treetop in Sierra Leone (right). Only large fruit bats do this, using their wings as protection from the elements.

in SIGHT

FRUIT BATS AND WATER

Fruit bats are often found near water. This is because large amounts of water are lost through evaporation from their wings and they must make up for that loss by having a readily available supply. Luckily bats are excellent swimmers, should they fall in, and are able to use their wings to push themselves along the surface.

Another benefit of being able to swim is that it allows the bats to grab fruit that falls into the water. However, they must always be on the lookout for crocodiles, which will not turn up their noses at such a tasty—and opportune—snack!

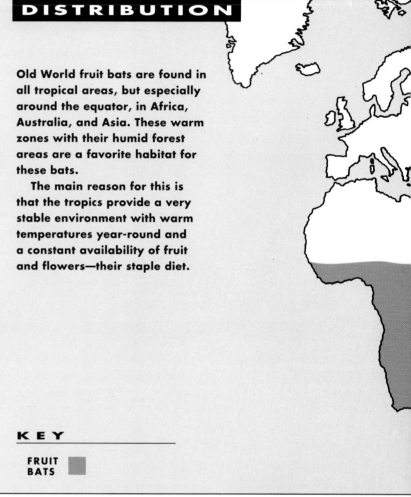

DISTRIBUTION

Old World fruit bats are found in all tropical areas, but especially around the equator, in Africa, Australia, and Asia. These warm zones with their humid forest areas are a favorite habitat for these bats.

The main reason for this is that the tropics provide a very stable environment with warm temperatures year-round and a constant availability of fruit and flowers—their staple diet.

KEY

FRUIT BATS ■

Nick Gordon/Ardea

● Some 70 percent of all the living species of fruit bat (over 200 species) are found in the tropical and subtropical areas of Southeast Asia and Indo-Australia alone.

● Old World fruit bats roost in trees and simply navigate by sight. The one exception is the rousette bat which roosts in caves and uses echolocation to move about.

● The larger flying foxes roost in exposed camps in trees, often stripping the leaves for improved visibility. They have no real natural enemies and use their wings against the elements.

Epauletted fruit bats in Africa hanging from wild gardenia (below). These shy creatures are only found singly or in small numbers.

long distances, coupled with the strong winds associated with the tropics, led to many bats being blown out to sea. Most would have perished, but occasionally some would have survived to colonize a new area.

But there are restricting factors to the range of the fruit bats, and one of these is their need for fresh water. Bats lose a lot of water through their wing membranes, especially in flight, so they must always have access to plenty of fresh water. They drink by flying down and dipping their mouths in water. But because larger fruit bats are less maneuverable in flight than smaller species, they need a reasonably large stretch of water to do this. Fortunately this is in abundance in tropical areas. ■

Peter Johnson/NHPA

GALAGOS

Galagos, pottos, lorises, and tarsiers are all adapted for lives spent sheltering in, and traveling around, trees and shrubs in the tropics. But between them, the various species show preferences for different types of habitat.

Some of the most elusive lorisids are virtually confined to closed-canopy primary rain forest, among them the needle-clawed galagos and the potto. Primary forests are those that have not been altered at all by man. Others prefer more open or modified habitats, though their habits still make them hard to find. Various races of the slender loris are associated with different forms of forest and woodland in India, including monsoon forests that shed much of their foliage in the dry season, and there is an especially thick-furred race that occupies cool, mountain forests in central Sri Lanka. The angwantibo of Africa is closely associated with natural forest clearings, where tree falls have opened up the canopy and there is plenty of dense undergrowth.

Tarsiers occupy a range of forest types in island southeast Asia, including primary rain forest, mangrove swamp, and thick scrub. The western tarsier seems to like secondary rain forest—that is, forest that has been partially cleared in the past by man and is in the process of regeneration. Compared with primary rain forest, such forest is characterized by

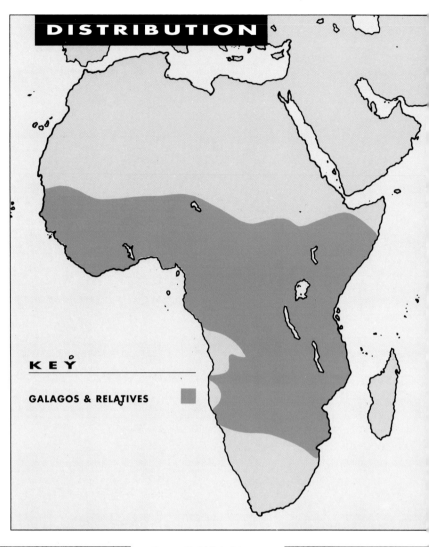

DISTRIBUTION

KEY

GALAGOS & RELATIVES

Nick Gordon/Survival Anglia

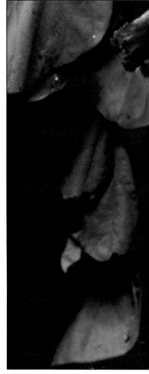

Pottos (left) inhabit the moist forests of equatorial Africa, where they share their home with the galagos.

No bigger than a man's hand, the dwarf galago (right) moves about by night, to avoid detection by the forest's predators.

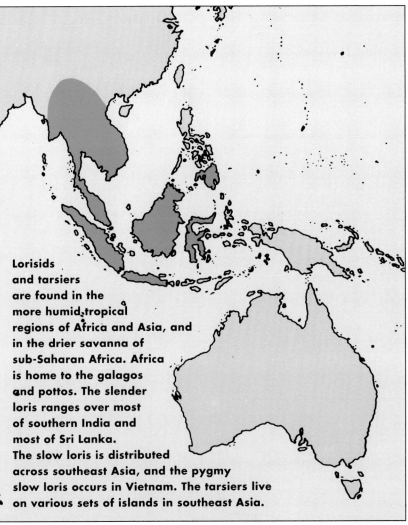

Lorisids and tarsiers are found in the more humid tropical regions of Africa and Asia, and in the drier savanna of sub-Saharan Africa. Africa is home to the galagos and pottos. The slender loris ranges over most of southern India and most of Sri Lanka. The slow loris is distributed across southeast Asia, and the pygmy slow loris occurs in Vietnam. The tarsiers live on various sets of islands in southeast Asia.

narrower, more closely spaced tree trunks. Similar habitats are provided by commercial plantations, and the western tarsier colonizes these, too.

Some widespread species of lorisids do not depend on forests and have consequently become more conspicuous. The lesser and the greater galagos of Africa—there are at least two species of both—are equally if not more at home in wooded savanna and dry bush, so long as there are enough trees or thickets in which they can take refuge and for them to avoid spending too much time crossing spaces at ground level. Of all the lorisids, these species are the most commonly seen. For lesser galagos, densities of up to 520 per square mile have been recorded in woodland savanna regions of East Africa, and in dense acacia thickets in South Africa the figure can reach 1,300. They can move easily among dense thorns, forbidding to most other mammals, and their orange eyes flash in car headlights on many an acacia-lined bush road.

These two groups of galagos are particularly hardy and adaptable compared to most other lorisids. Greater bush babies colonize pine, eucalyptus, and coffee plantations, and even appear in wooded suburban gardens. Their well-known wailing calls are probably the reason galagos gained their nickname of bush babies.

FINDING A NICHE

As well as occupying differing wooded habitats, lorisids and tarsiers also utilize habitats in different ways. Some species remain high up almost all of

Terry Mayes/Planet Earth Pictures

KEY FACTS

● With a head-and-body length of just 4.7 in (12 cm), dwarf galagos are among the world's smallest primates.

● Both galagos and tarsiers can leap several yards between the branches of trees. Tarsiers in particular can make giant leaps with seemingly little effort—jumps covering gaps of 20 ft (6 m) have been recorded. Lesser galagos can make upward leaps of up to 6.5 ft (2 m).

● Though they spend most of their time moving very slowly, pottos and lorises can sustain a faster pace for brief periods if they are forced to cross exposed passageways.

● Lorisids occasionally engage in serious fights if threat displays fail to sooth disputes. Greater galagos have been seen tumbling to the ground locked in combat.

● When fully extended, the powerful hind limbs of a tarsier reach almost twice the length of the animal's head and torso.

the time, in the dense tree crowns. This is the realm of the potto, which moves from outspreading branch to branch in the closed canopy searching for fruit and rarely descending to the floor. Tarsiers, on the other hand, spend much of their active time clinging to the lower portions of tree trunks, supported by their long fingers and bracing with the tail. Needle-clawed galagos are also adept at grasping trunks. Ridges in the center of their nails extend to form clawlike projections with which the animals can grip trunks too wide and smooth for other galagos.

Still other species live in the understory and in shrubs close to the ground. The angwantibo is the most restricted to this level. Adapted for clambering in dense vegetation over narrow stems and vines, it cannot climb trunks and larger branches and rarely crosses open ground.

Sleeping places also vary among the different species. Preferred sites for galagos and tarsiers may be within dense clumps of foliage, in the fork of a branch, in a tree cavity, or in an abandoned bird's nest. Some galago family groups build nests of leaves in these places. Pottos and lorises curl up hidden in dense foliage either in the understory or up in the canopy depending on where they feel most at home.

K. & K. Ammann/Planet Earth Pictures. Inset Ron Austin/Oxford Scientific Films

FOCUS ON

THE CONGO RAIN FOREST

Lorisids live in the rain forests of Africa and Asia. However, more species occur together in the equatorial rain forest of central Africa than in any other ecosystem. Here can be found dwarf galagos, needle-clawed galagos, Allen's galagos, and pottos, including angwantibos. The Congo rain forest is the most extensive of the regions of primary forest in Africa. A broad block of greenery 950 miles (1,500 km) long and 500 miles (800 km) wide around the mighty River Congo, it is watered by heavy rain for most of the year and bathed in tropical heat. There are several hundred tree species, among them ebony and mahogany, and some 400 types of orchid. Everywhere among the trees smaller plants take hold, among them ferns, lichens, figs, creepers, and vines. This mass of vegetation provides food and refuge for a fittingly diverse fauna.

The forest has no fewer than 700 species of ants. Even more numerous are beetles, which include the 4 in (10 cm) goliath beetle. Indeed, the African rain forest has more than its fair share of giants, including the largest land snail and the largest frog, along with outsized mantids, centipedes, millipedes, and flatworms. Other spectacular inhabitants include vipers, chameleons, hornbills, forest kingfishers, monkeys, leopards, and forest elephants.

RAIN FOREST LAYERS

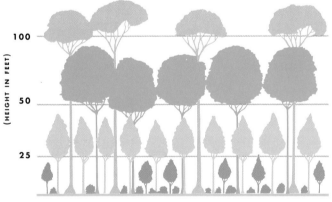

(HEIGHT IN FEET)

100
50
25

Rain forests comprise a number of vertical layers. The bulk of foliage is in the canopy. Above this stand a few very tall "emergent" trees, while directly below lies an "understory" of smaller trees with narrow crowns, palms, and shrubs. The ground cover of seedlings, herbs, and shade-tolerant plants is fairly sparse.

Differences in the ways in which animals utilize the same habitat for food and shelter make it easier for more than one species to live together without undue competition. This so-called "niche separation" is most marked in the rain forests of central Africa, where up to four species of galago may happily coexist—along with the potto and the angwantibo. Demidoff's dwarf galago, for example, generally keeps to the leafy cover of the tree crowns, while Allen's galago is largely active among ground vegetation. ∎

NEIGHBORS

The rain forests of central Africa are not as rich in species as those of Asia and South America, but nevertheless are home to a bewildering range of wild animals and luxuriant plant growth.

AFRICAN CROCODILE

Forest rivers are home for the dwarf crocodile, which has suffered greatly from hunting for its hide.

HIPPO

The hippo is primarily a savanna animal, but can be found in the Congo along rivers in forest clearings.

Illustrations Joanne Cowne/Cobra & Genet Edwina Goldstone

Rain forests in central Africa stretch several degrees north and south of the Equator, from Zaire, through the Congo, west to the Gabon coast. A narrower belt of rain forest continues, though patchily, along coastal West Africa as far as Sierra Leone.

GABON
CONGO
ZAIRE
Equator
Atlantic Ocean
ANGOLA

RAIN FOREST

FOREST HOG

The giant forest hog is the largest of the wild pigs. It roams around in family groups of up to twelve.

AFRICAN FISH EAGLE

This eagle often perches on a branch over a forest pool, and swoops to snatch fish with its fearsome talons.

COBRA

Known by their hooded head and deadly bite, cobras are common across much of Africa.

MANDRILL

The rain forest is home to the mandrill, its biggest and most bizarre monkey, with its vivid face mask.

GENET

A relative of the mongoose, the genet silently stalks its prey among the branches of rain-forest trees.

GAZELLES

These herbivores inhabit an astounding range of environments. Gazelles in particular span several climatic zones, from the southern tip of Africa, with its cool winters; across the forests, plains, and deserts of tropical Africa, North Africa, Arabia, and India; and into the arid steppes of China and Mongolia, where winters are bitterly cold.

Apart from the common duiker, which prefers bush and open woodland, all the duikers dwell in areas of dense cover—mainly forest, but also on wooded riversides, in thickets on savannas, and in tall grass. Several species, including the zebra duiker, Peter's duiker, and Abbot's duiker, occur in montane forest at altitudes of up to 12,800 ft (4,000 m). Some—including the white-bellied duiker, the black duiker, and the red-flanked duiker—prefer forest edges to the deep, dark interior of large forests, while the black-fronted duiker is found in swampy forests.

Among the dwarf antelopes, the royal and pygmy antelopes both inhabit lush forest habitats in Africa, while the suni lives in smaller forest and

Thomson's gazelle (below) is ideally suited to open plains, where its speed helps it escape predators.

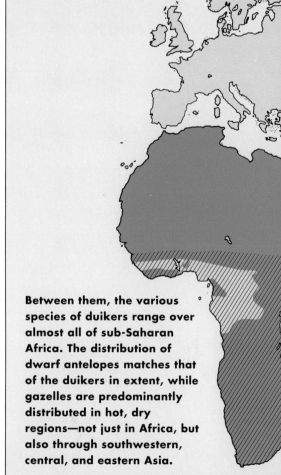

FOCUS ON

TSAVO NATIONAL PARK, KENYA

At over 8,000 sq mi (20,000 sq km) in area, Tsavo is Kenya's largest and wildest national park. Located toward the coast and bisected by the Nairobi–Mombasa railroad, the park is a dry, sparsely peopled wilderness, particularly toward the east. To the west, the plains are more dotted with low bushes, acacias, and baobab trees, framed against lines of rugged mountains. Yet everywhere the rich red soil shows through, not just on the ground but coating the hides of the park's elephant herds.

Here can be seen ostriches, buffalo, zebras, hartebeests, and warthogs, which all gather at dusk around water holes. The park is also a stronghold for the scarce gerenuk gazelle. Lions live here, along with leopards, genets, and mongooses. Verraux's eagles make breathtaking passes along stony crags inhabited by klipspringers, and the park's abundant bird life also includes several species of hornbills.

Between them, the various species of duikers range over almost all of sub-Saharan Africa. The distribution of dwarf antelopes matches that of the duikers in extent, while gazelles are predominantly distributed in hot, dry regions—not just in Africa, but also through southwestern, central, and eastern Asia.

Gerenuks (left) are fairly active throughout the day.

thickets outside the main rain-forest regions. Dik-diks favor fairly dry country with evergreen, shrubby ground cover. More open habitats with scattered trees and shrubs are home to the oribi, the steenbok, and the grysbok, while the beira dwells in dry, barren hills and mountains in the Horn of Africa.

The widespread klipspringer turns up almost wherever there are rocky outcrops with bushes as cover. It is well adapted for life among the rocks, cliffs, and massifs. Strong hind limbs help it negotiate slopes, and it can stand securely with hooves close together on tiny ledges. Its hoof tips wear down more rapidly on the inside, leaving ridges around the rim that give the animal better traction.

Gazelles are closely associated with open habitats such as savannas, steppes, and deserts, though Grant's gazelle may also be seen in lightly wooded country. Often their habitats have scant vegetation and stony or sandy ground. The relief is often hilly or mountainous, and the Tibetan gazelle occupies plateau land up to 19,200 ft (6,000 m) above sea level.

Several attributes fit gazelles for life in the bleak and open, including speed, stamina, and, for some, resistance to the cold. Perhaps their most impressive feature is their ability to withstand hot desert conditions. The slender-horned, dama, goitered, and dorcas gazelles all inhabit regions of the Sahara and Arabia, where they roam in search of plants. They conserve moisture by producing concentrated urine and dry feces and by minimizing sweating. When they need to cool off, they do so by panting through the nose with closed mouth—a process that wastes relatively little moisture. ∎

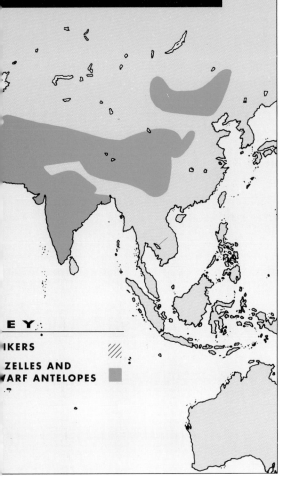

DISTRIBUTION

E Y

IKERS

**ZELLES AND
ARF ANTELOPES**

Unlike most gazelles, Grant's gazelle (below) often lives in wooded or marshy habitats.

Frank Schneidermeyer/Oxford Scientific Films

57

GIANT PANDAS & RED PANDAS

Szechwan, home to most of the giant pandas that survive today, is the largest and most populous province in China. Over 100 million people are concentrated in the low-lying plain, which has an area about the size of France.

The name Szechwan is Chinese for "land of the clouds." It is well named, for its lowlands are bordered by a dramatic landscape of cloud-enshrouded peaks and mist-filled, steep-sided river

---

THE PANDAS ARE JUST TWO OF THE MANY RARE SPECIES THAT SURVIVE IN THE REFUGE PROVIDED BY THE MOUNTAIN FORESTS OF SZECHWAN PROVINCE

---

valleys. The mountains, which form an almost complete ring, have existed for much longer than the Himalayas, far to the west across the great Tibetan Plateau. (Although they are the mightiest mountains on earth, the Himalayas are relative newcomers, being only about 50 million years old.)

MOUNTAIN RETREAT

During the last ice age, which was at its height about 18,500 years ago, Szechwan's ring of mountains prevented the southward advance of the great glaciers. Many species once widespread across northern Eurasia before the coming of the ice

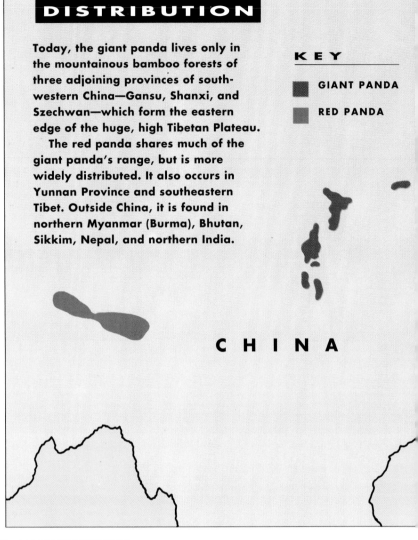

DISTRIBUTION

Today, the giant panda lives only in the mountainous bamboo forests of three adjoining provinces of south-western China—Gansu, Shanxi, and Szechwan—which form the eastern edge of the huge, high Tibetan Plateau.

The red panda shares much of the giant panda's range, but is more widely distributed. It also occurs in Yunnan Province and southeastern Tibet. Outside China, it is found in northern Myanmar (Burma), Bhutan, Sikkim, Nepal, and northern India.

KEY

■ GIANT PANDA
■ RED PANDA

CHINA

retreated there, surviving in the refuge created between the advancing walls of ice and the subtropical forests to the south. Others, such as pheasants, clouded leopards, and serows, were able to colonize the area once the ice sheets had retreated north with the warming of the climate, which occurred around 11 million years ago. In this way, a rich and unique mix of animals and plants came to thrive in the region.

VEGETATION ZONES

The giant panda's mountain habitat is divided into several vertical zones of vegetation, each with its own distinctive animal and plant communities. The zones are determined mainly by temperature, which drops by about 1.8°F (1°C) for every 330 feet (100 meters) increase in altitude. They are also dependent on latitude: the farther south you go, the

Michael Dick/Animals Animals/Oxford Scientific Films

This red panda (left) must remain alert to avoid the attentions of Szechwan's predators, such as weasels.

Timm Rautert/WWF/Bruce Coleman Ltd.

Liz & Keith Laidler/Wolfshead

flowers and ferns flourish.

At 1.5 to 1.75 miles (2,600 to 3,000 meters) there is a zone of almost pure conifers, mainly firs, which form a dense canopy. Here, a different slender-stemmed form of bamboo, also a favorite food of

The dense cover of the inaccessible mountainous forests of Szechwan (inset) provides a perfect hiding place for the giant panda (above). Researchers can spend months searching the panda's habitat without a single sighting.

GIANT PANDAS SPEND MOST OF THEIR TIME IN FORESTS THICKLY CARPETED BY MOSS, WHERE BAMBOO GROWS IN DENSE STANDS

pandas, makes up much of the understory. It forms thick stands and allows little chance for a variety of shrubs and flowers to grow, though rhododendrons are dotted about here and there. The ground is

higher up the mountain a particular zone is found.

On the lowermost slopes, below about 1.25 miles (2,000 meters), the land is cloaked with evergreen broad-leaved forest, containing trees such as oaks, birches, beeches, Chinese walnuts, maples, and poplars, though much of this has been cleared for agricultural land, which extends as high as 1.25 miles (2,000 meters) in some places. There is also, of course, a wide variety of bamboo species.

FOOD IN ABUNDANCE

At an altitude of 1.25 to 1.5 miles (2,000 to 2,600 meters) comes a mixture of broad-leaved and conifer forest. Deciduous maples, cherries, basswoods, and paper birches are mingled with coniferous evergreen spruces and hemlocks.

This is the zone of the most luxuriant bamboo growth, including the larger species, such as umbrella bamboo, that form the giant panda's main diet in spring. Away from the dense strands of bamboo, shrubs such as hazel and rhododendron grow beneath the trees, and numerous delicate

KEY FACTS

● **Bamboo is native to every continent except Europe and Antarctica. There are over 1,000 different species, of which 300—almost one-third of the world total—are found in China.**

● **Bamboo is the fastest-growing plant in the world. One stem in Kyoto, Japan, grew almost 4 feet (1.3 meters) in just 24 hours—an average of 2 inches (5 centimeters) an hour.**

● **Bamboo spreads so quickly and is so dense that it cuts off life-giving light to tree seedlings.**

thickly carpeted with moss and there are many fallen trees. This is where the giant and red pandas spend much of their lives.

Above the conifer zone, at up to about 2.5 miles (4,000 meters), there may be a scrub zone consisting of impenetrable rhododendron thickets, mixed with low-growing junipers and oaks.

AN UPWARD JOURNEY THROUGH THE BAMBOO FOREST'S VEGETATION ZONES REVEALS A CONSTANTLY CHANGING ARRAY OF PLANTS AND ANIMALS

Above this is the alpine meadow zone, containing rock and the small stones known as scree, interspersed with areas of grass. Covered with snow for more than six months of the year, it is transformed in spring, when a wealth of beautiful flowers bursts into bloom from the ground-hugging plants.

Finally, the tall mountaintops are forbidding,

FOCUS ON

THE BAMBOO FORESTS

The high mountain forests of Szechwan in southwestern China lie at the same latitude as subtropical Egypt or Florida, but the climate is very different. Although rainfall is not exceptionally high, the mountains are constantly damp, as clouds blanket the mountainsides.

Spring is the wettest season, though summer temperatures rarely rise above 50°F (10°C), and there are still frequent monsoon rains. Winters are long and cold, and temperatures drop well below freezing. Rivers are frozen and there is a thick blanket of snow from April to October.

The region is home to a large and unique community of animals and plants, isolated for millions of years by an almost complete ring of mountains.

Carnivores such as lynx, civets, and marten roam the forest, along with brown and black bears. Herbivores include the hardy sambar deer and three species of antelope. Rare plants, such as the gingko or maidenhair tree, are "living fossils," unchanged for 200 million years.

BAMBOO FEEDERS

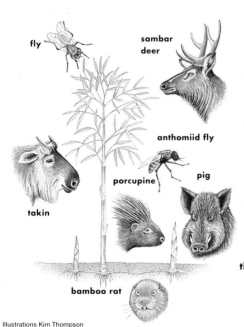

fly
sambar deer
anthomiid fly
porcupine
pig
takin
bamboo rat

Illustrations Kim Thompson

Although a number of creatures feed on bamboo, few eat it in sufficient quantities to threaten the panda's supply. Mammals such as the sambar and the takin feed on leaves, while pigs, porcupines, and other animals take the more nutritious option by feeding on bamboo shoots. Sometimes the flowers and shoots are destroyed by insects such as flies, which lay their eggs in them; anthomiid (an-tho-MIE-id) fly larvae make short work of the developing shoots. The only creature apart from the panda that is a specialist bamboo feeder is the bamboo rat, which feeds on stems and roots that it drags into its underground burrows.

desolate zones of rock and ice, almost permanently covered by a thick layer of snow.

There is a marked difference in animal life as one travels upward. For example, each species of pheasant, of which there is a rich variety, is restricted to a particular altitudinal zone. As one ascends the mountains, one first encounters the golden pheasant, then the white-eared pheasant, and, in the pure conifer belt, Temminck's tragopan. In the alpine meadows and up as high as the zone of perpetual snow lives the rare Chinese monal. ∎

NEIGHBORS

Along with the two panda species, Szechwan's mountainous bamboo forests are home to a wide range of animals —the greatest diversity of species to be found in a temperate latitude.

GOLDEN MONKEY

Named for its thick, glowing mane, this attractively colored monkey feeds on fruit, buds, bark, and lichens.

CLOUDED LEOPARD

A superb climber, the clouded leopard spends most of its life in the treetops. It feeds mainly on wild boar and deer.

Illustrations Rachel Taylor

Illustrations Chris Christoforou

Liz & Keith Laidler/Wolfshead

ENEMIES

MODERATELY DANGEROUS

DHOLE
Hunting in packs, these Asian wild dogs can easily kill young pandas and have even been known to attack and eat adults.

MODERATELY DANGEROUS

LEOPARD
Now rare in panda country, the few leopards that still survive present a threat to giant panda cubs and subadults.

GOLDEN PHEASANT

This distinctive and attractive bird lives alone or in pairs in rocky mountainous areas, feeding chiefly on plants.

SEROW

An aggressive member of the goat family, the serow is a surefooted animal, moving with agility on slippery rocks.

TAKIN

This large, heavily built goat antelope has an oily, shaggy coat, which protects it from the damp atmosphere.

GRASSHOPPER

A ground-dwelling insect, the grasshopper escapes predators by using its large hind legs to leap away.

GREEN TREE VIPER

A prehensile tail enables this snake to cling tightly to tree branches. Its prey includes frogs and small mammals.

GIRAFFES

Clem Haagner/Ardea

The giraffe and okapi occupy different areas of the African landscape, never crossing one another's path. The giraffe keeps mainly to the grasslands, although it ranges from those that are sparsely wooded to areas of more thickly overgrown scrubland or bush country. Very occasionally, giraffes are found at the edge of a forest, but they will venture into fairly dense vegetation only where it borders a river. Ill at ease in water, the giraffe stays clear of rivers—however shallow—so a stretch of water often marks the border of a home range.

There are two keys to a giraffe's environment: the presence of thorn acacia trees and firm ground. Acacia forms the giraffe's staple diet, and the trees grow up to elevations of about 6,600 ft (2,000 m). Firm ground is essential because—unlike its distant relative the camel, an even-toed ungulate that is well adapted to walking on soft, shifting sands—the giraffe's long legs have to support a relatively heavy body and the animal quickly becomes bogged down on soft or swampy terrain. Its enormous feet sink rapidly into soft ground, making movement difficult.

The giraffe is reasonably common south of the Sahara to eastern Transvaal, Natal, and northern Botswana, and it has been reintroduced to game reserves in South Africa.

 **S I G H T**

MUTUAL BENEFITS

The massive giraffe has one tiny but pernicious enemy—the troublesome tick that plagues it throughout its life. Its way of dealing with this is to stand over a 6-ft- (2-m-) high bush and rock itself backward and forward in an attempt to dislodge the ticks from its belly region, where the hair is at its thinnest. However, nature has provided another solution; oxpecker birds, also known as tick birds, are often seen perched on the backs and necks of giraffes, pecking at the ticks and other skin parasites—thereby gaining a tasty meal while fulfilling a much needed service to the giraffe. Such mutually beneficial relationships in the animal world are known as symbiotic partnerships. Besides ridding the host of the ticks, an oxpecker will also give an alarm call if a predator approaches.

K. & K. Ammann/Planet Earth Pictures

Animals converging on a drinking hole in the Etosha National Park, Namibia (above). The giraffe splays its legs awkwardly in order to reach the precious commodity. The elephant and ostriches will have no such problem.

A yellow-billed oxpecker helps itself to a meal of ticks (left), at the same time ridding the giraffe of an aggravating parasite.

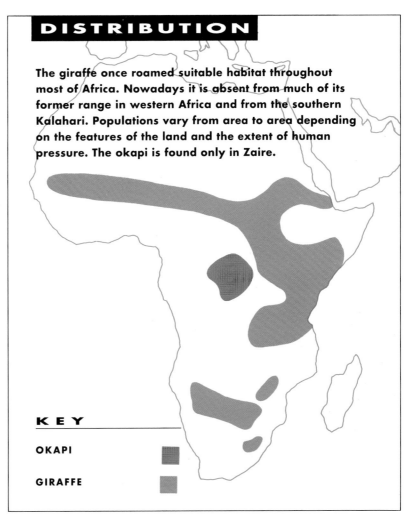

DISTRIBUTION

The giraffe once roamed suitable habitat throughout most of Africa. Nowadays it is absent from much of its former range in western Africa and from the southern Kalahari. Populations vary from area to area depending on the features of the land and the extent of human pressure. The okapi is found only in Zaire.

KEY

OKAPI

GIRAFFE

KEY FACTS

● At the end of the 1970s it was estimated that there were about 6,000 giraffes in some 5,000 sq mi (12,950 sq km) of the Serengeti.

● Some anthropologists believe that it was in the giraffe's homeland—the African savanna—that early man first adopted an upright stance. This enabled him to hunt more efficiently and to keep a lookout for predators above the tall grassland.

● The Serengeti is home to more than 100 species of mammals and some 200 species of birds.

● The acacia, one of the giraffe's favorite foodstuffs, is the most typical tree of the African grassland.

The okapi, on the other hand, lives only in Zaire, in the mixed forest belt of the northern, eastern, and southern Congo basin, bounded in the west by flood forest. Within the Ubangi, Uele, Aruwimi, and Ituri rain forests, it is found only at lowland depths, generally near streams and rivers. It tends to avoid very swampy areas, but it will splash across shallow water if need be. Within the dense, damp forests, it moves along regularly used, well-trodden paths, fleeing into the dense jungle at the least disturbance. With hearing the best developed of its senses, it quickly detects any danger.

HARMONIOUS GRAZERS

Not only does the giraffe share its environment with one of the richest diversities of animal wildlife to be found anywhere, but many of its fellow grassland dwellers are also hoofed animals—herbivores that could, therefore, compete with one another for available food. In fact, harmony reigns, for evolution has seen to it that the various species have different food preferences. The giraffe is exclusively a browser, plucking leaves from trees that are way out of reach of most other browsing animals.

Antelope and black rhinoceroses browse lower branches, while wildebeests and zebras—grazing animals—crop the grasses. Even at ground level, grazers feed on different types of grass, keeping competition to a minimum.

FORMIDABLE IN DEFENSE

The giraffe's great size, its superior eyesight (it has the greatest range of vision of any land animal), its surprising turn of speed, and the fact that its hooves are lethal weapons render it largely invulnerable to predators. The only time a healthy adult giraffe is at risk is when it splays its long forelegs by a watering hole to drink; then it is not unknown for a lion or even a crocodile to seize the opportunity to grab hold of the giraffe's head and strangle or suffocate it. While browsing, a group of giraffes is constantly alert, and if they spot a lion, they keep it in their field of vision, even moving around to insure it does not creep up on them unawares. A lion hesitates to attack prey that is aware it is being stalked.

If directly threatened, a giraffe kicks out with its legs to deliver a crushing blow capable, reportedly, of decapitating a lion. All its limbs make excellent defensive weapons, the hind feet delivering a conventional kick and the forelegs being used either to

give a forward chop-kick or a strike with the whole stiff leg. Calves are much more vulnerable than the adults and a considerable number are taken by lions, wild dogs, and hyenas. Young okapis fall victim to the golden cat, and also possibly to the shy serval, with which they share their forest environment. Only leopards are a threat to adult okapis.

Unlike many of the ungulates with which it shares its grasslands, the giraffe is not a migrant. Concentrations have been observed near rivers in the dry season, and their movement rarely exceeds a distance of 12–18 miles (20–30 kilometers). ■

FOCUS ON
THE SERENGETI

The Serengeti National Park is the largest and probably the best known of Tanzania's national parks. It is characterized by vast open plains, acacia and savanna woodland, and scrub areas, with tree-lined rivers and high rocky outcrops, and there is some swampy ground. There are two alkaline lakes in the south, which sometime dry up. In the wet season, their full waters attract a mass of waterbirds, including flamingos.

The Serengeti is home to the greatest concentration of game animals found anywhere in the world, including wildebeests, hartebeests, duikers, steinboks, gazelles, antelope, kudu, eland, buffalo, zebras, and rhinoceroses. There are all sorts of wildcats—the cheetah, caracal, African wildcat, serval, and leopard; above all, the Serengeti is renowned for its lion population. Visitors report seeing 40 or more lions in a day.

Many animals are migratory visitors, coming into the park when the seasonal rains have brought rich growths of short, succulent grass. The new growth is characterized by stems no more than 6 in (15 cm) long; it is particularly palatable to grazing animals. Naturally, the great droves of herbivores lured to this food also attract numbers of predators. Hyenas, for example, are common during the rains, but they tend to move on in search of other prey as the Serengeti dries out.

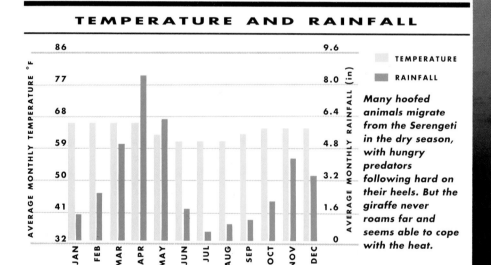

TEMPERATURE AND RAINFALL

Many hoofed animals migrate from the Serengeti in the dry season, with hungry predators following hard on their heels. But the giraffe never roams far and seems able to cope with the heat.

NEIGHBORS

The Serengeti is home to thousands of animals. Some of the hoofed species are annual visitors that take advantage of the lush grasses after the heavy rains.

GNU

Also called wildebeests, these grazing antelope flock to the Serengeti in thousands.

COBRA

Cobras are venomous snakes with front fangs. They are found all over Africa except in the Sahara

Illustrations Joanne Cowne. Elisabeth Smith: oxpecker, secretary bird, lion, and spotted hyena

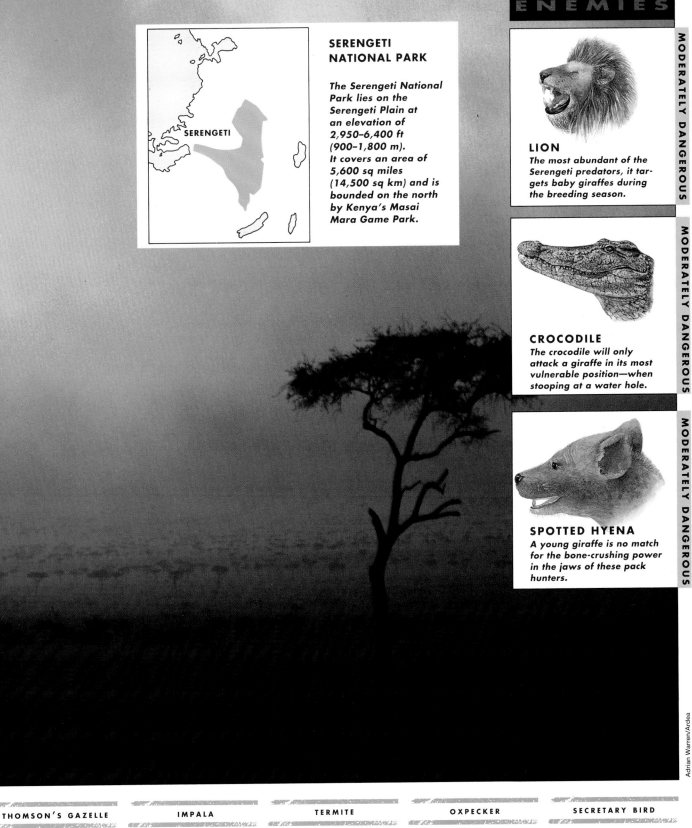

SERENGETI NATIONAL PARK

The Serengeti National Park lies on the Serengeti Plain at an elevation of 2,950–6,400 ft (900–1,800 m). It covers an area of 5,600 sq miles (14,500 sq km) and is bounded on the north by Kenya's Masai Mara Game Park.

SERENGETI

ENEMIES

LION
The most abundant of the Serengeti predators, it targets baby giraffes during the breeding season.

CROCODILE
The crocodile will only attack a giraffe in its most vulnerable position—when stooping at a water hole.

SPOTTED HYENA
A young giraffe is no match for the bone-crushing power in the jaws of these pack hunters.

MODERATELY DANGEROUS

MODERATELY DANGEROUS

MODERATELY DANGEROUS

Adrian Warren/Ardea

THOMSON'S GAZELLE
gile and graceful, this azelle is the favorite prey f many large predators, cluding lions.

IMPALA
Female impala live in large herds, accompanied by only one adult male. Young males often form bachelor herds.

TERMITE
The highly social termite is one of nature's great builders; its homes are often elaborate structures.

OXPECKER

This bird is a member of the starling family. It lives on a diet of insects that are parasitic on large mammals.

SECRETARY BIRD

This bird of prey feasts on snakes. Its scaly legs protect it from their bites.

GORILLAS

All three subspecies of gorillas live in the wet tropical forests of Africa. Within this environment, however, they exploit different habitat types. The mountain gorillas are restricted to semiopen forests on cool uplands, while the lowland gorillas, especially the western subspecies, have access to more dense forests.

LUSH LOWLANDS

The western lowland gorilla far outnumbers the eastern and mountain races and is correspondingly more widespread. It is, however, less well known in its habits. It has received a minimum of attention, at least when compared to the much-publicized events surrounding the work of Dian Fossey and other researchers among the mountain apes. The western race lives in the Central African Republic, equatorial Guinea, Gabon, and western Congo at least as far east as the Congo River. It also occurs in tiny, isolated areas of northwestern Cameroon.

This lowland distributional range constitutes a significant percentage of the Congo Basin—a vast area within which some four-fifths of Africa's tropical rain forests can be found. The moist jungles drain away into the mighty Ubangi and Congo Rivers, which reach the Atlantic coast at the northwestern

King of the hill: During mealtimes, the silverback often has first refusal of the choicest feeding spot.

Daniel J. Cox/Oxford Scientific Films

KEY FACTS

● The Parc des Volcans, which includes the southeastern sector of the Virungas, occupies only 0.5 percent of Rwanda's land area yet traps 10 percent of the country's total annual rainfall.

● In the Afro-alpine zone of the Virunga summits, giant plants abound. These include huge varieties of *Senecio,* which are tiny weeds in more temperate climates but reach heights of 20 ft (6 m) or more up on the volcanoes. They flower only once every ten to twenty years in the cold, wet climate.

● Mountain gorillas dislike crossing any watercourse larger than a stream. When forced to do so, they will either use any existing stepping-stones or even push tree ferns over to make a crude bridge. Lowland gorillas have no objection to water.

● The extinct crater of Mt. Visoke is now a lake, replete with alpine vegetation. The two newest volcanoes, Mt. Nyiragongo and Mt. Nyamuragira, are still intermittently active.

corner of Angola. Even today, access to the remotest parts of the Congo Basin is primarily up the rivers by boat, and the waterside vegetation is especially dense and primed with thorns. Here, too, lives the tsetse fly, a vector of lethal sleeping sickness. It comes as no great surprise, therefore, that humans had until fairly recently made few inroads on the western lowland gorilla's domain. The western lowland gorilla stays at altitudes no higher than about 6,000 ft (1,800 m), so its homeland is never too cold.

MOUNTAIN LIVING

Far away to the east, in and around the Great Rift Valley, can be found the other two subspecies. The Rift Valley is a series of ranges and depressions brought about by geological forces over the last 200 million years. There are two rifts—eastern and western. The former cuts through Ethiopia and Kenya and curls to a halt around Tanzania to the east of Lake Victoria. The western rift starts in the northwest of Lake Victoria on the Zaire-Uganda border, continuing south along Lakes Albert, Edward, Kivu,

Tanganyika, and Malawi (Nyasa) into Mozambique. Toward the northern end of this western rift, the Virunga volcanoes are strung across the valley to the north of Lake Kivu, forming a natural three-way border between Zaire, Rwanda, and Uganda.

Before the genesis of the Virungas, Lake Kivu drained northward via a river on the western Rift Valley floor. Then, maybe half a million years ago, the volcanoes started to erupt. The last two to emerge did so only 20,000 years ago. As the succession of craters spewed lava across the valley floor, they built up a huge dam some 1,800 ft (550 m) thick and 15 miles (24 km) wide. Prevented from draining, Lake Kivu's water level slowly crept about 400 ft (120 m) up the walls of the Virungas until finally, some 4,000 years later, it could drain south into Lake Tanganyika via the Ruzizi River.

The mountain gorilla is found today in two small islands of suitable habitat in the Rift Valley. These are the Virunga volcanoes themselves and the nearby Impenetrable Forest of Uganda. There are claimed sightings of mountain gorillas on the upper slopes of Zaire's Kahuzi-Biega National Park, northwest of Lake Kivu, but these are more likely to be eastern lowland gorillas.

The mountain gorilla's range has much to do with its diet. It has evolved to feed mainly on leaves—perhaps to avoid competition with its fruit-eating

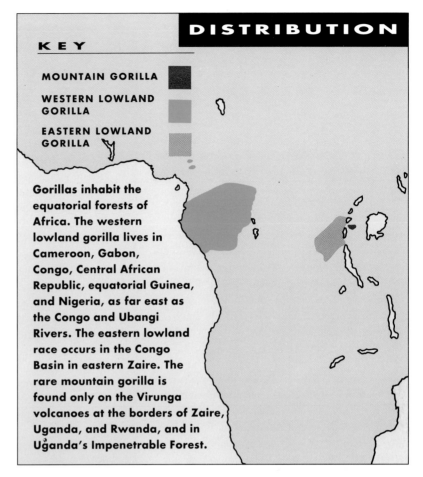

DISTRIBUTION

KEY

MOUNTAIN GORILLA

WESTERN LOWLAND GORILLA

EASTERN LOWLAND GORILLA

Gorillas inhabit the equatorial forests of Africa. The western lowland gorilla lives in Cameroon, Gabon, Congo, Central African Republic, equatorial Guinea, and Nigeria, as far east as the Congo and Ubangi Rivers. The eastern lowland race occurs in the Congo Basin in eastern Zaire. The rare mountain gorilla is found only on the Virunga volcanoes at the borders of Zaire, Uganda, and Rwanda, and in Uganda's Impenetrable Forest.

neighbor the chimp, or perhaps simply because the ecological niche presented itself. Whatever the origin of this diet, such food is scarce on the dimly lit floor of the densest primary rain forests—too scarce, at any rate, for a hungry group of heavy apes. The gibbons, by contrast, can manage very well in the lush evergreen rain forests of Asia, because they possess a winning blend of a compact, lightweight body and powerful forearms. These aerial acrobats swing hand over hand through the high canopy in search of ripe fruit, selecting fresh food trees at will. Not so the gorilla; although adventurous youngsters often take to the branches, such activity is unwise for a quarter-ton silverback. Therefore, gorillas stick to the habitat that offers the most abundant, easy-to-grasp supplies of food; in eastern Africa, this means secondary forest.

Secondary forest is that which has been partially cleared and has regenerated—unlike primary forest, which is wholly untouched, least of all by man. In some forests gorillas actually benefit by the consequences of human activity; where, perhaps, farmers once made a few clearings for crops or cattle but have long since left the area. In the absence of tall,

Gorillas thrive best in forests where sunlight can penetrate clearings to encourage ground cover.

shady old trees, sunlight reaches through and the undergrowth stakes its claim on the fertile soil, eventually becoming a supermarket of green fodder for the slow-moving leaf-eaters. In the eastern African mountains, fresh plant growth is generated through not only human inroads but also natural causes, such as volcanic activity, elephant damage, rockfalls, and the cyclical die-offs of the local vegetation, in particular the midslope bamboo forests. Coupled with all these agents is the pervading moisture on the high Virunga slopes.

EASTERN LOWLANDS

Ten times rarer than its western cousin, the eastern lowland gorilla occurs across a correspondingly smaller range. It lives in patches of lowland rain forest and in the western foothills of the Rift Valley, all within eastern Zaire. On Mount Kahuzi, it keeps to altitudes of around 6,560–8,200 ft (2,000–2,500 m), whereas mountain gorillas in the Virunga range live at altitudes of 9,200–11,150 ft (2,800–3,400 m).

If we were to track a gorilla group through the forest, there would be key signs to look for. Gorillas bulldoze, like elephants; they lumber ponderously through the undergrowth often in single file, leaving a trail of broken stems. Fronds and sprays of foliage are ripped or frayed where a huge hand has swiped

Steve Turner/Oxford Scientific Films

at a snack. There are circular nests on the ground or up in the trees—but these may not necessarily be recent, since such nests remain distinguishable for up to a year. A clear indication that gorillas have just passed by would be their smell—pungent, like human sweat. It is particularly noticeable when a male has been frightened, as glands in his armpits release the rank perspiration in an automatic fear reaction. Other key signs are the copious heaps of dung, with their distinctive three-lobed stools, littered at random along the way. ∎

FOCUS ON

THE VIRUNGA VOLCANOES

Rising to an altitude of 14,787 ft (4,507 m), the eight volcanoes of the Virunga range cannot quite match the 16,732 ft (5,100 m) of the Ruwenzori peaks to their north, but they have their own dramatic beauty. Like other African mountain ranges, they are an island haven for specialized, often unique plants and animals.

The lower slopes are clad in evergreen rain forest, where warthogs and bushbuck browse the vegetation. From an altitude of about 7,550 ft (2,300 m), bamboo thickets start to appear—these can grow to heights of 60 ft (18 m). Above the mixed bamboo and evergreen grow ancient forests of *Hagenia* trees. Around 50–60 ft (15–18 m) tall, the knotty boughs of this stocky species are draped in thick mosses and trailing lichens. Higher still lies a more open terrain scattered with huge heaths and lobelias. The bamboo and *Hagenia* forests are home to the mountain gorilla. On these subalpine slopes the atmosphere is thin, wet, and often freezing, but the ape has long, silky hair to fight the damp chill.

The entire Virunga range is now protected within national parks. Rwanda contains the Parc National des Volcans; Zaire holds the Parc National des Virunga; Uganda contributes the Kigezi Gorilla Sanctuary.

TEMPERATURE AND RAINFALL

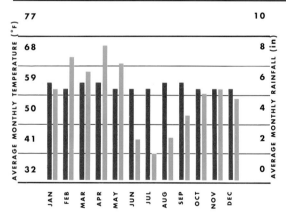

■ TEMPERATURE

▨ RAINFALL

Near the equator, lowlands remain warm throughout the year, but up on the high Virunga slopes it is often very cold and wet. Mean annual rainfall is 72 in (183 cm). There may be more than two hours of rain daily from October to December.

NEIGHBORS

The mammals of the Virungas include those that can live only in the forests and those that thrive also in open country. Some species have adapted biologically to suit the high-altitude climate.

BONGO

This forest antelope skulks among the bamboo, relying on its patterned coat to conceal it from view.

BUSHPIG

Bushpigs roam energetically through the forests in small bands, browsing on plants and foraging in the topsoil.

Neighbor illustrations Craig Robson/Wildlife Art Agency

THE VIRUNGAS

The Virungas lie strung across the Great Rift Valley at the northern tip of Lake Kivu, on the borders of Rwanda, Uganda, and Zaire. They are less than 125 miles (200 km) south of the equator. In Rwanda, the Virungas are officially protected within the Parc National des Volcans.

UGANDA

ZAIRE

RWANDA

Lake Kivu

PARC NATIONAL DES VOLCANS

RED COLOBUS MONKEY

p in the Virunga forests he red colobus grows an xtra-woolly coat to cope vith the cold conditions.

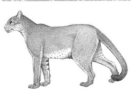

GOLDEN CAT

This cat preys on small mammals and birds in the forests and scrubland of West and central Africa.

CONGO PEAFOWL

This secretive cousin of the more familiar ornamental peacock was not known to science until 1936.

HAMMERHEADED BAT

Males gather at a lek to compete for mates. Their big heads naturally amplify their staccato mating calls.

CROWNED HAWK EAGLE

This supreme hunter can snatch monkeys from the forest canopy or swoop down upon duiker fawns.

GROUND-LIVING SQUIRRELS

Prairie dogs excavate their massive subterranean burrows in the open plains and plateaus in North America. Marmots also live mainly in the open habitats provided by steppes, alpine meadows, pastures, and some forest edges. Like prairie dogs, they spend most of their time underground. Their burrows are over three feet deep and up to 230–263 ft (70–80 m) long, although some hibernation burrows can be much deeper. Marmots are usually terrestrial, but occasionally they do climb into shrubs and trees, and the woodchuck, or groundhog, is known to be a good swimmer.

The woodchuck sometimes uses two sets of burrows. A winter burrow is often located on sloping ground in a wooded area, while the summer burrow is usually dug in a flatter, more open area, with a main entrance mound of freshly dug soil. The woodchuck has a different migration pattern than that of the prairie dog. In a more conventional style, it is the young woodchucks who migrate to establish their own home range when they are about three months old. They often dig temporary burrows within their home ranges and then, at a later time, head off to set up a permanent home.

In prairie dogs, however, it is the more experienced adults who migrate to new areas. The young remain in the burrows they know best. Quite often, the adults move to a territory that is already occupied, and in these cases it can take some time before they are accepted and able to establish themselves fully in the new home.

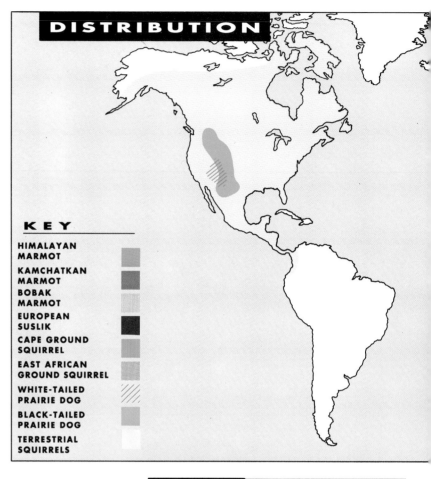

DISTRIBUTION

KEY

HIMALAYAN MARMOT	
KAMCHATKAN MARMOT	
BOBAK MARMOT	
EUROPEAN SUSLIK	
CAPE GROUND SQUIRREL	
EAST AFRICAN GROUND SQUIRREL	
WHITE-TAILED PRAIRIE DOG	
BLACK-TAILED PRAIRIE DOG	
TERRESTRIAL SQUIRRELS	

A white-tailed prairie dog (below) on sentry duty on the plains of its homeland in Wyoming.

KEY FACTS

● **The prairies and plains of North America once formed the greatest grasslands on Earth. They provided a source of food for an estimated 60 million bison, probably 50 million pronghorn antelope, and millions of elk and deer, as well as wolves and plains grizzly bears.**

Nowadays, cash-crop farming has completely changed the character of the Great Plains and of the animals that live there.

● **The Vancouver marmot is found only on tiny Vancouver Island, in British Columbia, Canada. It lives in forest clearings, high in the mountains above 3,300 feet (1,000 m).**

● **Menzbier's marmot is now restricted to very small areas of the Tian Shan Mountains of Uzbek and eastern Kazakhstan.**

Franz J. Camenzind/Planet Earth Pictures

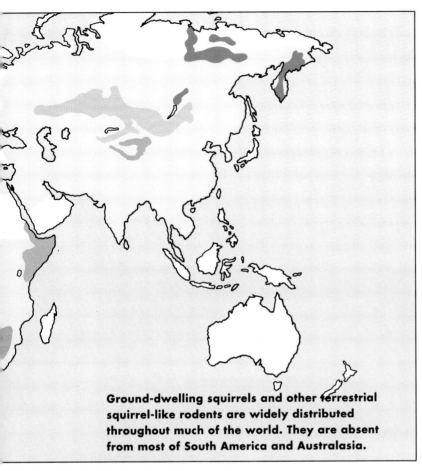

Ground-dwelling squirrels and other terrestrial squirrel-like rodents are widely distributed throughout much of the world. They are absent from most of South America and Australasia.

Anthony Bannister/NHPA

in S I G H T

ADAPTABLE RODENTS

Rodents have been successful because they are adaptable and opportunistic, exploiting almost any environmental condition to their own benefit. Rodents are an ancient order, with the oldest fossils being from the late Paleocene of North America some 50 million years ago. Many species have evolved from the original rodent design. Their ability to adapt in a number of ecological niches contributes to the fact that rodents are the most successful mammal order, representing over a third of all mammals.

The burrowing activity of ground squirrels and susliks can aerate and generally improve the condition of the land but may be a nuisance in an area where there is managed agriculture. The burrowing may even destroy or badly damage man-made irrigation channels. Other rodent activity can also be destructive: Chipmunks live in habitats where they can dig up newly planted corn seed in the spring and invade granaries in the autumn.

Rock squirrels are found only in China and comprise just two species, which some zoologists believe to be a link between the pouched chipmunks and the true squirrel species. Rock squirrels are

ROCK SQUIRRELS SHARE MANY OF THE CHIPMUNKS' BEHAVIORAL HABITS, ALTHOUGH THEY DO NOT HIBERNATE

extremely agile. They live on rocky, shrubby mountain cliffs, where they nest in crevices, and avoid dense forest habitats. Although they can climb trees, they prefer to move around in rocky terrain. They occasionally enter areas of human settlement in order to find food.

The Barbary ground squirrel inhabits Morocco and Algeria and was recently introduced on Fuerteventura, one of the Canary Islands. It is usually found in rocky areas, where it rests in its burrow, out of the hot midday sun. It emigrates to new regions when its population rises to a level that cannot be supported by the local habitat.

A Cape ground squirrel (left) uses its tail as a parasol to deflect the searing heat of the midday sun in Africa's Namibian desert.

Similar squirrels are found elsewhere in Africa but represent a different genus, *Xerus*. There are four species of African ground squirrels, and between them they inhabit Sudan, Tanzania, Morocco, Mauritania, Senegal, Kenya, Namibia, Botswana, Zimbabwe, South Africa, and Angola. These squirrels live in open woodland, grassland, or rocky country and dig burrow homes.

The long-clawed ground squirrel is found only in Soviet central Asia, near the Caspian Sea, and in northern Afghanistan and Iran. This species lives in small family groups in sandy deserts, where it digs its burrows among brushy vegetation. It will travel over half a mile (1 km) if there is little food to be found near its home, but it saves most of this activity for cooler periods of the day.

Western pocket gophers of the genus *Thomomys* are found in Canada and western and central North America. Eastern pocket gophers, genus *Geomys*, are found in central and eastern North America. *Thomomys* species inhabit areas with many soil types, from sea level to altitudes of about 13,000 ft (4,000 m). These areas include deserts, prairies, meadows, and open forests. *Geomys* species prefer loose and sandy soil in open or sparsely wooded regions, but gopher tunnels do cause soil

erosion on hillsides in these favored areas. Where the eastern pocket gopher lives in farmland, it often damages crops, either by feeding on them directly or by covering the plants with its mounds.

Taltuzas (genus *Orthogeomys*) and the single species of tuza, *Zygogeomys trichopus*, are found only in Mexico and Central America. Taltuzas inhabit a variety of terrains, from arid tropical lowlands to mountain forests at altitudes of around 10,000 feet (3,000 m). The tuza has a more restricted habitat. It lives in areas of deep, soft, and yielding soil in conifer forests that are located at altitudes above 7,000 feet (2,200 m). ■

FOCUS ON

THE GREAT PLAINS

To the west of the Appalachian mountains, there is an extensive eastern forest dominated by broad-leaved, deciduous trees. Beyond this to the west, the forest originally merged into prairies that were dominated by plants and grasses such as big bluestem and Indian grass. These have been replaced to a great extent by corn and soybean fields planted in recent times by humans. These tall-grass prairies change to mixed-grass prairies as one moves farther west because of the effects of lower rainfall.

Eventually these change to short-grass plains, which stretch to the Rocky Mountains. The plains are covered by buffalo grass and little grama grass. The short-grass plains were the home of the vast bison herds that were devastated by settlers' hunting and by the use of the land for grazing livestock. One of the few places left to see the original prairie plants is alongside railroads that cut through the original vegetation.

Escape from predators on these open grasslands is difficult for small mammals. Animals such as the prairie dog use burrows to avoid the coyotes, eagles, buzzards, and foxes that are their natural predators. The burrowing owl, too, nests in the prairie dogs' burrows because of the lack of suitable sites above ground.

TEMPERATURE AND RAINFALL

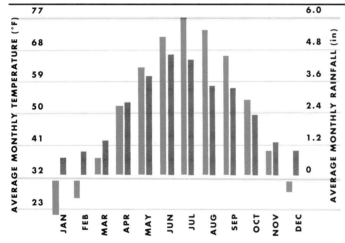

TEMPERATURE

RAINFALL

The eastern third of the Great Plains has about 30 in (76 cm) of rain each year. Farther west the rainfall drops, and the vegetation is lower in growth. Temperatures on the Plains can vary by more than 144°F (80°C) throughout the year.

NEIGHBORS

The Great Plains are rich feeding grounds for many herbivores, from the tiny prairie dog to the massive bison. Like all grazers, these animals attract predators, too.

BISON

Vast herds of bison once roamed the prairies but were exploited to near extinction.

INDIGO SNAKE

This nonpoisonous snake of North America is a lustrous blue-black in color.

Illustrations Joanne Cowne

ALBERTA TO TEXAS

The plains of North America now occur in patches, but the extent of potential grassland is much the same as it was before the railroads were laid. It stretches from Saskatchewan, Alberta, and Manitoba in the north, to Texas in the south, and from the eastern foothills of the Rockies in the west to Wisconsin and Illinois in the east.

ENEMIES

COYOTE
This versatile predator still thrives despite years of persecution. It eats mainly rodents and rabbits.

GOLDEN EAGLE
The golden eagle is found in America, Europe, Asia, and the Mediterranean. It eats mammals, birds, and snakes.

LEAST WEASEL
This weasel is found in woodland and farmland in North America, where it preys on rodents.

EXTREMELY DANGEROUS · EXTREMELY DANGEROUS · MODERATELY DANGEROUS

Photograph Leonard Lee Rue/Bruce Coleman Ltd.

COTTONTAIL

...ere are several American ...bbit species. The desert ...ttontail is a typical ...xample of a plains rabbit.

SWIFT FOX

This rare, cat-sized fox lives on the western plains. It can run fast and sometimes preys on prairie dogs.

BURROWING OWL

American burrowing owls often nest in old prairie dog burrows on the Great Plains.

PORCUPINE
The North American porcupine keeps mainly to the forests, but it ventures to grassy areas in summer.

GRAY FOX

This short-legged fox is a skillful tree-climber. It is a wily and elusive farmland predator.

HAMSTERS

The first hamsters probably originated in eastern Europe or western Asia. With the arrival of humans they were able to follow the spread of agriculture across Europe, as far west as Belgium and east into Russia. Although improved and mechanized farming methods are now destroying much of their natural habitats, hamsters are prolific breeders, and their survival is not yet threatened.

Hamsters generally live in areas with plenty of dry, sandy soil or clay, which they can dig through without too much effort. They often dig their runways through the complex systems of meadow plants' roots, ensuring greater stability. Hamsters

Raimund Cramm GDT/Bruce Coleman Ltd.

LIKE MANY RODENTS, FEMALE HAMSTERS WILL EAT YOUNG THAT DO NOT SURVIVE

---

are also found in grassy and cultivated land, and on lowland hills where they can survive at altitudes of over 1,968 ft (600 m).

Common hamsters were once found in abundance throughout central Europe, as well as parts of the former USSR. However, improved agricultural techniques that can damage and destroy their burrows, as well as the increasing need for more land to grow crops, have significantly reduced their numbers. Fortunately, they are still

P. Morris

The common hamster (above) was once plentiful throughout central Europe.

Dormice (left) are agile climbers and spend most of their time in the branches of trees.

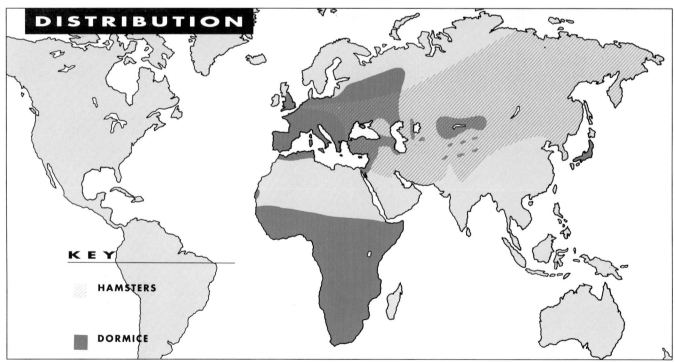

DISTRIBUTION

KEY

HAMSTERS

DORMICE

THE HAMSTER'S BURROW

Characteristics vary from species to species. Food supplies are usually stored in dead-end tunnels or widened areas. Some hamsters will build several food-storage burrows separate from their main living quarters. The amount of food stored also varies. Striped hamsters store about 7 oz (200 g), while migratory hamsters store 14–18 oz (400–500 g). Some species of ratlike hamsters take in large amounts of winter supplies, such as potatoes and soybeans that have been looted from nearby farms.

Angela Hargreaves/Wildlife Art Agency

KEY FACTS

● Hamsters belong to the largest order of mammals—the rodents. In total, there are nearly 2,000 separate species in this order, including lemmings, rats, voles, and gerbils.

● Despite the fact that they are called fat dormice, these athletic creatures are able to leap distances of up to 33 ft (10 m). The fat dormouse was introduced to England in 1902 by Lord Rothschild.

● During mating, common hamsters can emit high-pitched squeaks that cannot be heard by humans.

● A small number of golden hamsters were brought into the United States as laboratory animals in 1938, and by 1950 it was estimated that there were over 100,000 of them kept as pets.

● When hibernating, dormice sleep so soundly that they can be picked up and rolled across a table without waking up. This feature earned them their name from the French or Latin *dormire*, which means to sleep.

able to thrive in pastures, steppes, and along riverbanks. One naturalist noted how the common hamster was abundant in fields of lucerne in central Germany. This was because lucerne grows rapidly—within eight to ten days after the last crop has been mowed, a new crop has already become thick, providing the hamsters with constant cover. Lucerne also grows in dry habitats, and its green plant material is particularly rich in vitamins and minerals, so the hamsters can take advantage of a nourishing supply of food in autumn and spring when food is lacking in other fields. Plots of lucerne were found to have three times as many burrows as did neighboring fields of grain.

Other hamsters, on the other hand, remain true mountain animals, frequenting dry areas at the foot of mountains up to heights of 13,124–16,494 ft (4,000–5,000 m) and in belts of evergreen trees. Like most other hamsters, they avoid moist areas and areas built up by man. One exception is the Chinese ratlike hamster, which has been found living near moist meadow bogs.

Golden hamsters, which frequent desert regions (see right) where water is scarce, are able to survive by drinking tiny droplets of dew that form in the early morning. With the variation in temperature, some moisture from the air collects as dew, even when there is no rain. This is supplemented by what little moisture they get from their food.

Another species that is found in semidesert regions is the dwarf hamster, which has a particularly

---

IN MANY FARMING REGIONS HAMSTERS ARE REGARDED AS PESTS BECAUSE OF THE DAMAGE THEY CAUSE TO CROPS

---

good camouflage coloring that helps it blend in with the desert.

TERRAIN

The type of terrain often dictates how burrows are built. In central Europe, hibernating hamsters usually dig burrows in flat fields, keeping a good distance between each one. In some foothill regions of Asia, however, hamsters have been observed building burrows in groups on southeasterly slopes. The dense crowding is not due to a tendency to live

Gunter Heil/ZEFA

together in colonies, but to the limited number of sites suitable for burrow construction.

The natural habitat for dormice is in mature forests and rocky places. However, several species have been able to adapt to life in parks and gardens. They are found in most of Europe, through Asia, and into Russia. Dormice are becoming increasingly rare in the wild as their woodland homes are destroyed by deforestation. Some species, however, have benefited from human encroachment, stealing stored apples, plums, and other varieties of nourishing fruit. ∎

FOCUS ON
THE SYRIAN DESERT

Hamsters are remarkably adaptable animals, capable of living in extreme conditions. The golden hamster has adapted to life in the Syrian Desert. As in all desert habitats, temperatures vary widely from day to night and the hamster must be able to cope with both the extreme heat of the desert sun and the dramatic drop in temperature at night.

During the day, golden hamsters avoid the extreme heat by sleeping in their burrows. They dig down to a depth of about 39 in (99 cm), insulating themselves against the high surface temperatures. In this way they avoid dehydrating in the heat of the day.

In the desert, nighttime temperatures fall dramatically as there is no cloud cover to keep the heat in. As the temperature drops in the evening, golden hamsters emerge from their burrows to search for food. Here, once again, the desert is an inhospitable place and food supplies are scarce. The golden hamster's main diet consists of dry seeds that it sifts from the desert soil. It supplements its diet with green plants, whenever these are available, and may also feed on insects.

Hamsters travel long distances at night, gathering food in their cheek pouches for storage in their burrow. By storing food in times of relative plenty, golden hamsters are able to regulate their food supply.

TEMPERATURE AND RAINFALL

AVERAGE MONTHLY TEMPERATURE (°F)

AVERAGE MONTHLY RAINFALL (in)

■ TEMPERATURE
▨ RAINFALL

95 — 2.8
86 — 2.4
77 — 2.0
68 — 1.6
59 — 1.2
50 — 0.8
41 — 0.4
32 — 0

JAN FEB MAR APR MAY JUN JUL AUG SEP OCT NOV DEC

Summer temperatures in the Syrian Desert reach an average peak of 91.4°F (33°C) in July. From June to the end of September rainfall is virtually nonexistent.

NEIGHBORS

Hamsters share their desert terrain with a contrasting and colorful assortment of creatures that range from the camel and brown hare to the predatory scorpion.

CAMEL

Camels are supremely well adapted to life in the desert, being able to conserve water and food.

BROWN HARE

This species is related to the jackrabbits of the western United States.

Illustrations Kim Thompson

SYRIA'S DRY WILDERNESS

The Syrian Desert (Badiet esh Sham) lies to the east of the Ghab Depression, an extension of the Great Rift Valley. The main fertile areas in Syria—where most of the population is concentrated—are the coastal strip and the basin of the River Euphrates.

SYRIAN DESERT

GRAY WOLF
The wolf is a social animal and lives in packs. It will dig hamsters out of their burrows.

STRIPED HYENA
This mainly nocturnal carnivore lives in northern Africa and southern Asia from Turkey to India.

COMMON KESTREL
The kestrel hunts rodents, frogs, and small birds. It hovers in the sky, before diving onto its prey.

EXTREMELY DANGEROUS

MODERATELY DANGEROUS

MODERATELY DANGEROUS

Illustrations Kim Thompson

Inset picture P. Morris

FAT-TAILED SCORPION

ne of the most venomous orpions in the world, it eds on other vertebrates and lizards.

SOUSLIK

This squirrel feeds mainly on seeds, which it carries in its cheek pouches. It hibernates in the winter.

DESERT EAGLE OWL

Found in the northwest part of the North African desert, these birds are small and pale.

MONGOOSE

Most mongooses are carnivorous, but supplement their diet with plant material.

IBEX

Ibexes, wild goats capable of withstanding the harsh environment, can eat the toughest of browse.

HEDGEHOGS

Hedgehogs occupy a wide variety of habitats and can be found in the forests, plains, and deserts of Europe, Asia, and Africa. One species also occurs in New Zealand, introduced there by settlers in the last century, though there are no hedgehogs in Australia or the Americas.

THE EUROPEAN HEDGEHOG HAS ADAPTED
WELL TO THE CHANGING LANDSCAPE AND
IS ONE OF THE FEW MAMMALS TO THRIVE
IN AN URBAN ENVIRONMENT

Some species, such as long-eared and desert hedgehogs, have adapted to the hot and arid regions of Asia and North Africa. Others, such as the species found in western Europe, were originally animals of the deciduous woodland, and are scarce or absent in areas of mountain, moorland, and marsh.

WELL ADAPTED

Although much of Europe's deciduous woodland has been lost to cultivation, the European hedgehog has adapted well to the changing landscape and now frequents farmland and hedgerows. It is one of the few mammals that seem to thrive in urban habitats, inhabiting parks and gardens, even ones deep in the heart of cities.

Unlike many mammals, hedgehogs are also found in Ireland and on many of the offshore islands of Britain and Europe, though few of these can have

DISTRIBUTION

The European hedgehog inhabits woodland, grassland, and hedgerows throughout the British Isles and most of Europe, into Russia, around the Black Sea, in eastern China, and in New Zealand, while the Algerian hedgehog is found along the hot, dry Mediterranean coast of North Africa. The African species are found throughout much of Africa and the Middle East into Afghanistan and Pakistan and the long-eared hedgehog in desert and scrub throughout the Near and Middle East, southwestern Asia, across Russia, Mongolia, and China. Tenrecs can be found in Madagascar.

KEY

- EUROPEAN HEDGEHOG
- ALGERIAN HEDGEHOG
- AFRICAN HEDGEHOGS
- TENRECS
- LONG-EARED HEDGEHOG

been colonized naturally. It is much more likely that they found their way there by accident, scooped up with loads of thatching, peat, or animal fodder—though in some cases the animals were introduced deliberately to islands.

EXPANDED HABITAT

The territory of the closely related eastern hedgehog overlaps with its western European neighbor's along a rough line drawn from the Baltic to the Adriatic. Its range then extends into the steppes and forested plains of the east. In recent times it, too, has expanded its habitat to include cultivated land, villages, and towns.

In contrast to the wide distribution of hedgehogs, all the thirty-two species of tenrecs come from

Ashod Francis Papazian/NHPA

This long-eared hedgehog (left) lives in Syria and, to protect itself from the heat in summer, digs a burrow to provide a cool daytime resting place.

The European hedgehog (above) has a variable gestation period, which may be because of the unpredictable weather: A cold spring could lead to a food shortage and thus to the slower development of the embryo.

Madagascar alone, although the common tenrec has also been introduced to other islands in the Indian Ocean. Tenrecs occupy widely divergent habitats including both evergreen and deciduous forests, streams, rivers, and lakes.

HEDGEHOGS LIVING IN COOLER CLIMATES NEED NOT ONLY A WARM, SAFE PLACE FOR HIBERNATION, BUT A COOL NEST TO REST IN DURING HOT SUMMER DAYS

The aquatic tenrecs like fast-flowing freshwater streams and rivers, and are often closely associated with the iris plant. The rice tenrecs also tend to be found near water, particularly rice paddies (hence their name), freshwater streams, and large lakes. Most of the long-tailed tenrecs are confined to moist, forested areas. The common tenrec can tolerate a variety of habitats, both moist and dry, while the

lesser hedgehog tenrec is adapted to the dry southwest of Madagascar. Streaked tenrecs live in the moist lowland forests of eastern Madagascar.

Hedgehogs often build nests in hedgerows, clumps of vegetation, or piles of leaves where they rest during the day. Secluded places that provide shelter and warmth, such as dense vegetation, are vital in cooler climates because hedgehogs must hibernate in order to survive the winter cold.

COPING WITH THE CLIMATE

Elaborate nests are less important during the summer months, though females construct a large "nursery nest" for their families. If the weather is warm, hedgehogs may just rest in suitably thick vegetation or under a bush and not bother to build

KEY FACTS

● Long-eared and desert hedgehogs must avoid the heat of the day; they use their powerful legs and claws to dig burrows 16–20 in (41–51 cm) deep for a cool, moist resting place.

● Male hedgehogs, with their larger home ranges, travel farther and faster than females, sometimes as far as 2 miles (3 km) a night.

● The shrew hedgehog lives in cool, damp Far-Eastern forests at altitudes of over 6,560 ft (2,000 m).

a nest at all. So a good supply of leaves from deciduous trees is essential for survival in winter. Where there are no broad leaves there are rarely hedgehogs—so it is probably for this reason that they are rare or absent on mountains and in moorland and marshland.

> ONE ESSENTIAL FOR HEDGEHOG WINTER SURVIVAL IS A GOOD SUPPLY OF LEAVES SUITABLE FOR MAKING A NEST

Hedgehogs are not strictly territorial. The free availability of their food means that they do not need to defend a supply area. However, they often fight if they do meet, one animal attempting to butt another and bowl it over—which suggests that they do have some sort of social hierarchy.

Many hedgehogs tend to forage for food in the same area night after night. In males, the home

FOCUS ON

ENGLISH SUBURBAN GARDEN

Hedgehogs are familiar nighttime visitors to gardens, attracted by a diverse habitat which often contains a greater concentration of insects than nearby fields and woods. Foraging in a smaller area saves the hedgehog precious energy.

For instance, an English suburban garden may have flower beds in one place, long grass in another, and a compost heap teeming with insects. The nooks and crannies often found beneath a garden shed provide warmth and shelter: the perfect site for a hedgehog's daytime nap.

However, gardens are not without their perils. Many hedgehogs die in burning piles of refuse, drown in garden ponds, or are killed when the long summer grass is mown.

A NIGHT'S WANDERINGS

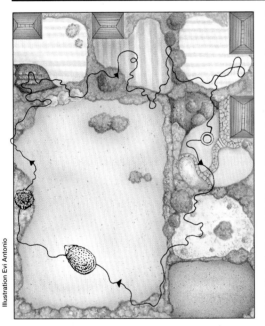

Illustration Evi Antonio

Hedgehogs are creatures of habit and return to the same foraging grounds night after night, covering a much broader territory than is usually imagined. On a typical night, a hedgehog will leave its nest at twilight and set out to visit as many different food sources as possible. These may include vegetable patches, orchards, woods, gardens, hedgerows, ponds, fields— and even houses in the hope of a saucer of food. The males range farther than the females—up to 2 miles (3 kilometers) from their starting point—and are less likely to return to their original starting point than to build another day nest elsewhere.

range is around 60 acres (about 20 to 30 hectares). This overlaps the ranges of several females, which are only around 25 acres (10 hectares).

With their larger home ranges, males are able to travel further and faster than females and, because of this extended traveling, male hedgehogs often do not return to the nest where they spent the previous day.

The size of the hedgehog's home range usually depends on the habitat: Hedgehogs in woodland areas move about less than those inhabiting more open places such as fields and parkland. ∎

NEIGHBORS

A surprising variety of wildlife shares the hedgehog's garden habitat. All of these creatures depend to some degree on the artificial environment created in towns and cities.

GRAY SQUIRREL

The town-dwelling squirrel eats nuts, bark, leaves, and roots but will also happily raid bird feeders and garbage cans.

EURASIAN ROBIN

In spite of its small size, the robin is fearless and will search for food in close proximity to people.

Illustrations Chris Christoforou

ENEMIES

MODERATELY DANGEROUS

RED FOX
Foxes hunt or scavenge at night, eating everything from hedgehogs to discarded human food.

EXTREMELY DANGEROUS

EUROPEAN BADGER
The powerful badger's sharp claws and pointed teeth can neatly peel a hedgehog.

Stephen Dalton/NHPA

TOAD
he toad is a nocturnal reature and has adapted to garden environment, even reeding in garden ponds.

WOOD LOUSE
The wood louse lives in dark, damp places—under logs and stones—where it feeds on rotting wood and leaves.

TAWNY OWL
The tawny owl is a nocturnal hunter, with sharp eyes in the dark, good hearing, and soft wings for silent flight.

RABBIT
With its diet of grasses, herbs, shrubs, and roots, the rabbit crosses easily from meadowland to gardens.

PEACOCK BUTTERFLY
The peacock butterfly feeds on the nectar from buddleia flowers and hibernates in garden sheds.

HIPPOPOTA-MUSES

U p until two centuries ago, hippos existed in suit-able habitats throughout Africa from the Nile delta south to the Cape. Their one essential require-ment being water, they have never inhabited the Namib Desert of southern Africa. There is some evi-dence, however, that populations once existed in the central Sahara and on the Moroccan coast.

Nowadays their range has contracted, and from a once-solid distribution they have been parceled up into thousands of isolated populations. There are vir-tually no hippos left in north Africa, or south of the Zambezi in southern Africa. Their distribution in West Africa is reduced, although a number of healthy populations exist in Guinea, Togo, and Benin.

Pygmy hippos have probably never been wide-spread, dependent as they are upon equatorial rain forests. Their stronghold is Liberia, but there are also fragmented populations in Guinea, Ivory Coast, Sierra Leone, and, possibly, Nigeria and Guinea Bissau. In the case of both species, geo-graphical distribution is very difficult to determine: Hippos move around a great deal, and pygmy hip-pos hide in the forests.

Richard Packwood/Oxford Scientific Films

HIPPOS ARE FOUND IN GREATEST DENSITY ALONG WINDING STRETCHES OF SMOOTH-FLOWING RIVERS WITH DEEP POOLS

An ideal habitat features rivers or lakes with firm, shelving borders, where hippos can kneel or stand in near-complete immersion. Gently sloping riverbanks also enable baby hippos to suckle in comfort. Fertile grazing pastures, or "hippo lawns," should be within easy strolling distance of the water. They like to wallow in company during the day; this requires space, and they therefore avoid thickly forested banks or stands of dense, high reeds, where space is limited. They will, how-ever, resort more frequently to thickets in areas where they are disturbed excessively by humans.

Hippos are found at altitudes of up to 6,560 ft (2,000 m), and even on seacoasts. Populations also exist on two islands, Mafia and Zanzibar. Hippos do not, however, enjoy excessively cold water.

Where they exist along rivers, it seems that hippos have distinct habitat preferences according to the group density. From a study of a section of the Nile, it was discovered that larger hippo

A heavily worn trail made by hippos on their nightly travels to their feeding lawns (right).

David Keith Jones/Images of Africa Photobank

FOOD FOR FISH

Because hippos graze from the land and return to the water, they excrete a fair amount of waste into the rivers and lakes. In the process they gradually transfer nutrients into the water. The waterways and aquatic plants are so enriched by the natural fertilizer that resident fish, such as tilapia and Nile perch, enjoy a feeding bonanza. This is much to the delight of local fisheries, since, in addition, the hippo groups at the shores tend to deter the more opportunistic fishermen from exploiting the fish species' shallow-water breeding grounds.

But the association also runs in reverse. A cyprinid species of fish, *Labeo velifer*, is known to nibble upon the hides of wallowing hippos, removing caked mud and scraps of vegetation. The fish receives a meal, and, in return, the hippo's skin is cleaned and conditioned. Out of the water, birds perform the same service for the hippo groups.

A large group of hippos (above) cooling off in the Mara River in the Masai Mara Reserve.

herds, containing two to five dozen animals, preferred the relatively shallow spits of land around estuaries, while solitary males and small groups of a dozen or so individuals were scattered somewhat at random along the banks.

FOOTPRINTS IN THE SAND

Hippos leave fairly obvious evidence of their presence by a river or lake, churning the sandy or silted banks into a marsh of mud. On their evening forays to the grazing lawns, they use regular routes up the bank and over the floodplains. These are soon worn down into twin ruts by the heavy foot traffic and are flagged at intervals by the animals' dung. These strong-smelling heaps seem to function as route markers for nighttime navigation, as well as reminders of a territorial bull's presence in the area. However, neither the paths nor the dung can be regarded as boundaries of a territory.

Territories, held only by high-ranking bulls, are usually pear-shaped, with the narrower end of the pear extending some way into the water. They can extend along the shoreline, from around 160–190 ft (50–60 m) to 800–1,600 ft (250–500 m), but they rarely penetrate further than six miles (10 km)

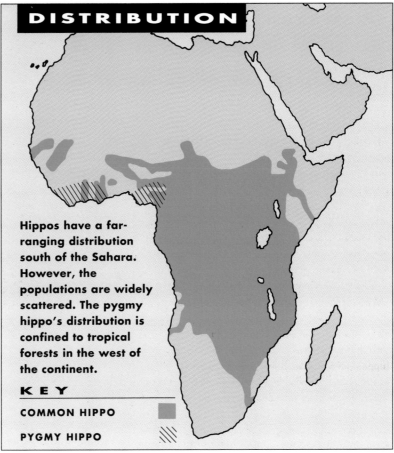

DISTRIBUTION

Hippos have a far-ranging distribution south of the Sahara. However, the populations are widely scattered. The pygmy hippo's distribution is confined to tropical forests in the west of the continent.

KEY

COMMON HIPPO

PYGMY HIPPO

inland: Water, after all, is the hippo's refuge in times of trouble. A bull may be ousted rapidly from his patch by an ambitious male, or he may hold it for several years, depending upon his fighting prowess.

The size of a male's territory depends largely on the density of the local hippo population, which itself varies constantly, according to climatic conditions and food supplies. When hippos were more abundant, one might easily have counted some 100 animals per mile (60 per kilometer). Nowadays, that number is usually a dozen or so, although groups of up to a hundred can occasionally be seen.

After a long period of hippo occupation, the bankside pastures are stripped of their grasses. Having naturally unstable groups, hippos tend to disperse—particularly during the wet season, when the widespread availability of food enables them to wander at will. As a result, the animals usually move on before they have eaten themselves into starvation. But these nomads do not leave a wasteland behind: The intense grazing clears the way for shrubs and thickets, which attract browsing mammals. At any one time, hippos may be found feeding alongside water buffalo, zebra, waterbuck, elephant, rhino, and many other savanna residents, not to mention the birds, fish, and crocodiles that benefit in various ways from the presence of hippos.

Alan Root/Survival Anglia

FOCUS ON

LAKES EDWARD AND GEORGE

The Ruwenzori, or Queen Elizabeth National Park, occupies 792 sq miles (1,980 sq km) of Uganda in the Rift Valley and is home to some of the richest, most diverse wildlife in all of Africa. The terrain is dominated by bush thickets, rich grasslands, savanna, tropical forest, and swamp, but it also includes the immense Lake Edward and much smaller Lake George. These bodies of water are linked by the 20-mile (32-km) Kazinga Channel, and between them they play host to probably 2,000 hippos—around one-third of Uganda's total complement. Indeed, some of the most detailed studies of hippos—their lifestyle and the ways in which they affect local ecosystems—have been conducted around Lake Edward and Lake George.

TEMPERATURE AND RAINFALL

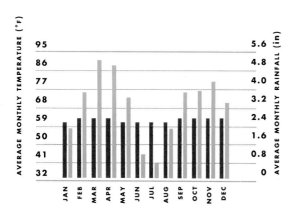

■ TEMPERATURE

▨ RAINFALL

The chart shows temperatures and rainfall for Kubali. Temperature is constant throughout the year at 61–63°F. Rainfall varies between 1 and 5 in, but one can almost set a watch by the time it rains—5:00–6:00 P.M. daily.

The pygmy hippo, too, is dependent on water, and its favorite habitat is a dense stand of forest containing plenty of streams or swampy patches. Here, each hippo occupies a home range. Bulls roam more widely than cows, and their ranges may encroach upon those of a number of cows. Within its home range, each individual wanders along set paths. These appear as beaten tracks in areas of thin ground cover and as leafy green tunnels in denser growth. These trails are marked, like those of the larger hippo, by scattered heaps of dung. ■

NEIGHBORS

Uganda is a prime stopover point for migrants, and over 500 species have been seen in Ruwenzori. The lions of the park are unusual in that they frequently climb trees to escape flying insects.

CARP

Introduced to Africa by European settlers, the carp has become one of its most common freshwater fish.

OXPECKER

This bird lives up to its name by perching on grazing mammals to peck parasites from their hides.

Neighbor illustrations Joanne Cowne/Oxpecker by Elisabeth Smith

RUWENZORI

The Ruwenzori National Park lies in the extreme southwest of Uganda, close to the Zaire border. It is flanked by the Ruwenzori mountains in the west and Lake Victoria in the east. To its north, Lake Albert is fed by the Albert Nile, the southernmost stretch of the mighty White Nile.

TERRAPIN	NILE CROCODILE	HAMMERKOP	THOMSON'S GAZELLE	AFRICAN WILD DOG

Sometimes scores of river terrapins are seen on a hippo's back, where they bask in the sun.

This deadly predator lurks in African waterways, waiting for unsuspecting mammals to drink.

This large wader is active mainly at night. It stirs up mud on the river bottom to get to its prey.

Slight of frame and elegant in profile, the "Tommy" is one of the savanna's fastest-running residents.

Also called the Cape hunting dog, this animal lives in strong family groups and hunts in packs.

HYENAS

Evolution has endowed hyenas with tremendous stamina, and despite their awkward appearance they can travel great distances without apparent fatigue. They have sturdy legs and toes with strong, nonretractile claws like those of a dog, adapted for running over level ground, and these factors make them well suited to life in open country, where food is often widely scattered.

The counterpart of the striped hyena in the south is the brown hyena, which occurs in southern Africa south of the Zambezi. These two species are much the same size and have very similar habits. It is significant that their ranges do not overlap: scavenging is a competitive trade, and two such equally matched rivals would probably spend their lives fighting if they were close neighbors.

The central and southern African range of the spotted hyena, however, overlaps those of both the

The pickings are rich for the spotted hyena during the calving season of the wildebeest (above).

others. Much bigger, and a killer as well as a scavenger, the spotted hyena's requirements are slightly different from those of its smaller relatives, so it can live alongside them in relative harmony. It will not hesitate to attack either in a confrontation, but there are sufficient alternatives available to make this a relatively rare event.

In particular, the spotted hyena concentrates on the larger herbivores that, in some areas, still teem on the African savanna. The largest populations of spotted hyenas occur on the east African plains of Kenya and Tanzania, in the game reserves of the Masai Mara, the Serengeti, and Ngorongoro, where wildebeests and zebras still roam in the thousands.

The savanna is a sea of grass, dotted with trees

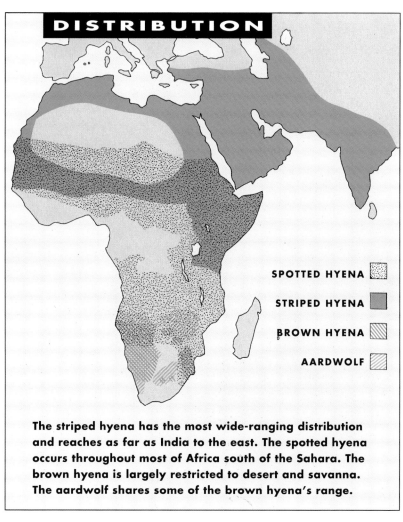

DISTRIBUTION

SPOTTED HYENA

STRIPED HYENA

BROWN HYENA

AARDWOLF

The striped hyena has the most wide-ranging distribution and reaches as far as India to the east. The spotted hyena occurs throughout most of Africa south of the Sahara. The brown hyena is largely restricted to desert and savanna. The aardwolf shares some of the brown hyena's range.

such as the great spreading acacias and the strange baobab, with its swollen, water-storing trunk. Water is at a premium on the savanna, because rain falls only during the rainy season from November to April; for the rest of the year it is hot and arid.

For the grazing animals, this seasonal cycle is crucial. In the dry season the grasses hardly grow at all, and in most areas the animals must keep moving to find suitable food. In the Serengeti, this continu-

---

THE AARDWOLF HAS A MOBILE TONGUE THAT CAN ROLL UP COMPLETELY WHEN IT CLEANS ITS MOUTH CAVITY

---

ous movement develops into a full-scale migration in May, when the herds finally exhaust the pasture in the dry southeast section of the reserve. Following some ancestral instinct, they head for the Mara in southern Kenya, where the grasses are still lush and green. By November they have exhausted the Mara, too, but by then the rains have brought a flush of green to the southern savannas, so the herds retrace their steps to the Serengeti.

These movements are naturally of the greatest interest to spotted hyenas, which prey on the grazing animals or scavenge their carcasses. So from November to May, when the herds are grazing the Serengeti, hundreds of hyenas feed within the reserve. When the herds move north, the Serengeti hyenas are left with no food supply except small

Clem Haagner/Ardea

Spotted hyenas at den site (left). This is the time to stretch, scratch, and groom themselves like cats.

A brown hyena (above) in the Kalahari picks over the bones of another animal's kill.

K E Y F A C T S

● The spotted hyena is the most abundant large carnivore in Africa today. Of no use to humans, it is not hunted for its fur or other properties like the big cats.

● The aardwolf prefers to live on grassland that has been overgrazed by hoofed animals such as wildebeests and gazelles, because the very short grass provides an ideal habitat for the harvester termites it preys upon.

● On the coast of Namibia the brown hyena is known as a beach wolf or beachcomber because of its habit of scavenging along the beachfront debris washed up by the tide.

● The striped hyena is the most widely distributed of all the hyenas, but it occurs at very low densities and is endangered in North Africa.

game. They cannot move north without trespassing on the territory of other hyenas, so they tend to make temporary forays, returning every day or so to the clan den.

Brown hyenas have a similar problem in the southwest arid zone of Africa, which includes the Kalahari and Namib Deserts. During the rainy season a host of grazing animals—wildebeests, red hartebeests, and springboks—migrate into the central Kalahari. They are accompanied by the lions, cheetahs, and spotted hyenas that prey on them, and the brown hyenas, being primarily scavengers, enjoy rich pickings from these kills. When the rains stop, the herds leave, but instead of chasing them the brown hyenas switch to a less ambitious diet of small vertebrates, insects, and fruits, which provide vital moisture during the dry months in the desert. In the Kalahari the animals may have to roam 30 miles (50 km) a night to get enough to eat.

In the far west of their range, on the edge of the Namib Desert, brown hyenas avoid this problem by scavenging along the beachfront of the Skeleton Coast. Here their diet is seasonally enriched by the mass breeding of the Cape fur seals, which haul out in vast colonies on the beaches. These colonies

offer unlimited food for a few months, after which the brown hyenas may have to make do with dead seabirds, fish, and marine debris.

The striped hyena is a solitary scavenger and small-time hunter. It will eat almost anything including carrion, small vertebrates, eggs, insects, and fruits. It will take advantage of the big kills if it can, but more typically it ranges widely in search of smaller prey and scraps, sometimes picking over garbage dumps. This enables it to survive in some of the most barren country of all. ∎

FOCUS ON

HYENAS IN THE NGORONGORO

The Ngorongoro Crater in Tanzania is shaped like a gigantic circular dish. Its rim completely surrounds an area of rich grassland, which feeds a variety of animals. The big animals that live on the crater floor can migrate in and out of the crater, but they often stay all year round.

About 25,000 hoofed grazing animals live within the crater. These make rich pickings for the lions and spotted hyenas that prey on them. The hyenas, some 400 of them, outnumber the lions three to one, and as a result they have become the major predators. This means that instead of scavenging lion kills, the hyenas generally kill their own prey and the lions do the scavenging—when they get the chance. The hyenas often hunt in packs of twenty or more, so although a pride of lions may win temporary possession of a carcass, the hyenas usually drive them away.

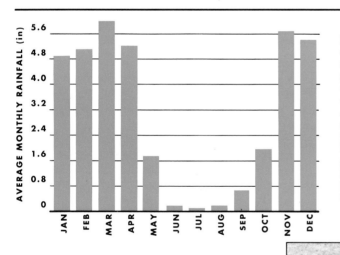

RAINFALL

During the rainy season from October to April, the grasslands are lush and green. In the driest months from July to September, the grasses scorch in the hot sun, making life difficult for the grazing animals that have to scratch a living anywhere they can.

NEIGHBORS

The Ngorongoro Crater supports a variety of wildlife. The largest grazers are the wildebeests and the largest predators are the lions.

PLAINS ZEBRA

Living in small groups, the plains zebras occupy a territory of 30–100 sq mi (80–250 sq km) in the crater.

ELAND

Elands are spiral-horned antelope that often form large groups, especially in the breeding season.

THE NGORONGORO CRATER

Situated in Tanzania, the Ngorongoro Crater rim stands about 2,300 ft (700 m) high and is 11 miles (18 km) across. The crater is actually a caldera—the collapsed, eroded remains of a vast, extinct volcano.

ENEMIES

EXTREMELY DANGEROUS

LION
A fierce competitor of the hyena, skirmishes often take place between them. Each will kill the other.

MODERATELY DANGEROUS

AFRICAN BUFFALO
Although hyenas feed on the remains of buffalo killed by other animals, they rarely attack this large, dangerous beast themselves.

THOMSON'S GAZELLE

bout 90 percent of this azelle's food is grass. It is n abundant species and a vorite prey of hyenas.

VULTURE

Quick to spot a kill, vultures wait for the predator to take its fill before stepping in to pick the bones clean.

COMMON JACKAL

Jackals live in small family units that hunt as a team. They often steal from hyenas and lions.

SOUTHERN REEDBUCK

A characteristic of the reedbuck is its leaping into the air when running. This species is the largest.

WILDEBEEST

The wildebeest, or gnu, has a relatively massive head and shoulders. Both sexes have horns.

JAGUARS

The jaguar is primarily an animal of lowland tropical habitats that offer plenty of cover and are remote from human disturbance. In the past it found suitable habitat over most of Central and South America, but the spread of settlement has pushed it from many areas it once inhabited. Its most secure refuges today are large tracts of dense tropical forest, particularly the forested areas of the Amazon and Orinoco river basins. Remnants of rain forest in the coastal zones of Colombia and Ecuador and of southeastern Brazil, along with some of the remaining forested regions of Central America and Mexico, also harbor some jaguars.

In places such as the Guiana highlands and the Andean rim of the Amazon Basin, jaguars range the forested lower slopes of mountains. Such montane habitats tend to be equally if not more humid than the rain forest proper, and though the trees are lower, the density and lushness of the

Jaguars still roam the grassy plains and steppe country of Venezuela (right), where habitats remain free from human intrusion.

The jaguar's strikingly patterned coat serves as superb camouflage (below). In the dim light of the forest floor, this big cat can simply melt into the scenery.

Jeanne Drake/Tony Stone Worldwide

ZEFA

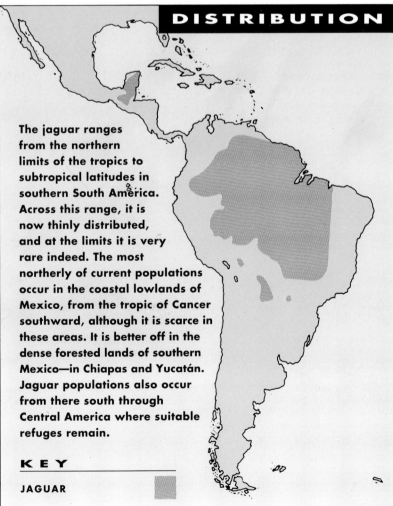

DISTRIBUTION

The jaguar ranges from the northern limits of the tropics to subtropical latitudes in southern South America. Across this range, it is now thinly distributed, and at the limits it is very rare indeed. The most northerly of current populations occur in the coastal lowlands of Mexico, from the tropic of Cancer southward, although it is scarce in these areas. It is better off in the dense forested lands of southern Mexico—in Chiapas and Yucatán. Jaguar populations also occur from there south through Central America where suitable refuges remain.

K E Y

JAGUAR

vegetation still provides generous cover. Records of jaguars living as high as 7,000 ft (2,135 m) in the Peruvian Andes are considered to represent the likely upper limit for the species, although there is an exceptional record of one occurring at 8,860 ft (2,700 m) in Bolivia.

But continuous humid forest is not the only remaining home of present-day jaguars. Some still survive in more open habitats, where their ancestors once flourished. The mixture of swampy grassland and forest in the Brazilian Pantanal, the seasonally flooded savanna of the Venezuelan llanos (grassy plains), and the mangrove swamps of the Orinoco Delta provide adequate cover and prey as well as places relatively distant from human settlements. Jaguars also inhabit the drier fringes of the Amazon—parts of the vast savannas or *cerrado* of central Brazil and the dry, thorny forests of the Bolivian Chaco. In the past they even ranged into the pampas, while in Mexico some still occur in rocky scrubland. Jaguars even once entered, though did not actually inhabit, the arid Sonoran Desert.

Though jaguars can survive in dry and open terrain, they seem to depend heavily on the presence of fresh water. In such habitats they are most likely to live close to permanent watercourses, and even in the rain forest they spend much of their time close to rivers and pools. Watercourses not only provide them with drinking supplies but are also good places to ambush prey that come to drink or

---

IT IS LIKELY THAT, IN THE PAST, THE JAGUAR ROAMED THROUGHOUT PARTS OF THE SOUTHERN UNITED STATES

---

to stalk semiaquatic animals, such as capybaras. During low water on the grassy seasonal floodplains that fringe some Amazonian rivers, jaguars sometimes search for tortoises. They hunt and perhaps play in the water's edge, and they are also prepared to swim across broad rivers, paddling in an almost straight line across the current.

Some low-lying forested zones of the Amazon Basin are steeped in floodwater for several months of the year. In these flooded forests the trees survive being immersed, in some cases up to their lowest branches. Jaguars that hunt in these forests therefore have little choice but to perch and climb through the branches. Some of the earliest reports of jaguars came from explorers traveling by boat who surprised cats resting on horizontal branches just above the floodwater level. Elsewhere jaguars sometimes climb up from dry ground to snatch monkeys, sloths, or birds. They can climb far better than tigers or lions, though not as adeptly as leopards or pumas. For the most part, however, they confine their hunting activities to ground level.

Jaguars share the bulk of their geographical range with pumas. Though the latter are more adaptable in habitat terms, they too dwell and hunt in forests and savannas. Since they share similar diets, both feeding opportunistically on small to large prey (a puma can tackle all but the biggest prey exploited by jaguars), competition between the two might be expected to lead to slightly different habits or habitat preferences. Few comparative studies have been made of jaguars and pumas residing in the same zones, but observations in Peru suggested that jaguars made more use of riverside areas than their fellow cats.

BLACK PANTHERS

As well as a few cases of albinism, melanism in jaguars is frequently observed—a trait whose presence may be linked with habitat. Melanistic jaguars are more or less uniformly dark brown or black, with markings only visible at close range or in oblique light. Such abnormal individuals have been noted across South America since the earliest records of jaguars and were at one time regarded as a separate race or even a separate species. Melanism is now known to be a product of the normal genetic

variation present in jaguar populations. The same phenomenon shows itself in leopards, producing the famous black panthers, particularly among populations in the Malay Peninsula and also in populations of the medium-sized African cat, the serval. But the more frequent occurrence of black jaguars in certain habitats implies that their appearance does not arise entirely at random. As with leopards, it is recognized that melanistic individuals are more common in dense, shady forests than in more open environments. ∎

FOCUS ON

THE COLOMBIAN AMAZON

Well over 90 percent of Colombia's human population lives in the mountain valleys and coastal lowlands of the west. By contrast, the country's vast eastern lowlands are scarcely populated. The wildest lands of all are those in the southeast, rolling lowlands drained by swollen rivers and blanketed with tropical rain forest. This is the northwestern corner of the vast Amazon rain forest. Most of Colombia's Amazon lands remain rich in forest life and are precious strongholds for the jaguar.

Tall tree trunks rise from the gloomy floor until they break into spreading branches. The tangled top layer of greenery, called the canopy, hosts the bulk of forest life, suspended 100 ft (30 m) or so above the forest floor. A few giant tree species push their crowns well above the canopy. Down below, there is a less crowded assemblage of young trees, palms, and creeping plants adapted to shade, which has its own distinctive fauna.

In the broad rivers and pools live an extraordinary variety of fish. Feeding on and alongside them are otters, herons, caimans, and river turtles. But, as in the canopy, the greatest diversity is shown by the invertebrates: the insects, crustaceans, and myriad minuscule creatures that are still unknown to science.

Jeff Foott/Survival Anglia

TEMPERATURE AND RAINFALL

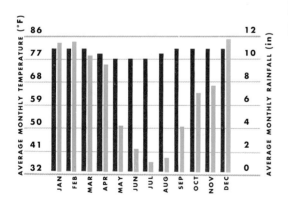

■ **TEMPERATURE**

▨ **RAINFALL**

The rain forest habitat is fostered by temperatures that remain high all year round, and by abundant rainfall in every month. Warmth, sunshine, and humidity combine to create ideal, fertile conditions for plant growth.

NEIGHBORS

Large carnivores such as the jaguar may be rare, but there are countless invertebrates in the lush rain forests. Colombia—and indeed South America as a whole—is also rich in bird and fish species.

GREAT TINAMOU

Shy birds   of the gloomy   forest undergrowth, tinamous are weak fliers but run well.

PIRANHA

Many species of piranha are in fact plant-eaters, and those that are carnivores feed primarily on other fish

THE COLOMBIAN RAIN FOREST

Colombia's rain forest stretches from the foothills of the Andes deep into the heart of Amazonia. Its southern and eastern limits are the borders with Peru and Brazil, and its northern limit is the valley of the Guaviare, which drains away into the Orinoco.

RAIN FOREST

POISON-ARROW TOAD

The bright coloration of these toads is a warning to enemies that they have poisonous skin secretions.

KING VULTURE

The bizarre head decoration of this big forest vulture is made up of patches and wattles of bare skin.

SNAPPING TERRAPIN

This predator lurks in streams, ready to snap up prey. It may feed on fish, frogs, birds, or mammals.

HUMMINGBIRD

The white-tipped sickle-bill hummingbird flits on rapid wing beats, sipping nectar from forest flowers.

ARMY ANT

Army ants live in vast, migratory colonies on the forest floor. They travel in spectacularly long columns.

KANGAROOS

Jean-Paul Ferrero/Ardea

The large kangaroos—the red and the western and eastern gray—are mostly confined to mainland Australia, although the western gray is also found on Kangaroo Island off Adelaide and the eastern gray occurs on the island of Tasmania. Tasmania has three kangaroo species, while New Guinea has seven species of wallaby and pademelon. Some of the smaller kangaroo species are found on a variety of offshore islands.

The ranges of the large kangaroos overlap to varying degrees but, though two or more species may occur in the same geographical area, they will

Red kangaroos (above) can travel with ease across almost any terrain.

THE ESSENTIALS OF GOOD KANGAROO COUNTRY ARE SHORT, GREEN VEGETATION, A REGULAR SUPPLY OF WATER, AND SOME FORM OF SHELTER FROM THE SUN

---

be ecologically separated because of their distinct habitat preferences. The various species of kangaroo and wallaby prefer different foods and also live in different types of terrain.

The red kangaroo is the most widely distributed and occurs in all the states. It is the kangaroo of the plains and is found throughout inland Australia. The plains—which are hotter than the coast in summer and colder in winter, and have very low, uncertain rainfall and intense evaporation because of the heat—have varying numbers of red kangaroos: The largest numbers occur in the better-watered, lusher regions.

However, the red kangaroo is not found in

AMAZING FACTS

HIGH FLYING

Red kangaroos can reach surprising speeds when they travel across open plains. Males can achieve speeds of 35 miles (56 kilometers) per hour in short bursts, though larger bucks are slower. The lighter females, or "blue fliers," can reach 40 miles (65 kilometers) per hour over short distances. Generally, though, red kangaroos prefer to cruise at a more comfortable speed of 12 miles (20 kilometers) per hour. When they are traveling, they use far less energy than other mammals moving at the same speed on four legs because the tendons in their hind legs act like springs.

Kangaroos have been known to clear fences 10 feet (3 meters) high, if trapped, and, when bounding at full speed, they can cover up to 29 feet (9 meters) in a single leap. The longest leap by any kangaroo was one of 44 feet (13.5 meters).

Hans Reinhard/ZEFA

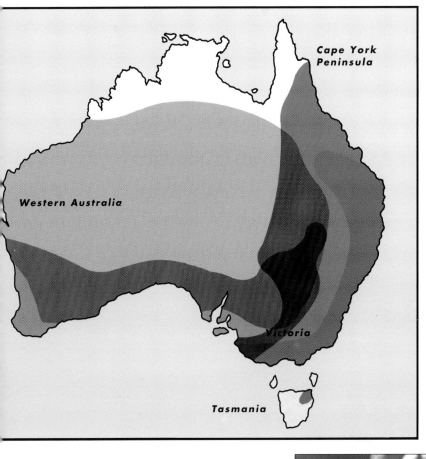

● The most widely distributed species, the red kangaroo, ranges throughout most of central Australia, covering an area of over 2 million sq miles (5 million sq km), though density varies from region to region.

● The red kangaroo thrives in regions that average less than 20 in (50 cm) rainfall a year, although it does not live in true deserts.

● The gray kangaroo is found in forest and scrub areas with average annual rainfalls of 10–40 in (25–100 cm).

● Kangaroos seem to have benefited from the additional water and pasture that European settlers created, moving into areas of eastern Australia from which they were largely absent in the 19th century.

Australia's forests. In the east, in New South Wales and Queensland, it stops short of the eucalyptus forests on the slopes of the Great Dividing Range and avoids large belts of dense scrub.

In southern and western Australia, the red kangaroo extends to the coast, except in those areas covered with dense scrub and forest. In the north, it is confined to the light acacia scrub and does not enter the eucalyptus forest beyond. This kangaroo has been recorded in all the Australian deserts but it is, most likely, not a permanent inhabitant of these very arid regions.

UNDER COVER

The gray kangaroo occurs in areas with relatively high rainfall where plant growth is more vigorous. There are two subspecies: The eastern gray is found in eastern Australia and the western—despite its name—along the southern belt of the continent. Both varieties are found in areas with an average annual rainfall of 10 to 40 inches (25 to 100 centimeters). The favored habitats of the gray kangaroo include

Living up to its name, the black-footed rock wallaby (right) is found among granite rocks in mallee scrub in southwestern Australia.

coastal heaths, temperate woodlands, subtropical forests, cool mountain forests, dry inland scrub, and the dense dwarf eucalyptus scrublands known as mallee scrub.

The wallaroo is found in rocky outcrops where there is daytime shelter in caves or crevices. In northwest and central Australia it is characteristic of areas where spinifex—a spiky type of grass— grows; in the southwest it occurs in mallee and mulga (acacia) scrub; the eastern inland wallaroo is found on bare rocky ranges with scattered mulga, while the more coastal colonies are located on grassed stony slopes in the eucalyptus forests.

ON THE ROCKS

The yellow-footed rock wallaby has a scattered distribution in New South Wales, Queensland, and South Australia. It occurs on the slopes of low tablelands and rocky hills, favoring areas with cliffs at least 6.5 feet (2 meters) high. These areas have open woodland with perhaps scattered acacia, lancewood, or mountain sandalwood trees above a low shrub layer on the slopes.

FOCUS ON

THE RANGELANDS OF NEW SOUTH WALES

New South Wales has 12,000 square miles (31,000 square kilomet of grazing land. The sheep rangelands of the inland area were created by Europeans in the 19th century. The grazers sank thousa of wells in this arid area to water their flocks and these watering points encouraged kangaroos to move out from the watercourses c the plains. Today, the plains cover nearly two-thirds of the state ar the sheep stations provide almost 40 percent of Australia's wool.

Before the sheep and cattle arrived, the plains were covered wit long, dry grass and, in some areas, saltbush. The flocks grazed the tall grasses and caused fresh perennial grasses to sprout—kangaro like these so much that they are known as "marsupial lawns."

The red kangaroo breeds when conditions are good and plenty food and water are available. There are almost certainly more kangaroos on the plains now than there were 200 years ago. They compete to some extent with the livestock for grass, but sheep and cows browse on a wider range of shrubs and other plants. Rainfall here is generally low, though it fluctuates widely from season to season and from year to year. A run of years with good rain leads to good pasture and a large increase in kangaroo numbers; drough leads to a large decrease.

VEGETATION ZONES

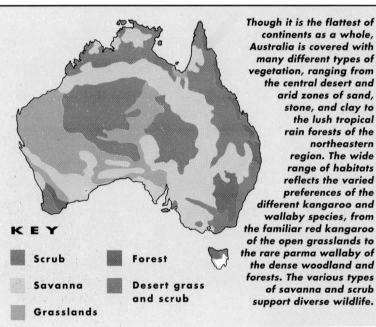

Though it is the flattest of continents as a whole, Australia is covered with many different types of vegetation, ranging from the central desert and arid zones of sand, stone, and clay to the lush tropical rain forests of the northeastern region. The wide range of habitats reflects the varied preferences of the different kangaroo and wallaby species, from the familiar red kangaroo of the open grasslands to the rare parma wallaby of the dense woodland and forests. The various types of savanna and scrub support diverse wildlife.

KEY

- ◼ Scrub
- ◼ Savanna
- ◼ Grasslands
- ◼ Forest
- ◼ Desert grass and scrub

Rock wallabies graze the sparse ground cover, particularly small tufted grass, spindly forb, and rock sedge. The species occur only where annual average rainfall is greater than 6 inches (15 centimeters), although they are quite adaptable. They can survive droughts by browsing on mulga, but in the drier parts of its range it is usually found around permanent water holes. ◼

NEIGHBORS

These fascinating creatures share their grassland habitat with kangaroos in New South Wales. A wide variety of native birds, from kookaburras to brilliant budgerigars, are abundant there.

TRAPDOOR SPIDER

This spider digs a burrow underground, with a pebble at the entrance as a trapdoor. It lies in wait for passing prey.

GOULD'S MONITOR

This lizard spends the nigh an underground burrow a emerges at dawn to hunt f birds, mammals, and repti

Illustrations Matt Lyon

ENEMIES

EUROPEAN RED FOX
Given the chance, the sly fox will take young kangaroos.

DINGO
A wild dog of Australia, the dingo will hunt roos in a pack.

WEDGE-TAILED EAGLE
This bird of prey swoops down on its victim from a great height.

Illustrations Matt Lyon

APL/ZEFA

THORNY DEVIL

e fierce-looking thorny evil feeds on ants and her insects, eating as any as 7,000 a day.

KOOKABURRA

A member of the kingfisher family, the kookaburra kills small rodents and reptiles with its strong beak.

EMU

This flightless bird can run up to 37 miles (60 km) per hour. Apart from the ostrich, it is the world's largest bird.

DEATH ADDER

One of the most venomous of snakes, the death adder hunts at night for lizards, rodents, and birds.

BUDGERIGAR

Distinctive in its brilliant plumage, the budgerigar feeds on the seeds of grasses and herbaceous plants.

KILLER WHALES

François Gohier/Ardea

Between them, the globicephalids live in almost every part of every ocean in the world. However, this widespread global distribution shows many local variations. The great killer whale is truly cosmopolitan: It has been sighted from the Arctic to the Antarctic, in the Atlantic, Pacific, and Indian Oceans. However, it shows a preference for coastal areas and cooler, shallower waters, including bays and estuaries. Killers can even leave the saltwater of the ocean and swim through estuaries up into rivers, though they rarely range very far into freshwater.

The killers may venture among the loose ice floes of the polar waters, searching for food such as seals and even polar bears. However, the denser the ice cover becomes, the less frequent the killer whales. Since they track the edges of the ice fields,

Killer whales (above) frequently swim just under the surface of the water, leaving only their long dorsal fins exposed from above.

A male killer whale breaching (right). In the final stage, the whale's body will be entirely clear of the water in a straight, horizontal line.

KEY

GREAT KILLER WHALE	
SHORT-FINNED PILOT WHALE **MELON-HEADED WHALE** **PYGMY KILLER WHALE** **FALSE KILLER WHALE**	
LONG-FINNED PILOT WHALE	

KEY FACTS

● Every single species of whales and dolphins has been known to strand or beach on the shore. Out of the water, which supports and buoys up the body weight, a whale soon suffocates under the weight of its own body.

● False killer whales have sometimes been seen swimming with dolphins, such as gray dolphins, with which they are often confused. Long-finned pilots sometimes travel with common and bottle-nosed dolphins. Short-finned pilot whales have been seen in mixed groups with bottle-nosed or Pacific white-sided dolphins.

● Pilot whales strand more often, and in greater numbers, than any other cetacean. False killer whales also strand frequently, while the killer whale and pygmy killer rarely strand.

Ken Balcons/Bruce Coleman Ltd.

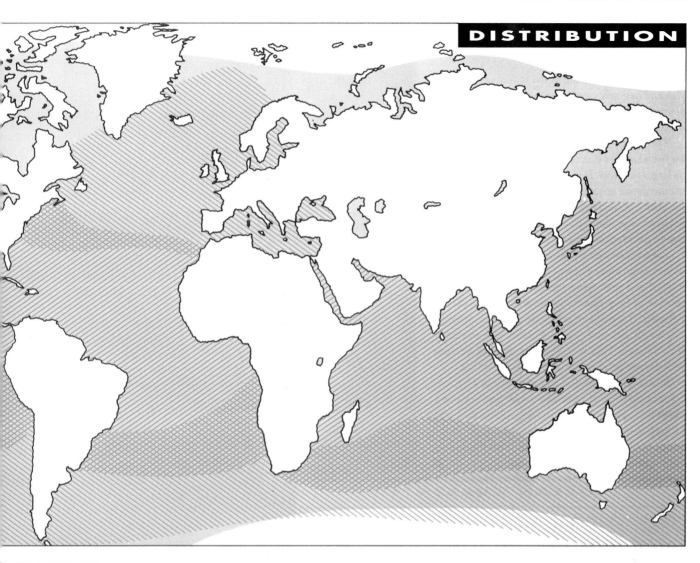

DISTRIBUTION

they move closer to the pole in spring and back toward temperate regions in autumn—simply following the retreat and advance of the ice. They are attracted to the polar regions because these waters are proportionally more productive in terms of life forms (cooler water contains more oxygen). The polar seas are especially rich in summer, when nutrients well up from the depths of the sea. The killer whales are at the summit of many food chains, so they are dependent on the rich web of life below them.

OTHER KILLERS

False killer whales live in all tropical, subtropical, and warm temperate waters. They tend to occur in the middle of the oceans. However, they have been seen in the Mediterranean Sea, Red Sea, and other partly enclosed seas.

False killers are fairly easy to identify by their habit of riding in the bow wave of a ship and their extraordinary porpoising abilities; it is also not difficult to locate them. They are the largest whales to enjoy bow-riding, but are also relatively slow. Any vessel going much faster than about 15 mph (25 km/h) will leave them behind—though they can still be seen playfully leaping in the waves of the ship's wake. They are very noisy, vocal whales. Their piercing whistles can be heard hundreds of yards away, even above the throb of a ship's engines.

The pygmy killer whale is even more at home far from land, in warmer, deeper seas than either of its larger relatives. It seems to occur in deeper tropical oceans all around the world. The pygmy killer's avoidance of land means that it rarely enters partly enclosed seas, although there have been some sightings in the Mediterranean.

Long-finned pilot whales like the cool, deep waters of temperate seas, whereas short-finned ones prefer tropical and subtropical regions. The northern subspecies of long-fins, *melaena*, lives in the North Atlantic. The southern subspecies, *edwardi*, inhabits the South Atlantic, South Pacific, and southern Indian Ocean. They seem to stay mainly within areas with a water temperature of 55–82°F (13–28°C).

Melon-headed whales probably live in all tropical and subtropical seas. However, less is known about this species than the others. At sea, they can be hard to distinguish from pygmy killers. At closer range, they lack the white "goatee" that the pygmy killer sports on its lower lip and chin. ∎

FOCUS ON

THE BAY OF PLENTY

For many years, killer whales have been sighted and monitored around the coasts of New Zealand. There are common sightings off Milford Sound in the southwest and Kaikoura in the northeast of South Island. Killers are seen virtually all year round in the wide, sweeping Bay of Plenty on the northeastern coast of North Island. These locations have one major feature in common: a richness of sea life, especially squid and fish, encouraged by the right combinations of water currents, nutrient availability, and seabed topography.

In the summer, warm ocean currents circulating counterclockwise from the tropical Pacific to the northeast bring schools of squid, fish, and other food. In the winter, the cooler waters of the Southern Current flow around New Zealand from the west. But the Bay of Plenty is largely sheltered from its effects, so life continues to thrive. There are resident pods of killer whales here, as there are off the coasts of British Columbia in Canada. The pods congregate when their food is concentrated, such as a school of fish or squid, or they spread out to forage for more scattered prey.

OCEAN CURRENTS

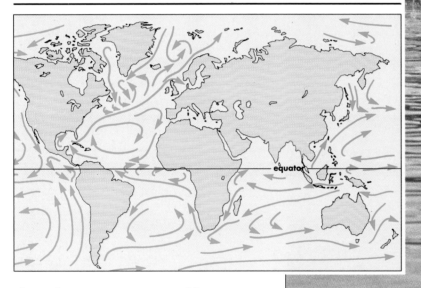

The surface ocean currents swirl clockwise in the Northern Hemisphere and counterclockwise in the Southern Hemisphere. Around New Zealand a warm current flows from the north between Australia and New Zealand and a cold current, called the West Drift, sweeps from west to east to the south of the islands. Because of the warm current, the North Island of New Zealand enjoys Mediterranean weather conditions.

NEIGHBORS

The oceans around New Zealand support a rich diversity of wildlife. In the Bay of Plenty, squid and fish abound, attracting many marine animals including dolphins and seals.

WANDERING ALBATROSS

This nomadic species has the largest wingspan of any bird. It spends most of its time at sea.

RISSO'S DOLPHIN

Living in pods of about a dozen or so, these robust mammals spend most of their time in deep waters.

NEW ZEALAND'S NORTH ISLAND

North Island covers an area of 44,297 sq miles (114,729 sq km) and is smaller than South Island. The two islands are separated by Cook Strait. The center of North Island contains New Zealand's largest lake, Lake Taupo. To its south there are geysers, volcanoes, and hot springs, which make the area very unstable.

SPERM WHALE

he largest of the toothed hales, sperm whales are ound in all the world's ceans.

MARLIN

A powerful and graceful swimmer, the marlin has a reputation for being the fastest of all fish.

OCEAN SUNFISH

This fish spends most of its time eating and breeding and is probably the most fertile of all fish.

MANTA RAY

This gigantic fish feeds on the smallest of ocean life. Because it lacks teeth, its mouth acts like a sieve.

GREEN TURTLE

One of the largest turtles, this reptile's head is so big that it cannot withdraw into its shell.

KOALAS

Some ten million years ago Australia drifted into collision with the islands of Indonesia, and was invaded by those placental mammals able to cross from the nearest of the Southeast Asian islands. Bats arrived first, then rats and mice riding on driftwood. Others followed, including, some 40,000 years ago, humans.

The land they found had moved through several climatic phases on its northward crawl. The ancient forests of the interior had given way to desert and semiarid savanna: a parched terrain of scattered trees, acacia, and tough grasses. The coastal lands still bore plenty of trees with small, leathery leaves adapted to retain water. Of these the most numerous by far were the various species of *Eucalyptus*, a genus virtually unique to Australia, found from the desert margins to the tropics. In the north, and on New Guinea, dense tropical rain forest prevailed.

The basic vegetation zones are similar today, but the plant life has been changed drastically by humans. With the arrival, in the late 18th and 19th centuries, of land-hungry European farmers, trees were felled on a huge scale to make way for crops and grass—not the bunchgrass of the interior but rich pasture suitable for grazing stock.

The big grazing kangaroos have benefited from the expanded grasslands. But the koala, among other species, has lost much of its habitat. As a eucalypt specialist, it was once widespread over eastern Australia, from the margins of the

Philip Chapman/Planet Earth Pictures

TAKING COVER

Dehydration can easily kill animals living in arid habitats. In the deserts and semiarid grasslands of Australia, hare wallabies survive by physiological adaptation and by moisture-conserving behavior. Being relatively small animals, they can hide from the sun by day, and on Barrow Island the spectacled hare wallabies tunnel into the spinifex grass. The spectacled hare wallaby can tolerate temperatures of up to 86°F (30°C) before it needs to lose heat—and water—by panting or sweating. It also conserves water by passing very concentrated urine. As a result the species has the lowest water turnover rate known among mammals of its size, and its moisture conservation is so effective that it never, ever drinks.

Jen & Des Bartlett/Survival Anglia Ltd.

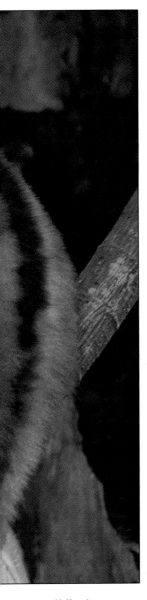

A Goodfellow's tree kangaroo (above). While the range of the koala has been fragmented, that of the Australian tree kangaroo has been concentrated.

The spectacled hare wallaby (left) is still relatively common across northern Australia. Its survival is due partly to its ability to conserve water —a vital weapon in the ceaseless battle against dehydration.

DISTRIBUTION

The koala is found in the eucalypt forests of eastern Australia. Tree kangaroos live in New Guinea and a small area of Queensland's coast. The banded hare wallaby is found only on Bernier and Dorré Islands, off Western Australia; the rufous (western) hare wallaby also occurs on these islands, and in the Tanami Desert. The spectacled hare wallaby inhabits central Queensland and Northern Territory, as well as Barrow Island, Western Australia. The eastern hare wallaby is now extinct, and there is some doubt whether the central hare wallaby ever existed.

KEY

TREE KANGAROOS

KOALAS

HARE WALLABIES

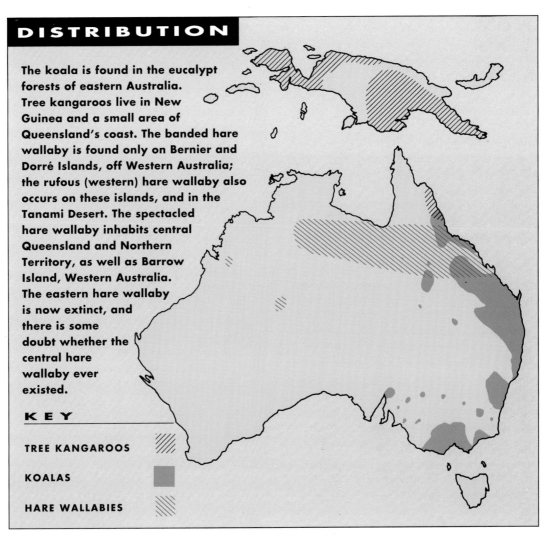

KEY FACTS

● Australian researchers have found evidence of a "new" species of tree kangaroo in the Torricelli Mountains of Papua New Guinea. Known as Scott's tree kangaroo, it is reported to be black with a bright orange streak at the base of its tail, but detailed studies of everything from behavior to anatomy have yet to be conducted.

● Fossil remains show that koalas were once common in southwest Australia. Since eucalypt woodland still flourishes in this region it is not clear why the koalas disappeared.

● Koalas are clumsy but strong swimmers, quite capable of escaping the occasional flash floods generated by tropical rainstorms.

Queensland rain forests to the cool-temperate coast of the Bass Strait in southern Victoria—originally one vast tract of eucalypt forest and woodland. Much of this forest has now gone, and many koala populations are now limited to small patches of habitat. Unfortunately, koala populations can easily outgrow restricted areas and run out of food, unable simply to disperse into neighboring tree cover.

TREE KANGAROOS

The two Australian tree kangaroos—Lumholtz's and Bennett's species—are now restricted to a patch of mountainous tropical rain forest on the east coast of northern Queensland. Lumholtz's tree kangaroo was once common in the coastal lowland rain forest, but much of this has long since disappeared. Similarly Bennett's tree kangaroo has had its habitat severely eroded, and is often seen crossing open woodland to reach isolated blocks of surviving rain forest. Northeastern Australia originally supported extensive rain forests comparable with those of New Guinea, where the ancestors of the Australian tree kangaroos probably originated. The

103

rain forests have survived well on New Guinea itself, and the seven native species of tree kangaroos are still found in their original habitat—one of the most productive in the world.

HARE WALLABIES

The hare wallabies live in the Australian deserts, tropical grasslands, and mallee scrub. Here, the vegetation consists of drought-resistant grasses, such as spinifex—which has hard, narrow, inrolled foliage and grows in low tufts—and scrub acacias and eucalypts. The vegetation provides food and daytime shade for the hare wallabies, which have also developed moisture-conserving adaptations of their own. These adaptations enabled them to thrive in these harsh lands for thousands of years before the Europeans arrived. Today, however, only the spectacled hare wallaby is still found throughout much of its original range, from the northeast coast of Queensland and across the tropical grasslands of the Northern Territory toward the Fitzroy River. It also occurs sparsely in the area to the west of the Great Sandy Desert, and is abundant on Barrow Island where it is free from introduced predators.

Islands have also provided refuges for the banded hare wallaby, originally widespread in southwestern Australia but now found only among dense

FOCUS ON

THE EUCALYPT FOREST

Aromatic and volatile, *Eucalyptus* trees and shrubs dominate the flora of Australia. They have freely diversified over millions of years into 500 or more species, each adapted to a particular set of conditions. They conserve nutrients and moisture within small, tough leaves, and are ideally suited to tropical areas with poor soils and prolonged droughts. They even evolved ways of exploiting the bushfires that punctuate the dry season. The volatile resins and oils in the eucalypts fuel the flames, which destroy competing plants. Naturally the eucalypt foliage is also burned, but the heat triggers the development of dormant buds. A potent poison in the new shoots enables them to sprout rapidly, without being nibbled by browsing animals—koalas included.

These forests support an abundant wildlife. Cockatoos, parrots, and honeyeaters flash between the trees, and bright flowers blossom in the undergrowth. Gliders and the nectar-feeding pygmy opossum forage in the branches; some fall prey to owls and wedge-tailed eagles. Yet nearly all the wealth of the habitat is invested in the trees; if they are felled, the poor soils are scorched to dust by the sun and swept away by the rains, transforming a rich, thriving natural community into a sterile wasteland.

TEMPERATURE AND RAINFALL

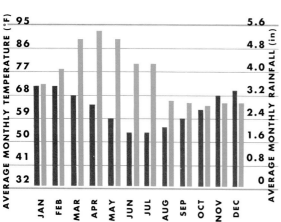

■ TEMPERATURE

▨ RAINFALL

These figures relate to the Sydney area, which enjoys a more moderate climate than the interior. Rainfall is highest in the autumn and winter (March to July); prolonged heat waves and droughts may occur in the summer.

acacia scrub on Bernier and Dorré islands, off Shark Bay. It shares the islands with the rufous (or western) hare wallaby, which otherwise occurs only in a small part of the Tanami desert in the Northern Territory: an area of sandy spinifex grassland interspersed with sand dunes and salt pans, supporting some 30–50 individuals. At one time this species was widespread throughout the deserts and dry grasslands of western and central Australia, and the exact reasons for its dramatic decline remain a disturbing mystery. ■

NEIGHBORS

Australia's wildlife today represents a combination of those species that evolved for millions of years in isolation, and those that invaded from Southeast Asia and, later on, Europe.

SNAKE-NECKED TURTLE

The neck of this aquatic turtle cannot be retracted; it is instead folded sideways under the shell rim.

FAIRY WREN

Although the drab female i hard to spot, the male is resplendent in his bright blue breeding plumage.

ENEMIES

MODERATELY DANGEROUS

DINGO
Introduced to Australia by humans some 8,000 years ago, this descendant of the wolf often preys on koalas.

MODERATELY DANGEROUS

WEDGE-TAILED EAGLE
This huge, dark eagle plucks young koalas from the trees, carrying them off in its talons to devour them at leisure.

The range of the koala (left) corresponds fairly closely with the distribution of eucalypt forests, although the species is not found in all eucalypt tracts. Much of Australia's eastern coastal region supports either this eucalypt forest or mixed broad-leaved and evergreen forest.

NEW SOUTH WALES

Sydney

VICTORIA

KOALA

Freddy Mercay/© ANT/NHPA

HORT-BEAKED ECHIDNA

his burrowing, spiny nammal catches insects vith its long, sticky tongue. also lays eggs!

SUGAR GLIDER

Sugar gliders sail among the treetops on flaps of skin linking their limbs. They eat sweet tree sap.

KOOKABURRA

A giant kingfisher of the forests, the kookaburra has a startling call resembling mad laughter.

BANJO FROG

The banjo frog is named for the twanging, banjo-string call of the male during the breeding season.

EMU

A powerful, flightless, ostrichlike bird, the emu lives mainly on open plains and semiarid scrub.

LEMURS

Madagascar is 226,657 square miles (587,040 square kilometers) in area, which is somewhat greater than the size of France, so its climate resembles that of a small continent rather than an oceanic island. Temperatures vary with latitude and also with altitude. Most of the island consists of upland plateau, and there are no peaks exceeding 9,840 ft (3,000 m). Rainfall varies enormously from region to region, with just under 200 in (5,000 mm) falling on the east coast rain forest near Toamasina to only 4.7 in (120 mm) in Morombé in the spiny desert region of the south. The dry season occurs during the southern winter (June to October), so pleasantly warm, cloudless days are the norm. These variations in climate and topography have created some distinct habitats.

SPINY FOREST

One of the oldest, strangest forests in the world lies in the south of Madagascar. In a semiarid zone, thickets of didierea trees push their prickly fingers toward the sky. Although they superficially resemble the

Ring-tailed lemurs (above) occupy the more open, scrubby areas in the south and north.

The red-bellied lemur (below) prefers the medium to high altitudes of the east coast rain forests.

The ruffed lemur (above) is sparsely distributed in Madagascar's east coast rain forest.

candelabra cactus of Mexico, they are not related. Didierea are deciduous and bear small leaves as well as spines, which cover the stems. The exterior layer of the sappy trunk disguises a stem of hardwood. The frequently impenetrable undergrowth of the spiny forest is a tangle of euphorbia shrubs. They are full of poisonous latex, one of the most effective weapons in the vegetable world, which is designed to repel browsing animals.

Today, the most arid areas of the prickly forest are

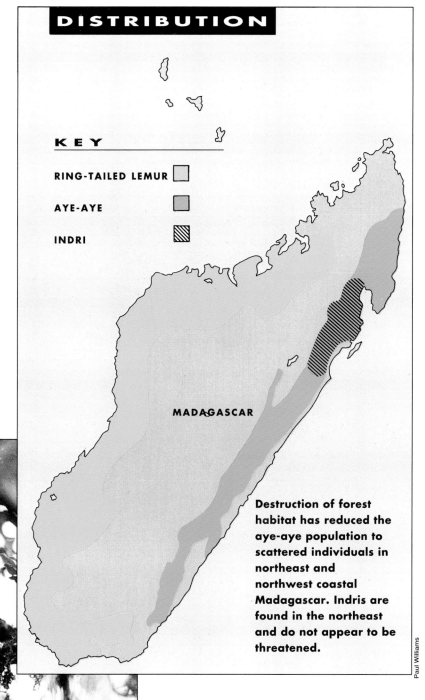

DISTRIBUTION

KEY

RING-TAILED LEMUR ☐

AYE-AYE ☐

INDRI ◪

MADAGASCAR

Destruction of forest habitat has reduced the aye-aye population to scattered individuals in northeast and northwest coastal Madagascar. Indris are found in the northeast and do not appear to be threatened.

Konrad Wothe/Bruce Coleman Ltd.

Paul Williams

the rains, which usually come in December and January in the form of torrential short-lived downpours, occasionally fail completely and there may be no moisture for eighteen months or longer. The baobab tree, which with its rootlike branches looks as though it is growing upside down, together with various species of Malagasy pachypodia, store water in their bottle-shaped trunks. Other trees combat

NINE OUT OF TEN OF MADAGASCAR'S WILDLIFE INHABITANTS ARE FOUND ONLY ON THIS ISLAND, MAKING IT ONE OF EARTH'S RICHEST AREAS OF UNIQUE FLORA AND FAUNA

water loss by shedding their leaves in the dry season, reducing the length of their branches, or transforming their leaves into thorns.

Large areas of the spiny forest have been cleared for the commercial production of sisal (a tough fiber used to make rope), as well as for subsistence crops such as sorghum and corn. Some areas of this fragile habitat are also under pressure from charcoal production, and Alluaudia trees are felled to provide timber for homes.

WESTERN DRY FOREST

Coquerel's sifaka is one of the most ostentatious residents in protected areas of dry deciduous forest like that found at the Ampijeroa Forest Reserve, south of Majunga. Lying in the rain shadow of the eastern ridge, this area suffers a prolonged dry season that runs for seven or eight months. Most of the trees shed their leaves during this period. Although lianas are abundant, there are no ferns or palms in this forest and epiphytes are rare. Many lemurs depend on the fruit of tamarind trees that grow

inhabited by troops of Verreaux's sifakas. *Propithecus verreauxi*, ring-tailed lemurs, sportive lemurs, gray lesser mouse lemurs, and fork-crowned dwarf lemurs, found throughout the prickly forest, live at higher densities in the gallery forest along the bed of seasonal streams, where they have better access to water. Ring-tailed lemurs and sifakas are particularly approachable at Berenty Nature Reserve, where they have become habituated to tourists. Gray mouse lemurs and fat-tailed dwarf lemurs are also present, and red-fronted lemurs have been introduced.

All the plants and lemurs of this area—especially the sifakas—are adapted to withstand drought, for along the banks of seasonal rivers.

Lying in a hilly area of north central Madagascar, the Sambirano forest contains plants that are typical of both arid and humid regions growing virtually side by side. Altitude and tropical climate combine to make the habitat one of the most complex in Madagascar. Black lemurs, aye-ayes, fork-crowned dwarf lemurs, greater dwarf lemurs, and gray-backed sportive lemurs have been found at Manongarivo Special Reserve.

TSINGY

A spectacular wilderness of limestone karst called *tsingy* is found in north Madagascar in the Ankarana Special Reserve, as well as in the west, in the Strict Reserves of Bemahara and Namoroka. The surface of the limestone has eroded over millions of years to form a corrugated surface of knifelike edges. Rising up to 400 ft (122 m) high at Ankarana, the walls of the tsingy massif present an almost impenetrable barrier.

The limestone is riddled with caves, hollowed out by floodwater. Some have collapsed to form deep canyons where trees and other plants flourish. Cut off from the outside world, they provide a last refuge for rare lemurs such as Sanford's and crowned lemurs, which have survived in the heart

of the Ankarana, although they have been virtually eliminated from the surrounding countryside.

Inside, the tsingy of Bemahara, 58 square miles (60 square kilometers) of needles up to 65 ft (20 m) high is interlaced with trees to form hanging gardens where Decken's sifaka, red-fronted lemurs, and fork-crowned dwarf lemurs live undisturbed.

Dramatic karst formations cover an estimated 12,750 square miles (33,000 square kilometers) in the west of Madagascar, and also include the Kelifely Plateau, Mahafaly, Majunga, Sitampiky, and Narinda Peninsula. ∎

FOCUS ON

MADAGASCAN RAIN FOREST

Most of Madagascar's 10,000 or so flowering plants are rain forest species and more than 80 percent of them can be found nowhere else in the world. Scrambling through a Malagasy rain forest is like walking back through time because many of the plants are extreme ancient—primitive palms and tree ferns that date back to before the dinosaur age. Lianas as thick as a human arm twist around trees th bear bean pods more than a yard long. Rare endemic orchids and clinging epiphytic ferns drip from the trees, helping to make up wha is probably the richest habitat on Earth.

The rain forest used to stretch all the way around the northwest coast and cover the entire eastern side of the island, cloaking the mountains in a lush tide of vegetation. But in the last 200 years, mo of it has vanished—although there are still areas of primary forest o steep and difficult land, some still waiting to be explored by scientis

In the northeast, the wettest area of Madagascar, moisture rots tr as they stand, held up only by virtue of the ropes of lianas that twis around their decaying trunks. The evergreen forest canopy is high— to 330 ft (100 m)—and is composed of vast numbers of different species. Aye-ayes poke to extract insects from under peeling bark, and mouse lemurs hunt beetles among the ferns, but the rain forest is also home to many vegetarian lemurs as well.

RAINFALL

ANNUAL RAINFALL IN MADAGASCAR (in)

60–120				
	60	37–60	20–60	
				0–14
THE EAST COAST	INTERIOR ESCARPMENT AND EASTERN PLATEAU REGION	THE WESTERN PLATEAU REGION	THE WESTERN PLAINS	THE EXTREME SOUTHWEST

Paul Williams

The prevailing influence on temperature and rainfall is the presence of the great north-south mountain ranges, which interrupt the moisture-bearing winds coming off the Indian Ocean. Temperature varies according to altitude and latitude.

NEIGHBORS

A colorful collection of insects, birds, and mammals coexist with lemurs in the forests of Madagascar. Many are unique to the island, making it a naturalist's treasure chest.

Illustrations Clive Pritchard/Wildlife Art Agency

PARSON'S CHAMELEON

In the male of the Parson's chameleon (Chamaeleo parsonii), the nose bears a pair of blunt "horns."

FOSSA

This catlike viverrid is at home in the trees or on the ground. The claws, like cats', are retractable.

EXTREMELY DANGEROUS

ENEMIES

The harrier hawk preys on
roll-tailed lemurs, which
they spot from high in the
Madagascan sky.

Silvestris Phototoservice/NHPA

LEAF-TAILED GECKO

oplatus fimbriatus—
obably the world's most
rfectly camouflaged
rk-living lizards.

FRUIT BAT

Madagascan fruit bats
often assemble in dense
roosts in tall trees and
in caves.

LYNX SPIDER

Peucetia madagascarien-
sis, an endemic creature,
is found in the eastern
rain forests.

PILL BUG

Pill millipedes the size of
golf balls (when rolled up
defensively) abound in the
west and in dry forests.

STREAKED TENREC

One of two species of
tenrecs found on the island,
the streaked tenrec has
detachable quills.

LEOPARDS

Eyal Bartov/Oxford Scientific Films

The South Arabian leopard (above) inhabits the Arabian desert, feeding on small mammals, birds, and reptiles.

The snow leopard (below) lives on rocky mountains. With its thick coat, it can survive extreme cold.

Michael Dick/Oxford Scientific Films

Leopards have a remarkable ability to survive, and even thrive, in just about any climate or habitat: They inhabit dense lowland rain forests, arid deserts, rocky mountains, low scrub, and even the suburbs of large cities.

This adaptability is due to several factors: the animal's ability to stalk its prey with only broken cover to hide behind, its taste for a wide variety of prey, and its solitary way of life. It means that leopards—with the most widespread distribution of all the cats—are found throughout Africa south of the Sahara, as well as in southern Asia; scattered populations live in North Africa and the Middle and Far East.

Wherever leopards live, two essential habitat elements will also be found: some form of cover, such as trees or bushes, and an adequate supply of prey. The cover provides places where the animal can feed and store its kill, undisturbed by predators, as well as acts as a screen when it stalks prey.

DISTRIBUTION

The leopard is found in Africa south of the Sahara (with small populations in North Africa); in southern Asia; and to a lesser extent in the Middle and the Far East and the islands of Java, Sri Lanka, and Zanzibar. Scattered populations of the snow leopard are found in the Hindu Kush, the Altai Mountains, and the Himalayas. The distribution of the clouded leopard ranges from India to southern China and Taiwan, to Malaya, Sumatra, and Borneo.

KEY

LEOPARD

CLOUDED LEOPARD

SNOW LEOPARD

LEOPARDS CAN LIVE IN ALMOST ANY HABITAT THAT HAS SUFFICIENT FOOD AND SOME FORM OF COVER

Perhaps surprisingly, water is not a necessity for the leopard. It drinks regularly when water is available, but in the desert the leopard gets enough moisture from the flesh of its victims and from a watery fruit called the desert melon.

COATS OF MANY COLORS

The seven subspecies of leopards have various thicknesses of coats and degrees of spotting according to where they live. For example, the coat of the Anatolian leopard of Asia Minor is

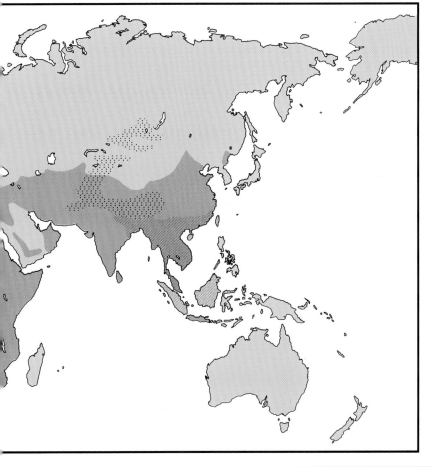

KEY FACTS

● One-third of all African leopards living south of the Sahara—nearly 200,000—are found in Zaire.

● The leopard is such an adaptable animal that it can, and does, live in temperatures varying from as high as 122°F (50°C) to well below freezing.

● There are approximately 25 times as many leopards per square mile in the African rain forest, where they are the only large predator, as there are in more open areas such as the Serengeti National Park, where competition for prey is much fiercer.

● The snow leopard usually lives at altitudes of about 9,800 ft (2,987 m) above sea level, though in the Himalayas it ranges up to 21,300 ft (6,490 m), and in Siberia in the summer it has been reported as low as 2,000 ft (610 m).

bright tan with gray patches, and the Sinai leopard, which inhabits the arid semideserts of the Middle East, has a light coat with large spots. The North African leopard, the most common subspecies, has a golden yellow coat, which provides excellent camouflage on the fringes of the Sahara.

SNOW LEOPARDS LIVE AT HIGH ALTITUDES IN THE SUMMER, DESCENDING DOWN THE MOUNTAIN IN WINTER TO FOLLOW THEIR PREY

These variations in coat color developed as the various leopard subspecies adapted to their own particular habitats. Varied background colors and spotting provide effective camouflage for each leopard in the different types of tree foliage or dense undergrowth it uses for cover.

KEEPING WARM

The length of a leopard's fur varies, too, and will often give an indication of the climate it inhabits. The longer the fur, the warmer a leopard will be. So the Amur leopard, found in the cold, mountainous areas of northern China, has a long, thick coat.

The melanistic leopard called the black panther

Tropical rain forest is home to the elusive clouded leopard (above). It chooses to dwell in areas of dense vegetation.

ZEFA/Photo Researchers

is frequently found in Asia—as many as half the leopards of the Malay Peninsula are black, and they are also common in southern India—but in Africa they occur only in the Ethiopian highlands, so it seems they thrive in humid habitats.

Sparsely distributed through the Himalayas of southern Asia, the Altai Mountains of Mongolia, and the Hindu Kush of Afghanistan, snow leopards are suberb rock climbers and live at varying altitudes according to the season.

> THE CLOUDED LEOPARD
> PREFERS AREAS OF DENSE VEGETATION—
> EITHER THICK EVERGREEN FOREST OR
> TROPICAL RAIN FOREST

In summer snow leopards are found high up in remote alpine meadows and scrub, high-altitude forests, and steep, rocky areas; in the winter they descend to low-lying forests in order to follow migrating prey and to avoid bad weather.

The coat of the snow leopard varies according to the seasons: It is fine in the hot summer, then grows thick for protection against the winter frost.

The clouded leopard is rarely seen in the wild, partly because it is largely nocturnal, and also

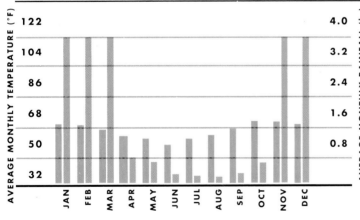

FOCUS ON

THE LEOPARD'S SAVANNA

The savanna, which consists of wide plains of tall grass with scattered bushes and trees, is an ideal place for a leopard to live. It is easy to take cover in grass that's as high as 10 feet (3 meters) tall. In addition, the occasional clumps of bushes and flat-topped trees such as acacias provide places to rest and to sleep, to keep newborn cubs safe, and to store food out of reach of other predators.

Lots of vegetation—a mixture of grasses and other plants, mostly red oat grass—means that there is plenty of food to support grazing animals, or herbivores, such as antelope and deer. These herbivores in turn serve as food for the carnivores such as the leopard. In fact, the savanna supports a complicated food chain, in which all the inhabitants, from the smallest beetle to the boldest lion, coexist by feeding on different types of food—including each other.

There are lakes and rivers in the savanna to provide drinking water, which the leopard will take advantage of whenever possible. Water levels may drop as much as 6 feet (1.8 meters) during the long dry season, but the leopard is able to survive for quite a while without drinking.

TEMPERATURE AND RAINFALL

AVERAGE MONTHLY TEMPERATURE (°F)

122
104
86
68
50
32

JAN FEB MAR APR MAY JUN JUL AUG SEP OCT NOV DEC

AVERAGE MONTHLY RAINFALL (in)

4.0
3.2
2.4
1.6
0.8

■ TEMPERATURE
■ RAINFALL

The climate of the savanna varies but is warm all year-round. There are two seasons: the dry, when there is often severe drought; and the wet, when the rains come. In the dry season the savanna looks parched but, when the rains come, it quickly blooms with grasses and other kinds of vegetation.

because it prefers areas of dense vegetation in which it can hide. Found in India, Nepal, southern China, Taiwan, Indochina, Sumatra, and Borneo, this cat inhabits thick evergreen forests and tropical rain forests, where it establishes its home range on sites close to riverbanks.

The blotchy pattern on the clouded leopard's coat resembles the pattern of light as the sun shines through the leaves of trees in the forests where it lives, and these markings break up its outline so it can remain hidden in the branches. ■

NEIGHBORS

These creatures coexist with the leopard and the other large carnivores, and all of them —flesh-eaters as well as grass-eaters—in the end depend upon the savanna grasses for their survival.

CHAMELEON

The chameleon lives in trees and eats insects, which it catches with its extremely long, sticky tongue.

GOLIATH BEETLE

The world's heaviest insect, this beetle weighs up to 3.5 (100 g)—8,000,000 times more than the lightest insect

Illustrations Elisabeth Gray

ENEMIES

THE AFRICAN SAVANNA

More than one-third of the African continent is covered by savanna vegetation.

To the north and south of the savanna lies desert—the Sahara, the Kalahari, and the Namib; to the west, an area of dense tropical rain forest.

SAVANNA

EXTREMELY DANGEROUS

LION
The leopard's most dangerous enemy, the lion will kill adult leopards as well as cubs.

MODERATELY DANGEROUS

HYENA
Spotted hyenas sometimes kill leopards, and they will often drive a leopard away from its kill.

MODERATELY DANGEROUS

BABOON
Male baboons will gather in a troop to mob—and possibly severely wound or kill—a single leopard.

WHITE-BACKED VULTURE	DUNG BEETLE	BABOON SPIDER	PANTHER TOAD	EGG-EATING SNAKE
The featherless head and neck of this vulture enable it to plunge deep into a carcass without getting dirty.	This beetle rolls herbivore droppings into a ball several times its own size, then eats it over several days.	This large, bird-eating spider gets its name from its hairy legs, said to resemble those of the baboon.	This toad is active only at night. Female panther toads lay long strands of as many as 24,000 eggs at a time.	The jaws of this snake are specially adapted to allow it to swallow bird eggs twice the size of its head.

LIONS

Lions' favored habitats are grassy plains, savannas, open woodlands, and scrubland. Although they range over a wide variety of habitats, including semideserts and mountains (at heights of up to 16,400 ft/5,000 m in Kenya), they avoid dense forests. Unlike the largely solitary tiger and jaguar, which tend to take smaller prey and thrive in such closed habitats, lions are adapted to hunting cooperatively for bigger prey; these are very scarce in thick forests, and the members of a pride of lions would find it difficult to keep in touch in close cover.

Within the grassy plains and savannas, lions make use of big outcrops of rock called kopjes. These prominent landmarks make ideal sites for groups of lions or individuals to lie up, hidden from the view of humans and prey alike, and to move around so that they stay shaded from the fierce heat of the sun. They also use other large objects such as anthills for this purpose.

GREAT WANDERERS

Lions are great wanderers, and they may turn up from time to time in areas where they were previously unknown for many years—often in places a long way from their present limits of distribution. Every so often, for instance, a few individuals wander onto the livestock farmland of the Zimbabwe plateau, from where they were driven out many years before. These nomadic lions generally kill a few cattle and then vanish as mysteriously as they

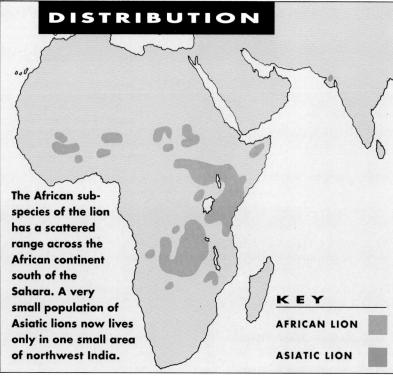

DISTRIBUTION

The African subspecies of the lion has a scattered range across the African continent south of the Sahara. A very small population of Asiatic lions now lives only in one small area of northwest India.

KEY

AFRICAN LION

ASIATIC LION

appear. Other wanderers have even ventured as far as the outskirts of large cities, such as Harare, the capital of Zimbabwe.

FOOD FOR ALL

The savanna grasslands are dominated by one group of plants: the grasses. Unlike many other flowering plants, the main growing parts of grasses are situated not at the tips of the stems, but at the bases of the leaves. This means that during the wet season, as fast as the great herds of zebras,

An Asiatic lion and subadults (left) stop for refreshments in the Gir Forest Sanctuary on the Gujarat peninsula in northwest India.

A pride of lions relaxes by water at the Ngorongoro Crater in Tanzania (right). In arid habitats they survive on the water that occurs in the intestines or in the blood of prey.

Joanne Vangruisen/Survival Anglia

Thomson's gazelles, and other grazing herbivores that wander these plains eat the leaves, the grasses grow again, thus providing a more or less continuous supply of food.

The east African savannas support the greatest remaining diversity and abundance of large grazing mammals in the world—over forty species of large grazing herbivores still live there, sharing a relatively uniform food supply. Rather than being spread evenly around the habitat, they mainly move in herds, constantly seeking nutritious new vegetation and water. During the dry season, when the savanna changes from a vast carpet of an intense green color to a parched, dusty expanse of rustling, dried-out, bleached-gold grass stems and leaves, huge numbers of wildebeests and other grazers are on the move, migrating from one area to another to find food and water.

DIFFERENT TACTICS

Although they all feed on the same food resource—grass—the many different species of grazers avoid competition by subtle differences in behavior. Three

@ SIGHT
THE WANDERING LIFE

Although in most habitats the majority of lions live in prides, there are always some that opt instead for a nomadic existence. Life is often hard for these homeless wanderers, which may roam over areas as great as 1,500 square miles (3,885 square kilometers). They are unable to kill very large mammals by themselves and are less likely to be able to subdue dangerous prey, such as buffalo or zebra stallions, so they are more likely to be injured. Their wanderings make them more likely to come into conflict with hunters or farmers. Also, a solitary male faces threats or attack from pride lions. He has little chance of usurping them and taking over a pride and enjoying the relative security of life with companions in a territory. On average, the death rate is bound to be higher among nomads than among lions living in prides. Unlike the territory-holding pride members, a nomad is usually remarkably tolerant of strange lions. Although it may spend a good deal of time traveling alone, it will often team up with one or more other lions if it gets the chance, even if only for a while. Such companions are usually of the same sex and roughly the same age.

Nicholas Parfitt/Tony Stone Worldwide

major species of grazers follow one another across the savanna. Plains zebras are the first to graze the long grass, eating the tougher parts of the plants. This makes the rest of the grass available to blue wildebeests or brindled gnu, which crop the living carpet shorter. Finally the diminutive Thomson's gazelles eat the short sward that remains, supplementing their diet by browsing on acacia bushes. Other large herbivores, such as

> A PRIDE'S TERRITORY HAS A CENTER OF ACTIVITY—AN AREA IN WHICH IT CAN FIND MOST OF ITS FOOD AND WATER

giraffes and elephants, are browsers, feeding in different ways on the foliage of bushes and trees.

These huge herds of herbivorous mammals provide a rich source of food for a range of predators, including lions, leopards, cheetahs, spotted hyenas, and hunting dogs. Just as their prey's different feeding techniques prevent them from eating one another out of house and home, these predators generally avoid competition by each hunting a different range of prey in a different way.

THE LION'S SHARE

Although all five of the predators listed above hunt mammals weighing less than 220 lb (100 kg), only the lion habitually kills prey heavier than about 550 lb (250 kg). Also, lions take a greater proportion of healthy adult prey than do the other species.

Lions specialize in hunting cooperatively, lying in wait for their prey at water holes or stalking it with great patience, using every available piece of cover in open habitats, until they are close enough to make a final brief dash. They are more successful when hunting at night.

Leopards, which are far smaller than lions but extremely strong and powerful predators nonetheless, tend to prey more on smaller creatures, such as Thomson's gazelles, wildebeest calves, and baboons. They hunt mainly in cover, especially in thickets and around kopjes, and are the supreme stalkers among the great cats.

Cheetahs—the most specialized of all the big cats—are by far the most lightly built of the great cats. Built for speed and not for stalking, they are the fastest of all land mammals. A hunting cheetah streaks across the open plains for short distances at speeds approaching 60 mph (100 km/h), running down Thomson's and other gazelles. In contrast to all other cats, it is almost entirely a daytime hunter.

PACK HUNTERS

The most powerful predator in Africa next to the lion is the spotted hyena. Once unjustly branded as a cowardly scavenger, it is bulky and powerful enough to attack wildebeest and other sizable

FOCUS ON

LIFE IN A NATIONAL PARK

Of all places where lions can be seen in numbers, the Serengeti National Park in Tanzania is a premier site. So many lions were being shot by big game hunters that the area was declared a game reserve in 1929. It became a national park in 1951, and in 1981 it—together with the adjacent Ngorongoro Conservation Area—was declared a World Heritage Site. It has been estimated that the total population of lions in the park needs to kill as much as 5,800 tons (5,890 tonnes) of prey every year to survive. This may seem like a great deal, but the predators do not endanger the continued existence of their prey. Lions, along with other predators, are an essential part of the savanna ecosystem, and the prey animals need the predators for survival just as much as the predators need the prey. The predators tend to take prey that is easier to catch, so that old, sick, or young animals are killed more often than healthy adults. Both predators and prey have shaped each other's evolutionary development. Prey has become fleet on foot, while the lions have attained a physical size and social structure ideally suited for exploiting a variety of large, grassland herbivores.

TEMPERATURE AND RAINFALL

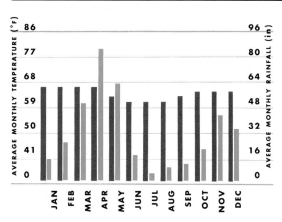

■ TEMPERATURE

■ RAINFALL

The Serengeti has an almost constant monthly temperature of 63–64°F (17–18°C) all year. After the November–May rainy season, the grasslands are arid, and most animals migrate elsewhere.

prey. And, like the lion, it has a highly evolved social system and is a very effective cooperative hunter. Packs of up to twenty-five spotted hyenas are capable of killing almost any prey, except for the real giants, such as elephants or rhinos.

Hunting dogs, though far less powerful, also benefit from hunting in packs. Capable of running fast for long periods, they can outpace and kill any sick or young animal, and sometimes tackle much larger healthy prey more than ten times their size, such as adult wildebeest or zebra. ■

NEIGHBORS

As well as immense populations of large grazing mammals and of lions and other predators, the Serengeti region supports a wealth of other animals and a rich plant life.

AFRICAN ELEPHANT

The African elephant is a generalist grazer, feeding on a wide range of plants according to availability.

DUNG BEETLE

Dung beetles perform a vital service by breaking down animal droppings, on which their larvae feed.

Illustrations Kim Thompson

SERENGETI NATIONAL PARK

Containing the greatest concentrations of large wild animals in the world, Serengeti National Park covers 5,708 square miles (14,783 square kilometers)—about three times the size of the Grand Canyon National Park. It lies in Tanzania, to the east of Lake Victoria, and extends as far north as Kenya.

KENYA

Serengeti National Park

TANZANIA

Purdy & Matthews/Survival Anglia

UPPELL'S GRIFFON VULTURE

his vulture is one of everal vulture species that east on the abundant arrion of the savanna.

CHEETAH

Cheetahs are vulnerable to other large predators, such as lions, which steal their prey and eat their cubs.

RED-BILLED QUELEA

Flocks of up to a million of these birds follow the rains, stripping the grain from crops.

COMMON JACKAL

Black-backed jackal pups are often guarded by adult "baby-sitters," usually their older siblings.

BLACK RHINO

The black rhino uses its highly mobile, elongated upper lip to pull leaves into its mouth.

MANATEES

All the living sirenians are aquatic animals, found only in warm tropical and subtropical waters. They rely on sea grasses or freshwater vegetation in order to survive, and their distribution therefore depends on where these plant materials are at their most abundant.

The two subspecies of West Indian manatees, although possessing different cranial characteristics, can be differentiated most easily by their range. As its name suggests, the Florida manatee can be found year-round off the coast of peninsular Florida in the United States. Its primary range along the Atlantic coast is from St. Johns River in the northeast to Miami in the south. On the Gulf coast it is abundant in Everglades National Park and extends northward to the Suwannee River. During the warm summer months, however, the Florida manatee may sometimes venture as far north as Virginia and as far west as Mississippi or Louisiana. Some animals have even been sighted in the waters of the Bahamas.

MANGROVES

The Florida Everglades are well stocked with distinctive mangrove swamps. Mangrove trees are evergreens with tough, leathery leaves and open-air root systems. These roots look and act rather like snorkels, enabling the trees to tolerate poorly

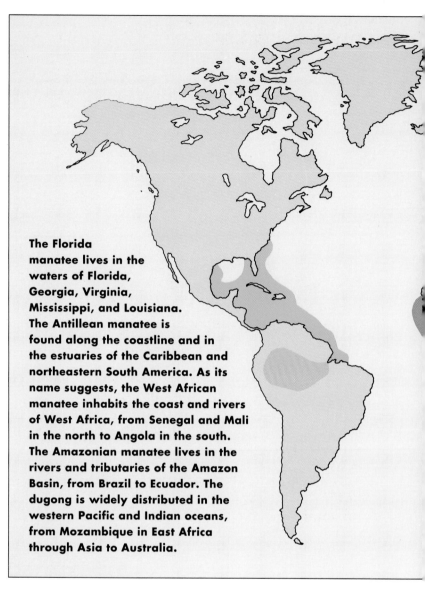

The Florida manatee lives in the waters of Florida, Georgia, Virginia, Mississippi, and Louisiana. The Antillean manatee is found along the coastline and in the estuaries of the Caribbean and northeastern South America. As its name suggests, the West African manatee inhabits the coast and rivers of West Africa, from Senegal and Mali in the north to Angola in the south. The Amazonian manatee lives in the rivers and tributaries of the Amazon Basin, from Brazil to Ecuador. The dugong is widely distributed in the western Pacific and Indian oceans, from Mozambique in East Africa through Asia to Australia.

Norbert Wu/NHPA

oxygenated soils, saltwater, and Florida's devastating hurricanes. There are three different types of mangroves. The red mangrove grows best in shallow salt water and spreads out into the sea. Its curving roots form a tough web that traps silt and, in time, creates a barrier against the sea behind which other plants can grow. The black mangrove grows in tidal zones. It has clusters of breathing pores that project into the air from the roots so that the tree can breathe during high tides and floods. The white mangrove is the most tolerant of freshwater and usually grows farther inland. It has few breathing pores and no supporting roots.

The Antillean manatee inhabits waters throughout the greater Caribbean area—including Mexico and southern Texas—and northeastern South America. Both subspecies can live in salt and fresh water, and any waterway that is over 3.3 ft (1 m) deep with a good supply of sea grasses or other vegetation can become home to a manatee. The West

The Lake Okeechobee-Everglades basin covers 17,000 sq mi (44,000 sq km), and the many rivers and connecting lakes are ideal for manatees (left).

DISTRIBUTION

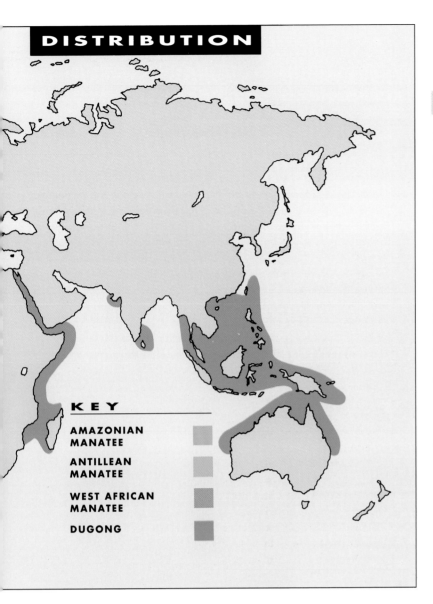

KEY

AMAZONIAN MANATEE	▇
ANTILLEAN MANATEE	▇
WEST AFRICAN MANATEE	▇
DUGONG	▇

in SIGHT

HEAT SEEKERS

Although the Florida manatee has always moved south to natural warm-water refuges for the winter, in recent years it has also been able to take advantage of man-made hot spots. The Florida coast is dotted with power plants that discharge warm water all year round. The manatees have become conditioned to expect warm water at these sites, and now many of them stay north of their historic wintering grounds, preferring instead to gather around these artificially heated sources. Sometimes, during especially cold weather, more than 200 manatees congregate at each water outlet. The power companies now find themselves laden with a huge responsibility toward the animals.

In December 1989, Florida experienced an unprecedented cold snap, with subzero temperatures lasting for several days. To escape the cold, many manatees headed for the warm outlets at the Florida Power and Light Company's power plants, instead of following their traditional migratory route south. Sadly, the air temperatures were so low that the water at the plants was not quite warm enough, and many manatees died. Now the company is looking into the possibility of creating a manatee "spa." This would be an enclosed area near the discharge, where the water could be kept at the correct temperature for the manatees without being cooled down by surrounding water currents.

Indian manatee can survive in bays, estuaries, rivers, and coastal areas, although it rarely ventures into deeper ocean waters.

During the winter, the Florida manatee migrates south to warmer water. The Blue Spring Run, a section of the St. Johns River in Blue Spring State Park near Orange City, Florida, is one of the most popular winter refuges. The attraction is the brilliantly clear water, which is kept at a constant 72°F (22°C) by warm water surging out of an underground spring at a rate of 100 million gallons (455 million liters) a day. Manatees have migrated here in the winter for thousands of years, and today the

Like other sirenians — and in fact like hippos, too — the Amazonian manatee possesses special valves that seal off its nostrils when diving (left).

park is an important winter refuge for over sixty individuals, many of which return every year and are well known to the rangers, who recognize them by scars on their backs. The manatees begin to arrive around mid-November, as soon as the water temperature in the main part of the river reaches 68°F (20°C), and they stay until sometime in March.

The West African manatee can also live in fresh or saltwater. It generally prefers quiet coasts, broad rivers, lagoons, and connected lakes. In Senegal, the manatee sometimes moves so far upstream in the Senegal River that it gets trapped in tributaries and lakes by dwindling water levels in the dry season. In these cases, staff from the Ministry of Water and Forests take the isolated manatees back to the river.

The Amazonian manatee is the only sirenian confined to freshwater. It lives in the myriad rivers of the Amazon Basin and is most abundant in floodplain lakes and channels in white-water (less acidic) river systems. Its preferred water temperature is around 77–86°F (25–30°C). During the wet season the manatee is widely dispersed throughout its range; but as the water levels drop during the dry season, animals begin to congregate in deep-water

Doug Perrine/Planet Earth Pictures

FOCUS ON

FLORIDA'S EVERGLADES

The Florida Everglades is an immense national park covering some 13,000 sq mi (33,670 sq km). It comprises various habitats including marshy grasslands, pine forests, and the mangrove swamps that are home to the Florida manatee. In addition to the manatee, the Everglades mangroves support the raccoon, coon oyster, roundtailed muskrat, sea turtle, tree snail, and many snakes.

The Everglades has a summer wet season from May to October and a winter dry season. During the former there is heavy rainfall and the atmosphere is warm and humid. This is also the hurricane season. During the dry season, water levels in the park fall dramatically, and the manatee migrates to deeper waters.

TEMPERATURE AND RAINFALL

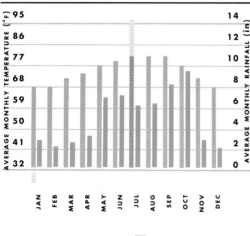

The data here apply to the Miami area, on the southernmost tip of Florida. Temperatures and rainfall peak in the summer months, but most months see an appreciable amount of rainfall. Florida is sunnier, and has more thunderstorms, than any other state in the United States. Although conditions are generally stable throughout the year, occasional cold snaps in January can cause problems for the manatees.

TEMPERATURE   **RAINFALL**

MINIMUM TEMPERATURE   **MAXIMUM TEMPERATURE**

lakes and deep parts of rivers, where they remain until the rains return and the water levels rise.

The dugong is chiefly a salt-water animal, but it is sometimes found in estuaries. It occurs in the waters of forty-three countries along the western Pacific and Indian Oceans and is most abundant in the northern half of Australia, where an estimated 70,000 individuals may live. Like the manatees, the dugong prefers shallow water, and although dives of up to 36–40 ft (11–12 m) have been observed, these are rare. ∎

NEIGHBORS   ROYAL TERN   AMERICAN ALLIGATOR

Florida's subtropical habitats are a rich, fertile environment for plants and animals. They are home to at least 100 different mammal species, including armadillos, bears, and big cats.

The royal tern feeds on fish and crabs. It breeds along the coasts of the Americas and West Africa.

A ferocious predator, the American alligator lives in the warm swamps of the southeastern United States.

FLORIDA
Much of Florida lies on a peninsula that projects some 500 mi (800 km) into the Atlantic Ocean and forms the eastern lip of the Gulf of Mexico. The land is low lying, the highest point rising only 345 ft (105 m) above sea level. South of the Everglades and Florida Bay lie the Keys, a long chain of tiny islands.

GEORGIA

Atlantic Ocean

Gulf of Mexico

FLORIDA

Everglades

SWAMPY AREAS

LEMON SHARK

e stealthy lemon shark uises the shallow coastal aters on the lookout for od-sized fish to eat.

SNAPPING TERRAPIN

The snapping terrapin possesses immensely powerful jaws that can kill even a baby alligator.

SPOTTED GROUPER

A master of disguise, the spotted grouper can change color in seconds to avoid its enemies.

MARSH HAWK

As hunters of frogs, small birds, and insects, hawks find a rich supply of prey in the Everglades swamps.

BELTED KINGFISHER

This winter resident of the Everglades is a solitary and deadly predator of freshwater fish.

MARMOSET MONKEYS

The Callithricidae monkeys live in a mixture of scrubland and rain forest areas in Central and South America. The Amazonian rain forest is probably the most exciting because it is like a hot-house world inhabited by a vast variety of birds, mammals, and insects. It is a threatened paradise that we have really only just started to explore. It is also of fundamental importance to the balance of the earth's atmosphere, because its trees are the largest oxygen producers on the earth's surface.

The rain forest contains about two-thirds of the world's freshwater, including the Amazon River and over 1,000 tributaries. It covers more than a third of South America and has over half the world's plant and animal species living in it. Within the Amazon Basin there are several hundred species of monkesy, more than 600 bird species, and over 40,000 species of flowering plants. Also, the vegetation supports millions of insects; 20,000 species can inhabit an area the size of a football field. Particularly in moist tropical rain forests, insects, amphibians, and fish have all developed unique, specialized lifestyles. This variation is partly due to South America's unusual geological history. The

---

THE UPPER AMAZON REGION CONTAINS THE GREATEST VARIETY OF TAMARIN AND MARMOSET SPECIES

---

fragmentation of the continents over 100 million years ago meant that its animals evolved in isolation for millions of years until the creation of the land bridge with North America, about 3.5 million years ago, allowed other species to enter.

SPECIES UNDER THREAT

This amazing diversity is only a part of an even greater variety spread across South America. There are about 800 mammal species and 3,000 bird species in South America, 80 percent of which are unique to the region. These bird species account for one-third of the world's total. Some 70 mammal, 300 bird, and over 80 other species are threatened. Surprisingly, only four mammal and two bird species are thought to have become extinct since 1600, including the glaucous macaw, Colombian grebe, and Falkland Islands wolf. Notable threatened endemic species, other than marmosets and tamarins, include the woolly spider monkey, maned wolf, giant otter, little blue macaw, South American river turtle, and the Galapagos land snail.

DISTRIBUTION

The various species of marmosets and tamarins inhabit different areas of the upper Amazon, but the family as a whole covers Columbia, Brazil, Bolivia, Peru, northern Paraguay, and Panama.

KEY

MARMOSETS & TAMARINS

Michael Freeman/Bruce Coleman Ltd.

The Geoffroy's tufted-ear or white-faced marmoset (above).

L. C. Marigo/Bruce Coleman Ltd.

Plants have adapted well to the rain forest environment, where there is plenty of heat and humidity. The tree canopy forms a layer 33 ft (10 m) deep, which captures about 95 percent of the available sunlight. Liana vines and other creepers struggle to reach this level to flower. Giant trees grow throughout the forest and most of these flower brilliantly, later producing fruit for fruit-eating creatures like the marmosets and tamarins, the cebid monkeys, and the fruit bats. A lot of the seeds from

BUSHY TREE GROWTH AND THICK TANGLES OF LIANA VINES PROVIDE GOOD SLEEPING SITES FOR THESE MONKEYS

the canopy level never reach the ground, but germinate in the moist cushion of debris and tree-living plants high above the ground. Ferns, large orchids, and bromeliad plants are epiphytes—plants that live high up on other trees, where they receive the light and water they need. The bromeliads collect rainwater and insects in cup-forming leaves, which provide them with both moisture and nutrients. Their sticky seeds are carried by birds to other trees where they germinate and grow.

There is an enormous population of platyrrhine (flat-nosed) monkeys in the forest canopy, and much of the large volume of dung that they produce is caught on the branches of the canopy. There it is disassembled rapidly by droves of dung

A pygmy marmoset (left) perches on grasses, easily justifying its status as the world's smallest monkey.

KEY FACTS

● The combined mass of all the tropical moist forests—Amazonia included—accounts for 80 percent of the earth's vegetation, even though they occupy no more than 7 percent of the planet's surface.

● The endangered buffy-headed marmoset survives only in Atlantic forest remnants in southeast Brazil.

● The Goeldi's marmoset is rare throughout its range, but especially so in parts of Colombia where the slash-and-burn style of agriculture has destroyed much of its habitat.

● The rain forest's soil is surprisingly poor in nutrients, tending instead to be thin and sandy. The organic debris that falls to the ground simply does not get a chance to leach into the soil, because it is recycled so quickly by the forest's flora and fauna. For this reason, most attempts to graze cattle or grow crops on cleared rain forest land fail within a couple of years, when the nutritive value of the land peters out.

beetles. Millions of ants and termites devour any decaying logs, leaves, or corpses of other animals. These and other insects are eaten by marmosets and tamarins. The canopy provides a complete food chain, with monkeys, tree-climbing rats and mice, sloths, birds, and insects feeding on fruits and seeds, and in turn becoming food for other animals. Spiders, too, feed on small invertebrates—and they themselves fall prey to the monkeys.

LIVING IN A PERFECT NICHE

The tropical rain forests provide a rich and varied environment, and the animals living in this hot-house environment have specialized to fill every tiny habitat type and to exploit every possible food source. Yet some ancient species have survived from before the region's early period of isolation. One of these is the velvet worm, which has short, thick legs and a segmented body like a fleshy milli-pede, and which seems to be a form intermediate to annelid worms (such as earthworms and leeches) and arthropods (insects and crustaceans). In partic-ular, the rain forest has allowed the evolution of an amazing range of animals with grasping tails. As well as monkeys, porcupines, mice, rats, opossums, the fruit-eating kinkajou raccoon, and even some

FOCUS ON

BRAZILIAN COASTAL FOREST

The tropical forests of northeastern South America lie mostly within Brazil. Passion flower and bougainvillea sprawl through the trees where the marmoset lives. Pollinated by countless small birds and bats, these vines provide a lot of the monkey's food—in the form of fruit, flowers, and nectar, or the small invertebrates and insects sheltering there.

Animals in the forest rivers range from clouds of tiny biting insects to large alligators. Many river species once inhabited the ocean; these include sharks, sawfish, sole, needlefish, and rays, as well as large marine toads and the manatee. Riverine predators include the piranha fish and the caiman, which itself falls prey to the anaconda snake. Birds, such as the scarlet ibis, the spoonbill, and the hoatzin, visit the rivers to feed. Unique species include the world's only aquatic marsupial, the water opossum, and the basilisk lizard, which can run over the surface of the water.

In higher regions, few plants grow at ground level, but at low altitudes, the forest floor is barely penetrable. Most of the mammals, such as the monkeys, live up in the tree canopy. Ground-level animals include the tapir, the swamp deer, the paca, and the capybara, which is the world's largest rodent.

TEMPERATURE AND RAINFALL

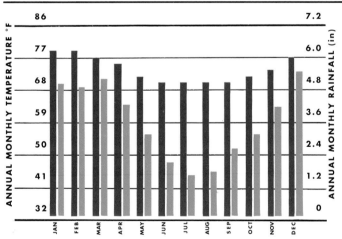

- TEMPERATURE
- RAINFALL

The climate of the Brazilian coastal forest varies with the location. The rainfall is heaviest, and the temperature most constant, in the Amazon Basin at the equator. Farther south, the rainfall is lighter and the temperature more variable.

tree snakes, have this useful "extra limb." One rea-son for this may be the frequency of flooding in large areas of rain forest at specific times of the year, forcing animals to travel from branch to branch instead of along the ground.

A wide variety of monkeys can coexist in the rain forest by feeding on different kinds of food at different levels of the forest trees. These monkeys include the callithricids, but because the tamarins and marmosets hate water, they have evolved into many different species separated by the rivers and tributaries that divide up the rain forest. ∎

NEIGHBORS

Animals living in the South American forests have many neighbors—some of which, such as the pampas cat, ocelot, and jaguar, are highly dangerous to small tree-living monkeys.

OCELOT

Itself hunted mercilessly for its fur, the ocelot is an occasional predator of marmosets and tamarins.

RED HOWLER MONKEY

One of the largest New World monkeys, the red howler utters deafeningly loud calls.

Illustrations Kim Thompson

COASTAL BRAZIL

Brazil comprises almost half the land area of South America and a high proportion of the world's rain forests. Along the coast to the east of Rio de Janeiro is situated some of the fine coastal forests of the country. The area shown on the map is home to the rare golden lion tamarin.

RIO DE JANEIRO

Martyn Colbeck/Oxford Scientific Films

OOLLY SPIDER MONKEY	AGOUTI	FIELD MOUSE	THREE-TOED SLOTH	TREE ANTEATER

OOLLY SPIDER MONKEY
lso called the muriqui, this ow endangered species habits the forests from ahia to São Paulo.

AGOUTI
These large but secretive rodents help to disperse the seeds of rain forest trees by feeding on fallen fruit.

FIELD MOUSE
The South American field mouse spends most of the night in trees, where it feeds from plants.

THREE-TOED SLOTH
Some sloths never leave the trees; this species descends to defecate. It eats leaves, tender shoots, and fruits.

TREE ANTEATER
Active at night, the tree anteater or tamandua climbs around with the help of its prehensile tail.

MARTENS

Although martens are adaptable enough to thrive in a wide variety of habitats, their strongholds lie in the great conifer belt of the north: the boreal forest, named after Boreas, the Greek god of the north wind, and known in Siberia as the taiga.

The taiga is the biggest forest in the world. In the former Soviet Union it stretches over 10,000 miles (over 16,000 km) from the Pacific to the Baltic, and extends west through Scandinavia to the shores of the North Atlantic. In North America, the forest covers much of Alaska and sprawls eastward across Canada to Labrador and Newfoundland. It is an immense ocean of trees, flanked to the south by the grassy steppes and prairies and to the north by the bleak, half-frozen swamplands of the Arctic tundra.

ALL-WEATHER MAMMALS

In the continental heart of the taiga the climate is testing in the extreme. In eastern Siberia the temperature may fall to –76°F (–60°C) in winter, yet in summer it may reach almost 100°F (38°C). There is little rain; even in wetter areas the rain often falls as snow and remains locked up as ice for much of the year. The conifers of the forest—pines, firs, spruces, and larches—are well equipped to survive these conditions, with tough, spiny leaves that resist water loss and drooping branches that shed snow before its weight builds up to timber-cracking levels, and they shield the animals of the forest from the worst weather. Even so, the animals need to be tough. The pine marten, the sable, and the fisher are among the

Mink (above) rely on their coat of guard hairs and underfur to keep them warm.

MINK AND OTTERS

In Britain the introduced American mink has been implicated in the decline of the native otter population. It is assumed that, as a semiaquatic hunter, the mink competes with the otter for food and territory, and has driven it out of its old haunts.

This is unlikely. At 22 lb (10 kg) the otter is ten times the size of the 2.2 lb (1 kg) mink, and accordingly it concentrates on much larger prey. Otters studied in Scandinavia fed mainly on large fish, while mink living alongside them preyed on small mammals such as water voles. Both will catch small fish and frogs, but as an underwater specialist the otter is more likely to take them in deep water while the mink scoops them out of the shallows. Mink tend to prefer overgrown waterways that are unsuitable for the otter's underwater hunting technique. Where the two occur together they can usually live in harmony, for an otter will have no objection to an animal of a different species occupying part of its territory.

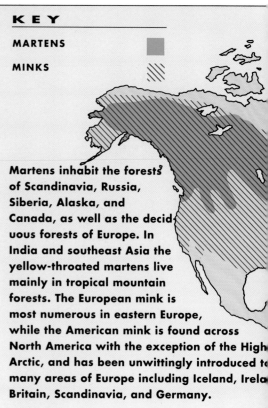

KEY

MARTENS

MINKS

Martens inhabit the forests of Scandinavia, Russia, Siberia, Alaska, and Canada, as well as the deciduous forests of Europe. In India and southeast Asia the yellow-throated martens live mainly in tropical mountain forests. The European mink is most numerous in eastern Europe, while the American mink is found across North America with the exception of the High Arctic, and has been unwittingly introduced to many areas of Europe including Iceland, Ireland, Britain, Scandinavia, and Germany.

toughest, thanks to the superb insulation provided by their legendary silky fur. The fur comprises two distinct layers: Long guard hairs cast off the rain and protect against physical damage, and a denser underfur retains an insulating blanket of air around the animal's body core. In spring much of the fur is molted to leave a shorter, coarser summer coat, but in autumn the thick pelt grows again to see the animal through the winter.

Although quite capable of bearing the Arctic cold, martens rarely stray north of the tree line into the tundra zone, even in summer when prey is abundant on the grasslands. They are forest-hunters, and although species like the sable and the fisher hunt mainly on the ground, rather than in the forest canopy, they rely on the trees to provide cover—both for them and for their prey. To the south they readily colonize deciduous forest, and in western Ireland, for example, pine martens flourish in the hazel woodlands of County Clare. In Britain they were common in the oak woodlands of southern England as recently as the mid-18th century, and there are records of martens being trapped in woodland near Arundel, near the south coast, in the 1840s. Their disappearance from such regions had more to do with persecution than a preference for more rigorous habitats, and today pine martens still flourish in the deciduous forests of France, Germany, and central Europe, occurring as far south as Sicily.

A fisher (above) eating a rare meal of fish. This species is better known for its prowess in penetrating the spiny defenses of the North American porcupine.

In general the pine marten seems to prefer scrub woodland with plenty of fruit-bearing bushes, abundant prey, and good ground cover; it is rarely seen in the open, and even individuals that live on heather moors take care to stay out of sight. Martens do not have many enemies apart from humans, but they are regularly caught and eaten by eagles, the only birds of prey that are powerful enough to carry them aloft. Wolves may take them, but the strong smell of their scent glands—although not unpleasant to us—tends

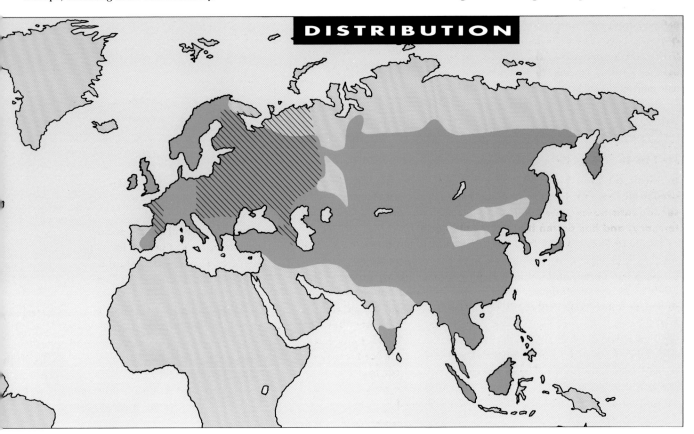

DISTRIBUTION

to discourage all but the most determined mammal predator. Since birds cannot smell, eagles are not deterred in the same way.

Most habitats support only one marten species at a time. In the forests of North America, however, the fisher may share territory with the American marten. This works because the bigger, more powerful fisher tends to concentrate on prey that the smaller marten could not tackle. The size difference also means there is no competition for den sites, for the American marten can squeeze into crevices that the fisher would not consider.

In Europe a similar size differential reduces the potential rivalry between the introduced American mink and the Eurasian otter (see box, page 126) but there is little difference between the newcomer and the native European mink, which occupies exactly the same ecological niche. Consequently it is feared that the now-rare European species has been displaced by its more vigorous cousin in some regions. In others, however, such as Britain, the absence of the European species left the niche vacant, and the American mink simply filled it.

Both species of mink commonly live along riverbanks and in reedbeds, swamps, and marshes; like martens, they like to keep close to cover. In winter mink may abandon their summer hunting grounds if

Manfred Danegger/NHPA

FOCUS ON

CALEDONIAN FOREST

Some 2,000 years ago the great boreal forests extended across Europe to northern Britain. The ancient Caledonian forest has now largely disappeared from Scotland, its place taken by heather moorland. The fragments that remain are the strongholds of the pine marten in Britain.

The dominant tree in these primeval woodlands is the Scots pine, one of only three species of conifer native to Britain. Scots pine is a common tree on acid soils throughout Britain, but it achieves a particular majesty in the Caledonian forest. The trees provide food for a variety of birds, such as the goldcrest, siskin, crested tit, and crossbill, as well as the red squirrel—all potential prey for the pine marten and the sparrow hawks, kestrels, and buzzards that patrol the skies. The surrounding scrub of heather, bilberry, and bracken provides cover for gamebirds such as the blackcock and the mighty capercaillie, red and roe deer, and small mammals and the carnivores that stalk them such as the red fox, weasel, marten, and, in some areas, the wildcat. In the valleys there may be otters fishing the clear waters of the Highland rivers, adding a finishing touch to a scene that, in these fragments of ancient forest, has barely changed since the end of the Ice Age.

TEMPERATURE AND RAINFALL

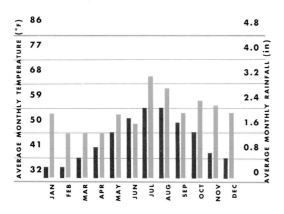

■ TEMPERATURE

▨ RAINFALL

Winter brings frosts and deep snowfalls, obliging all but the hardiest birds and mammals to migrate or hibernate. The summer is mild and moist, and, in typical Scottish style, heavy rains persist through the autumn.

the water freezes over and move on to fast-flowing streams where the water moves too rapidly for ice to form. This may involve moving uphill, unlike most other animals which tend to move downhill into the valleys in winter to take advantage of the milder climate. Such considerations are irrelevant to a mink, for like the sable it has a luxuriant fur coat with up to twenty-four underfur hairs for each guard hair. The American mink thrives as far north as northern Alaska, and the European mink may hunt over the tundra on the icy coast of the Arctic Ocean. ■

NEIGHBORS

Some of Britain's rarest mammals can still be found in the cool, fragrant glades of the Caledonian forest, while the pine seeds provide a rich source of food for the many birds.

WILDCAT

The wildcat looks like a domestic cat but for its more massive head, thick coat, and bushy, blunt tail.

CROSSBILL

The crossbill uses its bizarre beak and thick, leathery tongue to snip out and eat the seeds from pine cones.

Neighbor illustrations Ruth Grewcock. Crossbill and moth Andrew Robinson/Wildlife Art Agency

CALEDONIAN PINES

Naturally regenerated from strewn seeds, Scots pine trees are broadly spaced like oaks in an English woodland, and grow to a similar size. The remaining stands of Caledonian forest are scattered throughout the Highlands and along the valleys of rivers such as the Spey.

ANCIENT FOREST

RED DEER

[...]is deer is widespread in [...]tain, but its strongholds among the Grampians [an]d Highlands of Scotland.

WOOD ANT

These ants forage along paths up to 100 ft (30 m) from their nests among the fallen pine needles.

RED FOX

Now common in our cities and suburbs, the red fox preys upon the voles and rabbits of the pine forest.

CAPERCAILLIE

Now sadly rare, the magnificent capercaillie cock lures his mate with a raucous, thrilling call.

PINE BEAUTY MOTH

This moth blends well with the bark of pine trunks, and its caterpillars look rather like pine needles.

MOLES

Of the two mole families, the Talpidae—the moles, shrew-moles, and desmans—have a much wider world distribution than the golden moles. Whereas the Talpidae are spread throughout Europe, Asia, and North America, the golden moles are restricted to sub-Saharan Africa.

Golden moles originated in Africa, probably from a tenreclike ancestor, and have never managed to expand beyond this dry continent. They are confined to areas south of the equator. Golden moles have changed little over time; fossils have been found from 27 million years ago in Kenya, and

---

MOLEHILLS CAN BE MISTAKEN FOR NEST HILLS OF THE YELLOW ANT, BUT THESE ARE LARGER AND MORE STEEPLY SIDED

---

over two million years ago in South Africa. They occur in a wide range of dry habitats, from scrub and swamp edges to dry forests. Many of the species are poorly known and the classification of the group remains provisional.

FOOD-BASED TERRITORIES

Adapted for a digging lifestyle underground, moles can make their home anywhere where the soil is deep enough to support both a tunnel network and sufficient prey animals. If the soil is waterlogged or subject to permafrost, this will limit the moles' distribution. Suitable habitats differ greatly in the

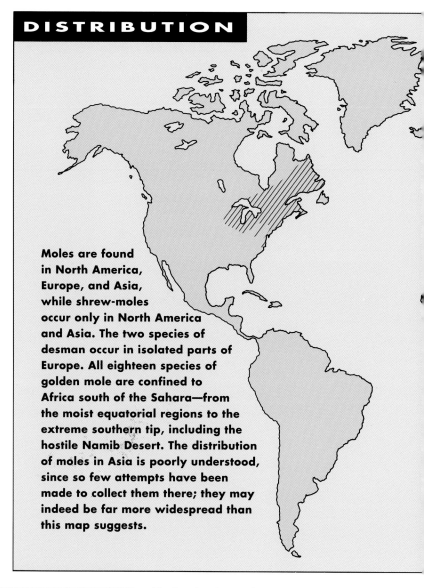

DISTRIBUTION

Moles are found in North America, Europe, and Asia, while shrew-moles occur only in North America and Asia. The two species of desman occur in isolated parts of Europe. All eighteen species of golden mole are confined to Africa south of the Sahara—from the moist equatorial regions to the extreme southern tip, including the hostile Namib Desert. The distribution of moles in Asia is poorly understood, since so few attempts have been made to collect them there; they may indeed be far more widespread than this map suggests.

John Hartley/NHPA

The Russian desman lives in burrows or natural hollows beside slow-moving rivers and lakes (left).

amount of food that they can supply, and typically include deciduous woodlands and permanent pastures at one extreme to coniferous forests and near-barren sand dunes at the other. Moles living in habitats with high prey densities—in the order of 0.7–0.8 oz of invertebrates per square foot (200–250 g per square meter) occupy small ranges of 3,228–4,304 square feet (300–400 square meters). In contrast to this, some individuals have been found living in sand dunes where prey is a hundred times more scarce. In this case individual moles had territories a dozen times larger, at more than 1.24 acres (5,000 square meters) in area.

Although moles are rarely seen, every proud gardener whose lawn has been turned overnight into a mountain range will know that they betray their presence in grand style. Molehills lack any

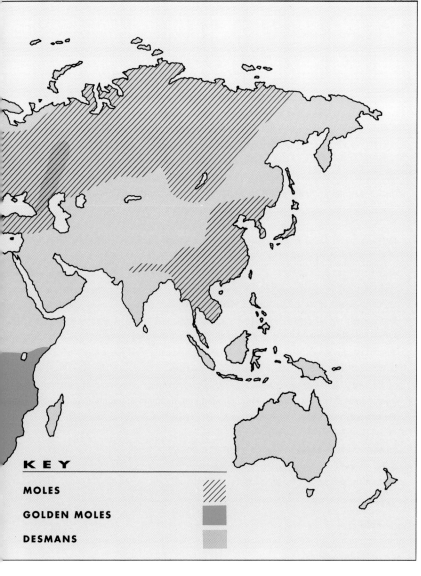

KEY

MOLES

GOLDEN MOLES

DESMANS

KEY FACTS

● Russian desmans face competition from introduced coypus and muskrats in their native habitats, in addition to the drainage of wetlands. Furthermore, particularly heavy frosts may trap desmans beneath the ice.

● The central Pyrenean subspecies of desman is extinct, probably as a result of competition with, or direct predation by, the introduced American mink.

● The giant golden mole of South Africa occurs locally in remnants of forests and in open grasslands. Such habitats are rapidly being converted into grazing and arable pasture.

● Pyrenean desmans are confined to small, fast-flowing watercourses; they rely particularly on the smallest mountain streams bordered by deciduous vegetation, which casts only limited shadows onto the water surface, and allows enough light for both the desman and its prey to survive. In many parts of its range, reforestation with fast-growing coniferous trees has caused dense shade and soil acidification, driving the desmans away.

The European mole (right) has a penchant for pastures, which are rich in earthworms.

kind of entrance hole, as they are merely the spoil heaps ejected by the animals in the construction of their tunnel networks. In due course, vegetation, the wind, and the rain leave their mark upon the mounds of loose, rich soil, softening them gradually into the contours of the terrain.

The layout of a tunnel system depends on the soil type, but typically consists of a horizontal network roughly 3–8 in (8–20 cm) beneath the surface, with another horizontal network some 12 in (30 cm) below this. The two networks are linked by a series of shafts. From the lower network, irregular, blind shafts may penetrate to depths of 47 in (119 cm).

Moles do not dig new tunnels every time they go in search of food. Rather, they repeatedly use a series of tunnels over a long period of time for feeding, and several generations of moles may use the

131

same series of tunnels, particularly if there is a rich and dependable supply of food, such as is found beneath old pastureland.

DENIZENS OF STREAM AND LAKE

The two species of desman inhabit very different watery homes. The smaller Pyrenean desman, weighing a mere 2 oz (56.7 g), lives in the Pyrenees and parts of northern Iberia, along rushing mountain streams that are well oxygenated and contain high levels of nutrients. This combination supports plenty of aquatic insect prey. The desman may nest in natural hollows among roots; usually, however, it excavates a tunnel with an underwater entrance and an uphill slope to a snug, grass-lined chamber. Highly territorial, a pair of Pyrenean desmans will stoutly defend stretches of stream up to 650–1,300 ft (198–396 m) long against intruders. Within this zone, however, the male and female lead mainly solitary lives.

The Russian desman is a bulky, rat-sized creature by comparison. It lives along slow-flowing or even stagnant watercourses, such as ponds, canals, and lakes. The fossil record for this species suggests that at one time it was distributed right across Europe, from southern Britain in the west to the Caspian Sea in the east. It has become progressively

M. Walker/Frank Lane Picture Agency

FOCUS ON

THE SOUTH DOWNS

The chalky South Downs in Sussex and Hampshire, England, are broken into five main blocks by four rivers—the Cuckmere, Ouse, Adur, and Arun—which drain southward over the chalk scarp to the coast. While large parts of the eastern end of the downs are short-tu grasslands, the western hills support beechwoods and, more recentl, introduced conifer plantations. Dry valleys are a common feature; these are old river valleys that no longer contain rivers or streams a. the level of the water table has dropped within the soil.

The close-cropped turf of these southern chalk downs are among 1 richest botanical habitats in Europe: Over twenty species of flowerin, plant may be found on an area of turf 12 in (30 cm) square. Over th last few decades, however, much of the downs has been reseeded t, create better quality grazing for sheep, and large areas have been turned over to arable land. Hawthorn scrub has invaded many form, pastures; its spread has been exacerbated by the decline of rabbits, which used to provide a natural control on the vegetation. In additio, chalklands have succumbed to the general "tidying up" of Britain's countryside, particularly hedge removal.

Chalky soils are favored by moles, being firm and free draining, and permit these burrowers to dig an extended network of permane or semipermanent tunnels.

TEMPERATURE AND RAINFALL

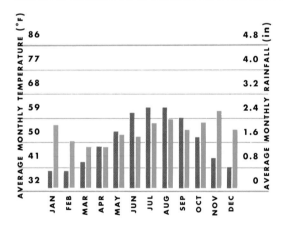

■ TEMPERATURE

■ RAINFALL

The southeast coast is one of England's sunniest regions. It receives less rainfall than the north and west. However, the windchill factor can be severe in winter, as the airstreams blow practically unimpeded from as far afield as the Urals in Russia.

more restricted in range, mainly to large river basins in parts of the former USSR.

The Russian desman is an enthusiastic digger, and will often make its nest deep within the root systems of bankside plants. The nest has two or three entrances, all of which lie well below the water level, ensuring safe and easy access even in winter. The entrances rise to the nest chamber, which is lined with moss and leaves and lies very close to the soil surface. In this way, the chamber is naturally ventilated from above. ■

NEIGHBORS

Chalk grasslands support a particularly rich and diverse flora, which attracts insects, small mammals, and their predators. The bird life includes seasonal migrants from overseas.

BARN OWL

This pale owl hunts over open country in the twilight and night. It preys on small rodents, birds, and insects.

GRASS SNAKE

This nonvenomous snake, with its pale yellow collar, feeds on frogs and is often found in damp locations.

Neighbor illustrations Joanne Cowne, except barn owl by Kim Thompson and rabbit by Chris Christoforou

SOUTH DOWNS

The chalky hills that form the South Downs rise to a modest 850 ft (259 m) above sea level and stretch for 56 miles (90 km) along the south coast of England, from Beachy Head in East Sussex through West Sussex to the border with Hampshire in the west.

SOUTH DOWNS

Inset photograph ZEFA

RABBIT

Introduced to Britain by the Normans, the adaptable rabbit lives colonially in a range of habitats.

SKYLARK

Generally heard before it is seen, the skylark is famous for its twittering song given from high in the sky.

COMMON FROG

Found in damp, shady areas, this frog hibernates in mud at the bottom of ponds during the winter.

HEDGEHOG

Hedgehogs feed mainly on earthworms, but also eat beetles, slugs, millipedes, larvae, seeds, and berries.

PAINTED LADY BUTTERFLY

This common butterfly is a noted migratory species. It has a distinctively fast and erratic flight pattern.

OLD WORLD RATS & MICE

Almost all the world's main land habitats have mouse and rat inhabitants. These ubiquitous rodents survive in alpine pasture, rocky uplands and moors, temperate and coniferous forests, shrubland and grassy savannas, arid scrub and semidesert, steamy tropical rain forests, marshes, and banksides. The distribution of the house mouse, the brown rat, and the black rat has been further increased by their links with humans; they travel by ship, road, railroad, and even airplane.

THE DRY SAHARA SUPPORTS VERY FEW RATS AND MICE, BUT IN THE GRASSLANDS OF AFRICA THERE MAY BE 10 OR 15 SPECIES IN ONE SMALL AREA

In Europe, there are only about eight species of mice, five of which—the wood mouse, the rock mouse, the pygmy field mouse, the yellow-necked mouse, and the striped field mouse—belong to the genus *Apodemus* (app-o-DEE-muss).

Each of these species has its own habitat preferences. The wood mouse is probably the most common and adaptable, ranging from dry sand dunes to parks and gardens, scrubland with bracken and brambles, woods, and farmland. It eats almost anything at any time of year.

In slightly more specialized habitats, however, the other species flourish at the expense of the wood

DISTRIBUTION

KEY

■ HOUSE MOUSE & BROWN RAT

WOOD MOUSE

STRIPED GRASS MICE

▨ RUFOUS-NOSED RAT

Opportunists in the extreme, the house mouse and the brown rat have spread throughout the world with very few exceptions. They are absent from the extreme polar regions, which are too cold, and areas where competition from other small mammals is too fierce, such as central Africa.

The wood mouse is found in various types of woodland habitats throughout the British Isles and Europe, except for Scandinavia and Finland, and is found through the eastern Altai and Himalayan mountains.

Striped grass mice live in central and southern Africa, where they thrive in grasslands, prairies, dry wooded areas, and savannas.

The rufous-nosed rat is found in the forested regions and dense woodlands of western Africa, the Congo Basin, and bordering areas.

With a taste for almost any type of food, the wood mouse rarely has trouble finding enough to eat in its woodland habitat, even during the winter months. Here, a small piece of fungus makes a tasty snack (left).

mouse. The determining factors include types of food, food availability through the season, and types of shelter and nesting sites.

The rock mouse thrives in dry, rocky places in southeastern Europe, such as stony hillsides, dry scrubland, and even stone walls. The yellow-necked mouse is found across Europe and can live in many of the habitats occupied by the wood mouse, but it is a better climber and thrives also in conifer forests.

The striped field mouse, widespread in eastern Europe, prefers damp, lowland places, where it digs in the soil and spends most of its time underground. It eats worms, grubs, and small snails, specializing in animal food more than its relatives do.

East and south from Europe, the numbers of Old

ZEFA

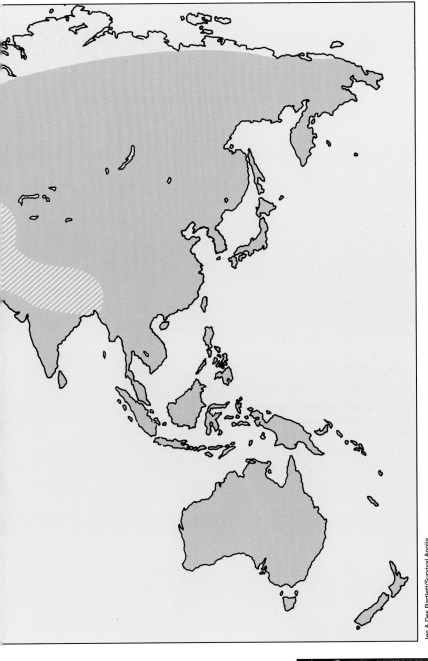

Jane Burton/Bruce Coleman Ltd.

KEY FACTS

● Adaptations to habitat shape physical characteristics, from the strong claws of Peter's arboreal forest rat for gripping trees to the huge ears of hopping mice, which give off excess heat.

● Highest densities of Old World rats and mice species occur in countries with tropical forests. For example, the Philippines has 32 species; Uganda, 36; and Zaire, 44.

● The most successful of all mammals, Old World rats and mice are found in Europe, Asia, Africa, and Australia.

Jen & Des Bartlett/Survival Anglia

World rat and mouse species rise rapidly in their main habitat—tropical woods and forests. Countries such as Uganda and Zaire have around thirty to forty species, as do India, the Malaysian region, Papua New Guinea, the Philippines, and Australia.

OUT OF SIGHT

Being small and fairly defenseless, rats and mice rely on their senses, agility, and camouflage to escape detection. As with many hunted animals, the color of their fur blends in with their surroundings.

Many scrub and semidesert species, such as the hopping mice of Australia, are light brown, fawn, or yellow to blend in with the light, sandy soil and pebbles. The hopping mice also show other

The stripes on the back of this Cape striped mouse (above) are clearly visible; they act as camouflage in its grassland habitat.

An African giant pouched rat (left) decides whether cocoa pods are good enough to eat.

135

adaptations to their semidesert habitat, including large hind legs for leaping across the open terrain and big ears—not only for acute hearing, but also to give off excess body heat in the hot conditions.

In contrast, the African swamp rats of the genus *Malacomys* (mal-a-CO-miss) are adapted for a watery life. Their hind feet have long, widely splayed toes for walking on soft ground, and their fur is thick and well coated with natural skin oils to repel water. Their coat is also dark brown to merge with the shady, muddy environment.

HOMEMAKERS

Most rats and mice build nests, the site and construction of which vary according to habitat. In grassland, nests are usually made in burrows and lined with shredded grass and other plant matter. The four-striped grass mouse of central and southern Africa digs a burrow up to over 3 feet (1 meter) long. This mouse has dark lines along its back, which camouflage it among the grass stems.

In woodlands, nests may be made in trees. The yellow-necked mouse often makes its nest in the crook of a branch or under a log. Peter's arboreal

FOCUS ON
THE MAYANJA FOREST

The lush, tropical habitat of Uganda's Mayanja Forest is not only home to some of the most varied and unique wildlife, but it is also a place where more than a dozen rat and mouse species thrive.

Here, competition is reduced by the way each species prefers a different minihabitat and has its own particular requirements. These minihabitats range from high tree branches, to bushes, to the ground, and spread from thick forest, to forest edge, to grassy clearing, to the bank of a pool or stream. Where two or more species occupy the same minihabitat, they coexist by eating different types of food.

The punctated grass mouse, for example, lives mainly on the ground alongside Peter's striped mouse; but the grass mouse is found in open, grassy areas, while the striped mouse prefers the forest interior. The long-footed rat ventures into swamps and streams to catch insects, frogs, and toads, while the climbing wood mouse feeds on seeds, fruits, and shoots in bushes and undergrowth.

TEMPERATURE AND RAINFALL

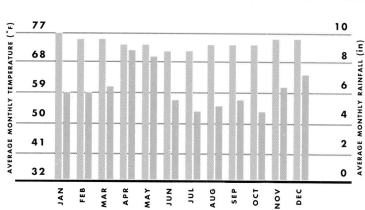

■ TEMPERATURE
■ RAINFALL

AVERAGE MONTHLY TEMPERATURE (°F): 77, 68, 59, 50, 41, 32

AVERAGE MONTHLY RAINFALL (in): 10, 8, 6, 4, 2, 0

JAN FEB MAR APR MAY JUN JUL AUG SEP OCT NOV DEC

The temperature in African tropical forests ranges between 68°F (20°C) and 77°F (25°C) all through the year. Rain falls in all months, though it is concentrated in two periods, from March to May and October to December. Plentiful rainfall results in constant flowering and fruiting and rapid plant growth.

forest rat usually makes its nest in a tree hole and weaves it from creepers, twigs, leaves, and vines.

The pencil-tailed tree mouse lives in a variety of habitats, including bamboo thickets and plantations, where it nests in the hollow stems of the bamboo plant. It gnaws a hole about about 1 inch (25 millimeters) in diameter in the woody outer layer, cleans out the interior, collects various dry leaves for the nest, and sets up a home.

In contrast, the marmoset rat of Southeast Asia lives only among bamboo. It nests inside the stems, lines its nest with leaves, and feeds on all parts of the bamboo plant. Its wide-splayed toes are ideally suited for gripping the slippery stems. ■

NEIGHBORS

Tropical conditions in Uganda's forests promote rich and varied flora and fauna. These creatures, from insects to exotic birds to grazers, share their homes with the numerous rats and mice there.

GIANT SNAIL

The giant snail feeds on forest vegetation, scraping off bite-sized pieces of leaves with its rough tongue.

TREE PANGOLIN

The scaly skin of the tree pangolin acts like a suit of armor, protecting it from its enemies in the trees.

Illustrations Peter Bull

THE MAYANJA FOREST

UGANDA

Mayanja Forest

Lake Victoria

Uganda is situated in central Africa between the Congo Basin and the Great Rift Valley. It is bordered by Kenya, Zaire, Tanzania, and Sudan.

To the west of Uganda's Lake Victoria lies the Mayanja Forest —a tropical region where rainfall and temperatures are high throughout the year.

ENEMIES

PYTHON
This extremely long snake grabs small mammals in its jaws and swallows them whole.

EXTREMELY DANGEROUS

GABOON VIPER
This extremely poisonous snake injects its venom into its victim using 2 in (5 cm) long fangs.

EXTREMELY DANGEROUS

GOLIATH FROG
Up to 12 in (30 cm) long, this huge frog sits patiently waiting for its unsuspecting prey.

MODERATELY DANGEROUS

Ardea

LUNA MOTH
[t]his huge moth wards off [e]nemies with the eyespots on [it]s wings, which look like two [se]ts of staring eyes.

WATER CHEVROTAIN
This shy little creature rests by day and grazes at night. It is always found near water, hence its name.

GRAY PARROT
With a screeching call, the gray parrot flies swiftly and skillfully through the high canopy of the forest.

MILLIPEDE
The millipede has an unusual defense: When threatened, it oozes a foul-smelling liquid from its exoskeleton.

CROWNED EAGLE
An awe-inspiring predator of the forest canopy, the crowned eagle swoops down on monkeys in the branches.

OPOSSUMS

Opossums are infinitely adaptable: They inhabit great swaths of North America and nearly all of South America, except for the highest Andes. The ability to thrive in such diverse surroundings is remarkable, particularly when compared with the marsupials of Australia. There, humans have become a serious threat and many marsupials have been forced back to small centers of their ranges or into sanctuaries. By contrast, many opossum species have dramatically widened their ranges since the arrival of large-scale human settlement.

GENERALIZED OR SPECIALIZED
Besides the official classification, opossums can be divided into two general groups depending on their habitat. Generalized species, such as the Virginia and southern opossums, are the real survivors, adapting to the widest range of climate and landscape. Specialized opossums have adapted to particular conditions, such as highlands or tropical riverbanks, where they flourish. These latter opossums are more threatened by humans because they occupy fragile environmental niches.

The Virginia opossum is the most familiar and widespread species, ranging from southeastern

(in) SIGHT

"SHREW" OPOSSUMS

Seven species of "shrew" opossums live in the wet, cold cloud forests of the highest Andes. These opossums are only about 8 in (20 cm) long, half of which is tail. Fossils indicate that the "shrew" opossums, with no pouch and only a few incisors, diverged from the family tree even before the Australian marsupials did. They are now classed in their own family, Caenolestidae (kie-no-LEST-id-ie).

The "shrew" opossum lives chiefly on the ground, using its long tail mainly as a balance as it bounds along well-marked trails in the undergrowth. It prefers mossy slopes and ledges protected from winds and cold rain. The "shrew" opossum feeds mainly on insects, earthworms, and other small invertebrates.

Canada and the eastern United States all the way south to the River Plate in Argentina. It has been introduced, and thrives, in scattered pockets along North America's Pacific coast.

Opossums generally favor forested or brushy areas, although they also live in more open country as long as there are wooded waterways nearby. The Virginia opossum prefers moist woodlands or thickets near swamps and streams. That type of

Woolly opossums (below) live in trees in the equatorial forests of America. They are highly agile, searching the branches for fruit, leaves, and live prey.

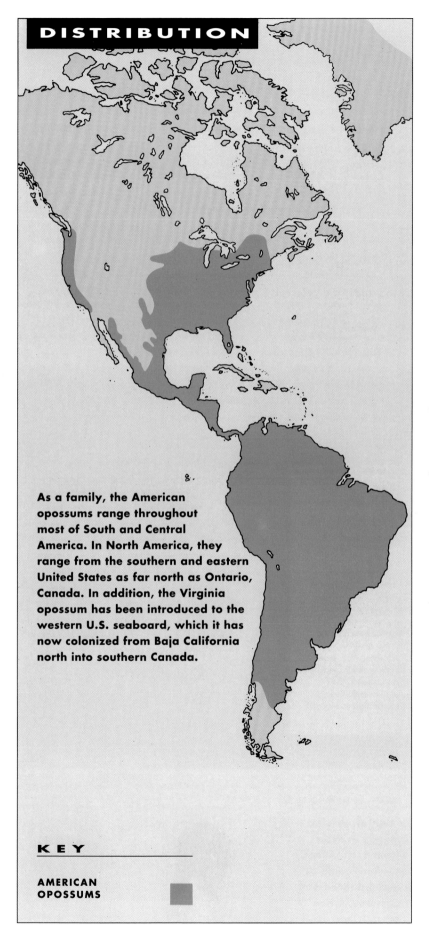

DISTRIBUTION

As a family, the American opossums range throughout most of South and Central America. In North America, they range from the southern and eastern United States as far north as Ontario, Canada. In addition, the Virginia opossum has been introduced to the western U.S. seaboard, which it has now colonized from Baja California north into southern Canada.

KEY

AMERICAN OPOSSUMS

landscape is common in Virginia, where the species was first studied closely.

THE GREAT COLONIST

Virginia, apart from lending its name to the common opossum, also marked the northern edge of the opossum's territory when the first settlers arrived in North America in the 1600s. The opossum has steadily spread north and west since that time. After being introduced to a pocket of California in 1890, the opossum went on to occupy the whole U.S. Pacific Coast and into southwestern Canada. It is estimated that in the last fifty years alone, the Virginia opossum has extended its range by more than 800,000 sq mi (2,000,000 sq km).

This expansion is almost certainly a result of the opossum's ability to coexist with humans. Despite being trapped for their pelts and eaten as a delicacy in the South, opossums have matched the westward expansion of American settlers almost step for step. Garbage cans, dumps, farms, and poultry houses have become traditional food sources.

IT MAY BE THAT THE VIRGINIA OPOSSUM'S RANGE EXPANSION WAS AIDED BY HUMANS, WHO KILLED OFF MANY OF ITS PREDATORS

In southeastern Canada—the northern limits of the Virginia opossum—winter temperatures commonly fall to –22°F (–30°C). Deciduous trees have largely yielded to pines at this latitude, and snow covers the ground for more than five months a year. It is here that the opossum's resilience is stretched to breaking point, with ears and tail falling victim to frostbite. Yet conditions well within its established range can be nearly as hostile. Consequently, it could be argued that the sparseness of the human population, rather than the harshness of the climate, dictates the opossum's northern limit.

OPOSSUMS IN SOUTH AMERICA

The southern opossum is equally at home with humans; it has been seen nesting in trees along some of the busiest city streets in South America. The southern opossum's territorial range and pattern of behavior in the wild resemble that of the Virginia opossum. These opossums seem most prolific in moist broad-leaved forests of tropical and semitropical South America.

The Andes host a number of South American opossums. Five species of shrew opossums live in the high forests and meadows of the Andes; they thrive in altitudes of up to 13,200 ft (4,000 m). They prefer cool, damp, densely vegetated areas and use runways along surface vegetation to go from one feeding territory to another.

The "shrew" opossums share their Andean range with some of the forty-six species of mouse, or murine, opossums. These distinctive opossums have prominent eyes that reflect light as a deep ruby red. In some species the tail is twice as long as the rest of the body. As a result, most mouse opossums live in trees, using their strong, prehensile tails to anchor themselves when feeding. Other mouse opossums make their homes in Mexican cacti or in the banana plantations of Central America.

Many opossum species inhabit the tropical low-lands east of the Andes. The woolly opossum, southern opossum, and Virginia opossum are gener-alized species that range throughout the region. Other opossums, such as the tree-dwelling ashy murine opossum and the aquatic yapok, focus on one aspect of this rain forest. Abundant food makes this region densely populated with opossums, but different species coexist with little competition.

The thick-tailed opossum is well suited to the vast, grassy pampas of South America. Its hairy tail does not grip well and the "thumb" on each foot is not fully opposable; but these shortcomings do not trouble it in a land of so few trees. Thick-tailed opossums are also less solitary than other species.

FOCUS ON

WEST VIRGINIA

West Virginia is one of the northernmost of the "southern" states in the United States. The Allegheny mountains, part of North America's Appalachian Range, cover two-thirds of the state. Slopes, many of which exceed 4,000 ft (1,250 m), are heavily wooded. Forests cover 62 percent of West Virginia, yet the state's human population is less than two million. The forest cover is mixed, with oaks and maples sharing space with hardwood nut trees such as hickory and walnut. Peach, apple, and cherry trees grow well in West Virginia, and fruit cultivation is the main farming activity in cleared land.

The climate is humid, with the Atlantic influence slightly modifying the continental extremes. These conditions, which encourage a profusion of wildlife, particularly favor the Virginia opossum. Its arboreal, nocturnal lifestyle is well suited to the forested landscape, while fruit orchards provide rich pickings in times when animal prey is hard to find.

Once considered Virginia's "poor relation" because its land is less arable, West Virginia is now promoting itself as a wilderness playground. Opossums, although occasionally the victims of hunters, thrive on the scraps left by human interlopers.

Erwin & Peggy Bauer/Bruce Coleman Ltd.

TEMPERATURE AND RAINFALL

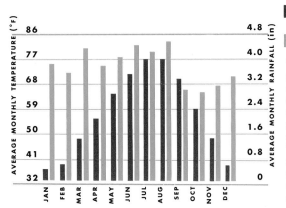

■ TEMPERATURE

▨ RAINFALL

The data here apply to West Virginia's capital, Charleston; the Appalachians have a similar, but slightly cooler and drier, climate. Temperatures and rainfall peak during the summer, but most months see appreciable rainfall.

The Patagonian opossum lives farther south than any other marsupial. The landscape near the extreme tip of South America is nearly treeless, so this opossum has become a ground-dwelling preda-tor. Its toes are stronger and more pronounced than those of other species, making it easier to scamper along the grassy pampas. As in some other species, its tail thickens with fatty deposits at cer-tain times of the year as a reserve for lean times. Its short, broad skull and long canine teeth suit its role as a hunter of small birds and mice. ■

NEIGHBORS

In the forests and uplands of West Virginia, the black bear and eagle are potential threats to opossums, while raccoons and squirrels often compete with them for food.

AMERICAN BLACK BEAR

The black bear is the largest carnivore of the Appalachians, measuring up to 5 ft (1.5 m) long.

AMERICAN BEAVER

The amphibious beaver is easily recognized by its long, sharp incisors and broad, flat tail.

Illustrations Joanne Cowne

WEST VIRGINIA

The Appalachian Range forms most of the border between West Virginia and Virginia. Most of the state's unspoiled forests and wildlife are in this Appalachian area. The mighty Ohio River, which forms most of the state's western border, also marks the beginning of the rich farmlands of the U.S. Midwest region.

STRIPED SKUNK

med with its repellent ent glands, the striped unk is a fearless denizen the American forests.

BALD EAGLE

The bald, or American, eagle is a large, fish-eating raptor and the national bird of the United States.

BULLFROG

The largest of all North American frogs, this species is named for its size and its deep voice.

GRAY SQUIRREL

Always alert, the gray squirrel seems poised for escape, even when stuffing its mouth with nuts.

BLACK WIDOW

One of the few poisonous spiders of North America, the female is jet-black with distinctive red markings.

ORANGUTANS

Orangutans were once found all over Asia. Today, they are restricted to just two areas of Southeast Asia—the islands of Borneo and Sumatra. The subspecies *Pongo pygmaeus pygmaeus* is found in Borneo; *Pongo pygmaeus abelii* lives in Sumatra. On both islands, the orangutan's habitats are being destroyed at an alarming pace to clear space for building and agriculture.

In Borneo and Sumatra, the orangutans inhabit small patches of tropical rain forest, mountain forest, and mangrove swamps. Their main requirements of their habitat are fruit trees as their chief source of

Konrad Wothe/Oxford Scientific Films

Orangutans are arboreal (tree-dwelling) animals (right and below). They swing slowly through the trees in search of food and remain there to sleep and breed. Only adult males spend much time on the forest floor.

C. & R. Aveling/ICCE

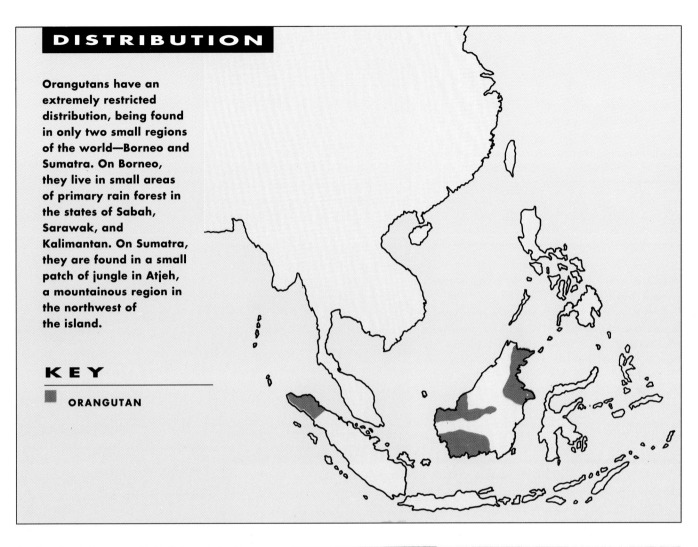

DISTRIBUTION

Orangutans have an extremely restricted distribution, being found in only two small regions of the world—Borneo and Sumatra. On Borneo, they live in small areas of primary rain forest in the states of Sabah, Sarawak, and Kalimantan. On Sumatra, they are found in a small patch of jungle in Atjeh, a mountainous region in the northwest of the island.

KEY

■ ORANGUTAN

food and suitable trees for building their sleeping nests. Nests are made of branches and leaves and are usually built about 33–66 ft (10–20 m) above the ground. The nest is occupied for only a few nights before a new one is built elsewhere.

The orangutans spend most of the time in the lower to middle branches of the trees, although they do venture higher up from time to time. Their huge size means that, apart from humans,

---

ORANGS USUALLY REACT TO HUMAN INTRUDERS BY SHOWERING THEM WITH BRANCHES—DIRECT ATTACKS ARE RARE

---

they have almost no natural enemies. Sumatran orangutans are occasionally hunted by tigers, but there are so few of these cats left that they do not pose a serious threat.

The rain forest provides a very stable environment for the orangutans. It is hot and humid all year round, with very little difference in temperature between the seasons. Rather than seasons, the

KEY FACTS

● If an orangutan cannot reach the next branch with its hands, it rocks the tree it is sitting in to and fro until the branch is within grabbing distance.

● In general, primates are concentrated in the tropical parts of the world. Large areas of the globe have no nonhuman primate representatives at all.

● Most orangutans make only rare excursions down to the forest floor. But older, heavier males sometimes find it easier to "fist-walk" along the ground than to find branches strong enough to bear their great weight.

● There is evidence to suggest that adult males continue their aggressive behavior even after they have ceased to be sexually active after about thirty years. The reason for this is thought to be to enable males to defend their territory until their eldest offspring are old enough to take over the same space in the forest.

year can be divided into hot and wet times, and hot and even wetter times. The average annual temperature in the rain forest ranges from about 68°F (20°C) at night to 86°F (30°C) during the day. An average of 9.8 in (25 cm) of rain falls every day. Most of this falls during the afternoons, in spectacular thunderstorms. During such a downpour, orangutans have been known to cover themselves

---

ORANGUTAN DENSITY VARIES BETWEEN 0.25 TO 1.25 ANIMALS PER SQUARE MILE, DEPENDING ON HABITAT QUALITY

---

with large leaves—with all that fur, getting soaking wet is no fun at all.

Orangutans wander through the rain forest, searching for food. But they do not roam completely at random. They follow well-established travel routes that, combined with their vast knowledge of the forest and the fruiting habits of the trees in it, lead them to the trees most likely to provide them with a decent meal. They also follow the movements of other animals, such as hornbills, which share their liking for fruit and can lead them to a

good source of food. Because of their bulk and weight, orangutan movements are normally slow and deliberate, and they only travel a few hundred yards a day through the trees.

When several adult orangutans meet, because they are attracted to the same food source such as a fruiting fig tree, they show no social interaction and depart separately after they have had their fill. However, orangutans do recognize other animals whose ranges they overlap, and have a good knowledge of the whereabouts of other individuals. ■

FOCUS ON

THE JUNGLE OF BORNEO

The rain forests of Borneo are famous for their huge butterflies, gigantic trees, hanging lianas (vines), buzzing insects, and, of course, for their orangutans. Despite their huge size and brightly colored coats, they are surprisingly difficult to see among the lush foliage of the forest. A grunt or the creak of a tree branch may be all that gives them away.

Borneo is the third largest island in the world. It lies across the equator in Southeast Asia. Although its tropical rain forest is fast disappearing, patches still remain along the coasts and on the hills inland. There are also mangrove swamps along the coasts. The Bornean rain forest contains thousands of different species of tree. Among the most common are the dipterocarp trees, with their two-winged fruits.

ANNUAL RAINFALL

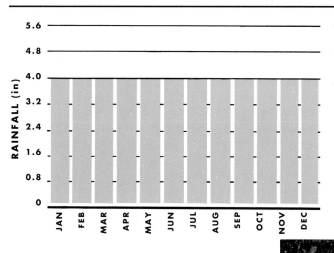

RAINFALL (in): 5.6, 4.8, 4.0, 3.2, 2.4, 1.6, 0.8, 0

JAN, FEB, MAR, APR, MAY, JUN, JUL, AUG, SEP, OCT, NOV, DEC

There is no distinct dry season, though the least amount of rain tends to fall in July, August, and September (when areas of felled jungle are burned off). The average rainfall in most localities is about 150 inches a year, most of which falls between late afternoon and early morning.

NEIGHBORS

Orangutans have no shortage of neighbors in their forest homes, as the rain forests of the world contain at least half of all the species of plants and animals on earth.

HORNBILL

The hornbill's huge, bony casque may help to amplify its calls so that they carry through the forest.

BIRDWING BUTTERFLY

The Bornean jungle is home to birdwing butterflies, which have wingspans of up to 7.8 in.

Gerry Ellis/Nature Photography

RESERVES
Orang populations are protected in the Gunung Palung and Bukit Raja Reserves in Indonesian Kalimantan (in the southeast) and in the Lajak Entimau Reserve in Sarawak (in the northwest). A further reserve is proposed for Sabah (in the northeast).

| COLUGO | FLYING FROG | FLYING SNAKE | CENTIPEDE | BROWN TORTOISE |

...lugo, or flying lemur, ...s flaps of furry skin ...etched between its front ...d back limbs.

Wallace's flying frog is able to glide by stretching out the webbing between its fingers and toes.

The golden flying snake is able to escape predators and pursue its prey through the trees.

These creatures are active predators, hunting insects, spiders, worms, and other small prey.

Like other species of tortoise, the brown tortoise withdraws into its shell when faced with predators.

PLATYPUSES

as well as on live termites. The termites build their nests underground or in dead wood—just where the echidna, which cannot tolerate very high temperatures, can find them.

Surrounding the outback and spread over much of the lowlands of Tasmania are areas of savanna and grassland. Climate in these areas ranges from seasonal wet and dry periods to Mediterranean and monsoon conditions. Termites are plentiful, and here species such as the compass or magnetic termite *(Amitermes meridionalis)* build their nests in the form of huge earth mounds that rise like tombs above the flat landscape. These wedge-shaped mounds are up to 11 ft (3.4 m) high and 10 ft (3 m) long but only about 3 ft (1 m) across. They usually point north/south with the broad sides facing east/west, so that they are mainly exposed to the cooler morning and evening

Short-nosed echidna (left) on stony ground. In such a habitat the echidna rests and hides under rocks.

The environments of Australasia are many and varied, ranging from the high equatorial mountains of New Guinea to the vast, dry desert of the Australian interior, which is popularly referred to as the outback. Echidnas have adapted to most of these environments.

The short-nosed species of echidna even survives in the heart of the outback, where the rainfall from the monsoons of New Guinea fails to reach inland, and the highlands in the east of the continent—the Great Dividing Range—act as a barrier to the moisture-bearing Pacific winds.

THE SHORT-NOSED ECHIDNA IS THE MOST WIDELY DISTRIBUTED OF ALL THE MONOTREMES

Here midday temperatures sometimes reach over 100°F (40°C) continuously for weeks on end and annual rainfall rarely exceeds 10 in (25 cm). In this harsh climate, vegetation is sparse, with low-growing acacia trees and species that have developed water-storing roots and flattened green stems instead of true leaves to minimize loss of water.

Mammals in the outback are few and far between, in terms of both numbers and variety of species, but there are rich supplies of termites and ants to be found, and these are the short-nosed echidna's main food. The termites feed on plant debris, and the ants on plant and animal remains,

The platypus (right) lives in a wide range of temperatures, from near tropical to below freezing.

KEY FACTS

- Because the platypus is such a highly specialized mammal, particularly when it comes to feeding, any change to its habitat renders it vulnerable.

- Echidnas often sleep under rocks and in hollow logs, but they also dig burrows. If they are disturbed they roll into a ball like a hedgehog. When living in soft-soil areas, they burrow rapidly into the soil and cling to the sides by using their spines and claws.

- The platypus was once found in streams and rivers throughout eastern Australia, but hunting reduced its numbers. Now its numbers are increasing once more.

- The short-nosed echidna is a strong swimmer and will often cross water to reach a supply of food.

sun, and get the least sun at midday, when the sun's heat is fiercest, to keep the inside of the nest cool. The termites often top their mounds with tall, thin "chimneys" to ventilate the chambers deep within. The echidnas use their claws to dig into these nests for food. They also eat other species of termites, which forage for food in the open, providing easy pickings for the short-nosed echidnas.

Where ants and termites are plentiful, short-nosed echidnas do not roam far. Each has a living area of not more than 124 acres (50 ha), which is the equivalent of about 50 soccer fields. Within this area, the animal uses a variety of shelter sites. It usually feeds first thing in the morning and late in the afternoon, when it is less hot. During very hot periods it may feed only at night, spending the day in the shade of a clump of plants.

In New Guinea, echidnas are most plentiful in the central-highland forest regions, where the long-nosed, earthworm eating species is most prevalent.

ANT/NHPA

DISTRIBUTION

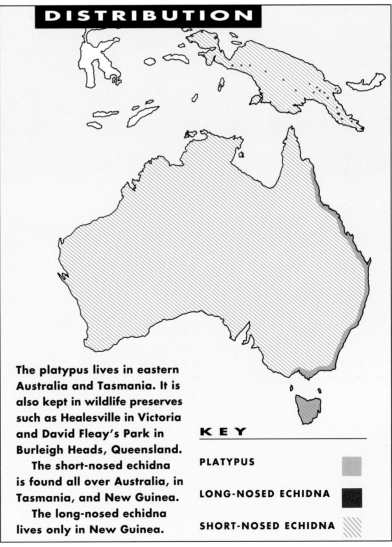

The platypus lives in eastern Australia and Tasmania. It is also kept in wildlife preserves such as Healesville in Victoria and David Fleay's Park in Burleigh Heads, Queensland.
The short-nosed echidna is found all over Australia, in Tasmania, and New Guinea.
The long-nosed echidna lives only in New Guinea.

KEY

PLATYPUS

LONG-NOSED ECHIDNA

SHORT-NOSED ECHIDNA

With mountains reaching 14,000 ft (4,267 m) or more, the cooler climate of these regions, although variable, is always wet. Rainfall can average 400 in (1,016 cm) in a year and there can be frost and even snow on the highest peaks. The long-nosed echidna avoids any extremes of climate, and in cold conditions, or during long periods of rain, it enters a dormant state. Like the Australian echidnas, these long-nosed species have a living area that is smaller the more plentiful the food supply. Generally, this area is no more than 25 acres (10 ha).

The earthworms they eat are abundant in the soil of the forests, and some reach lengths of 10 ft (3 m) or more. They feed on leaves, which they pull into their burrows, or digest organic material in the soil or on its surface, thus helping to recycle nutrients and aerate the soil.

The short-nosed echidnas feed on ants within and beneath the forest floor. In these forest areas are other invertebrates including huge numbers of ants and termites—the ants generally being the more widespread. They mainly inhabit the forest floor, although leaf-cutter and weaving ants forage in the trees, where they are safe from the echidnas (which do not climb). The leaf-cutters dissect green leaves with their scissorlike mandibles and carry them back to their underground nests to eat. The weavers construct their nests by binding leaves

FOCUS ON

THE RIVERBANK WORLD OF THE TASMANIAN PLATYPUS

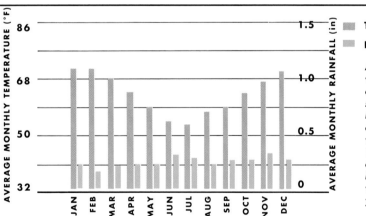

The duckbilled platypus is an Australian and Tasmanian original. It exists nowhere else in the world, looks and acts like nothing else, and in fact there was a time when it was not believed in anywhere else.

Separated from southeast Australia by the Bass Strait, Tasmania is the perfect setting for such an unusual animal. The island state is fortunate in having large areas almost empty of people. As a result, the government has been able to set aside about 30 percent of the land for national parks. These include the Western Tasmania National Parks Wilderness, a group of national parks that together form a World Heritage site. The wilderness covers 2,972 square miles (7,697 sq km) and contains rugged mountains, fast-flowing rivers, eucalyptus, and forests.

For the platypus of Tasmania, there is a plentiful supply of food in the clear waters. This is important to the platypus, because it probably needs more food relative to its body weight than any other mammal. Platypuses burrow extensively into riverbanks, usually leaving an entrance below water and another above.

TEMPERATURE AND RAINFALL

■ TEMPERATURE

■ RAINFALL

Australia is the world's largest country, but it is the smallest continent. Hobart, the capital of Tasmania, is a port with a population of 179,000. It is the coolest part of the island, with westerly winds blowing all year round.

together with strands of silk.

The world is divided into ten major biomes, or divisions of flora and fauna. Australasia is made up of six of these: tropical rain forest, desert, temperate grassland, savanna, scrub, and temperate rain forest. The short-nosed echidna is found in all of these contrasting regions. The long-nosed echidna lives only in tropical forests. The platypus can be found in regions of tropical and temperate forest and savanna.

NEIGHBORS

These animals coexist with the monotremes and depend on some of the same food supplies. They include marsupial mammal species, birds, and reptiles.

KOOKABURRA

The kookaburra has a noisy, laughing call that it uses to tell rivals to keep out of its territory.

TASMANIAN DEVIL

The Tasmanian devil will hunt prey but prefers carrion. As a result, it is n[e] a threat to monotremes.

Illustrations T. A. Sitch/Wildlife Art Agency

TASMANIA

Tasmania is an island state of Australia lying to the southeast. It is the smallest state of the country and the least populous. Once called Van Diemen's Land, Tasmania has a flourishing tourist industry due to its natural beauty.

Alan Root/Survival Anglia

COPPERHEAD

...e the platypus, the ...pperhead eats frogs. It is ...ually coppery brown and ...out 5 ft long.

BLACK SWAN

About 3 ft long, both sexes have a pure black plumage, a red bill, and a trumpeting call.

WOMBAT

Like its relative the koala, the wombat looks like a small bear but is more like a badger in its habits.

NATIVE HEN

One of the 14 species of birds unique to Tasmania, the Tasmanian native hen is aquatic by nature.

QUOLL

This pouched mammal is arboreal and a carnivorous, nocturnal predator. Its jaws can open very wide.

POLAR BEARS

Despite their name, polar bears rarely visit the North Pole itself, although they are found throughout the arctic regions, particularly on the Arctic Ocean pack ice—thick and heavily ridged ice—and along the surrounding coasts. Individual bears have even ended up as far south as Iceland, northern Japan, and Newfoundland, Canada.

The Arctic can be a stunningly beautiful place. In summer, the intense blue of the sky contrasts dramatically with the dazzling white of the vast expanses of ice and snow. In the clear air, the only sounds to break the silence over this great wilderness may be the rushing of a distant river or the occasional eerie howls of a wolf pack. The word *Arctic* comes from *arktos* (ARK-toss), the Greek name for "bear," because it is the land where the constellation of Ursa Major, the Great Bear, shines

Johnny Johnson/Bruce Coleman Ltd.

Well adapted to its harsh environment, the polar bear can weather almost any storm. Its thick coat and layer of insulating fat protect it from the cold (above).

At the mercy of the winds and sea currents, this polar bear (left) is following the shifting pack ice as it melts, breaks up, and refreezes.

brightly in the night sky directly above.

The Arctic is a frozen ocean encircled by the northern fringes of the continents of Europe, Asia, and North America and the island of Greenland. Here, animals have adapted over the slow process of evolution to a harsh world of ice, rock, and permanently frozen soil. In summer, the pack ice covers about 45 percent of the ocean, over 2 million square miles (about 6.6 million square kilometers); it covers more than 85 percent in winter.

ALTHOUGH IT LOOKS LIKE LAND COVERED WITH SNOW AND ICE, THE ARCTIC IS ACTUALLY A FROZEN OCEAN, BORDERED WITH FRINGES OF LAND

During the grim Arctic winter, when temperatures plummet to below -40°F (-40°C), the sun remains below the horizon for months on end, and the only source of heat is the inflow of air from lower latitudes. Even during the summer, the sun never rises far above the horizon and brings little heat—the average highest temperature does not exceed 50°F (10°C)—though slopes facing the sun

Bryan and Cherry Alexander

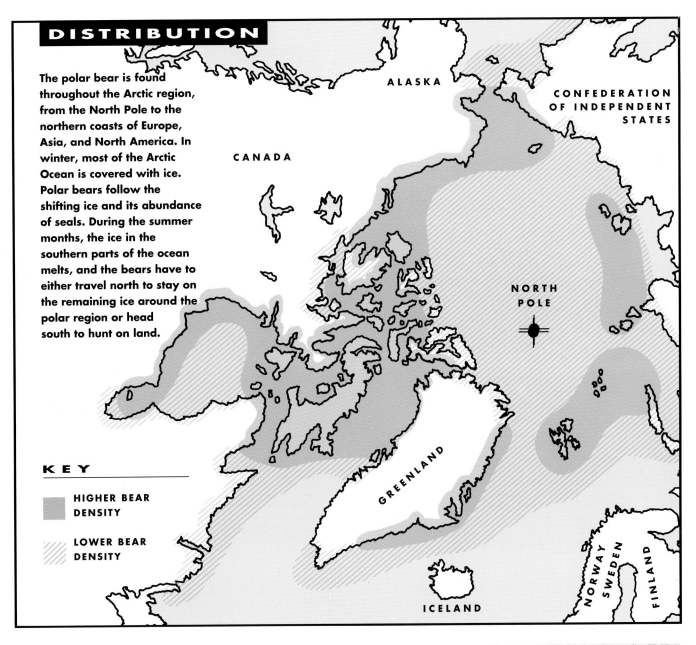

DISTRIBUTION

The polar bear is found throughout the Arctic region, from the North Pole to the northern coasts of Europe, Asia, and North America. In winter, most of the Arctic Ocean is covered with ice. Polar bears follow the shifting ice and its abundance of seals. During the summer months, the ice in the southern parts of the ocean melts, and the bears have to either travel north to stay on the remaining ice around the polar region or head south to hunt on land.

ALASKA

CONFEDERATION OF INDEPENDENT STATES

CANADA

NORTH POLE

GREENLAND

NORWAY SWEDEN FINLAND

ICELAND

KEY

- HIGHER BEAR DENSITY
- LOWER BEAR DENSITY

can be surprisingly warm. Polar bears in more northerly areas—both males and females—may dig out dens in the snow in winter to survive the fierce blizzards and bitter cold.

In the Arctic region, the great northern conifer forests gradually give way to the vast open spaces of the tundra. Though the tundra is dotted with lakes, ponds, and winding rivers, chill winds and a covering of snow and ice for much of the year allow only very hardy, stunted plants to grow.

The life of the polar bear is one of adjustment to a constantly changing environment and a moving food source. Winds keep the pack ice in almost constant motion in a giant clockwise spiral—it may travel up to 50 miles (80 kilometers) a day. This eternal drifting means that, to stay in one feeding area, polar bears must compensate for

KEY FACTS

- The Arctic is a frozen ocean encircled by Europe, Asia, North America, and Greenland. It stretches for over 5 million square miles (almost 15 million square kilometers).

- Despite their name, polar bears rarely visit the North Pole itself, as much of the polar basin is covered by thick ice built up over several years and there is not much to eat there.

- In winter, when howling winds and fierce blizzards add to the icy chill, Arctic temperatures may plummet to below -40°F (-40°C). Even summer temperatures do not rise above 50°F (10°C).

- Floating ice packs, pushed along by winds and currents, may travel as much as 50 miles (80 kilometers) a day.

the drift by moving in the opposite direction. How they do this in an environment devoid of landmarks remains a mystery.

Winds and currents also break up the ice to form long stretches of open water called leads. Such areas are important to polar bears because seals, the bears' main prey, are more abundant there. The bears also use systems of leads as migration routes.

HIDDEN DEPTHS

Pressure ridges, which are usually found along coastlines, in fjords, and in large bays containing islands, are formed when areas of ice are forced together. They may snake across the ice for many miles. In areas where snow can accumulate in drifts along these ridges, ringed seals make breathing holes in the ice. Here, in spring, the female seals dig out lairs in which to give birth to their pups. Polar bears, particularly females with young cubs, are attracted by this supply of food.

The bears are forced to move as the ice shifts, breaks up, and refreezes. In some places, such as the Greenland and Bering Seas, their distribution changes dramatically over the course of the year. In other areas to the south, notably the Hudson and James Bays, the ice melts completely in summer.

FOCUS ON
THE HIGH ARCTIC

To the north of, and overlapping, the tundra zone lies the High Arctic, where summer temperatures do not exceed 41°F (5°C) and only the most specialized plants and animals can survive. This is a world of stony or gravelly polar deserts and extensive areas of land buried by ice caps. The huge ice cap covering much of the interior of Greenland extends far to the south. In some places the flat Arctic landscape is broken by mountain ranges with peaks permanently covered in dazzling snow and ice.

With large areas devoid of land vegetation, the animals living in the High Arctic mostly depend, directly or indirectly, on the sea for their food. Food chains start with the simple organisms that drift passively with the ocean currents and are collectively known as plankton. The plant plankton is eaten by the animal plankton. Animal plankton, in turn, provides food for the great baleen whales, such as the bowhead whale. Arctic cod feed on both plant and animal plankton and are in turn eaten by other, larger fish. Fish are preyed on by various seabirds, seals, and toothed whales such as belugas and narwhals.

Land-based predators in the High Arctic include the wolf, Arctic fox, and stoat. At the top of the food chain, feeding almost entirely on seals on the ice and at the ice edge, is the polar bear. The killer whale is the top predator in the open sea, feeding on other whales as well as on fish and seals.

HIGH ARCTIC TEMPERATURES

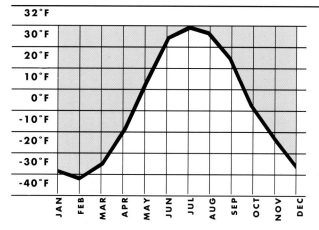

Although there is some seasonal variation in the climate of the High Arctic, temperatures rarely rise above 32°F (0°C). In the depths of winter, average temperatures are recorded as -33°F (-36°C), but on occasion they may plummet to as low as -40°F (-40°C). The relative warmth of late spring and summer promotes a new flush of vegetation.

This forces the bears ashore, where they remain, roaming inland into coniferous forests, until the winter comes and the sea refreezes; then they return to hunt seals again.

Although the salt in the seawater becomes trapped as the ice freezes, it gradually melts down through the ice, so that ice a year or more old is almost salt-free. This is an advantage to polar bears because they do not need to visit land for freshwater; they can drink from puddles that form as the surface of the ice melts. ∎

NEIGHBORS

These creatures coexist with the polar bear and other predators of the High Arctic, though some, such as the fox and the mosquito, are limited to the areas covered by tundra, not by ice.

ARCTIC TERN

This bird breeds in the Arctic and then migrates to spend the summer in the Antarctic. It feeds on fish and plankton.

ARCTIC CHAR

A member of the salmon family, this fish ranges arou... the whole of the High Arctic, returning to rivers to spawn.

Illustrations Elisabeth Smith

THE HIGH ARCTIC

The Arctic is roughly divided into three zones—Low, Middle, and High—according to the amount of plant life present. The Low Arctic has plenty of year-round vegetation; the Middle has some, usually in low-lying areas; whereas the High, where it is not covered by ice, is mostly rocky with scattered vegetation.

High Arctic

ENEMIES

KILLER WHALE

The ferocious killer whale eats mostly fish, seals, and whales but will seize the chance to attack an unsuspecting bear.

WALRUS

Weighing up to 1.5 tons (1.6 tonnes), the walrus is a powerful enemy, and its long tusks can be lethal weapons.

Illustrations Matt Lyon

Jeff Foott/Survival Anglia

SNOWY OWL

owl feeds mainly on mings, and the number of ng it produces depends ow well lemmings breed.

ARCTIC FOX

This wily predator hunts a variety of small prey. It has a dense white coat and can survive extreme cold.

GREENLAND SHARK

About 10 ft (3 m) long, this harmless shark swims slowly near the seabed and feeds on fish and crustaceans.

IVORY GULL

A year-round resident of the High Arctic, the ivory gull survives the winter by scavenging polar bear kills.

MOSQUITO

The mosquito is abundant in the Arctic summer, but spends most of the winter as a cold-resistant egg.

RACCOONS

An expert's advice: "If men cut a raccoon's wood down to build a summer cottage, they can expect the animal to come and live in the fireplace chimney. Fill in the creek where raccoons catch shiners and chubs, and you will hear your garbage cans go rattling over at midnight. Pour concrete, and raccoons will make themselves at home in the culverts under the road. Raccoons take civilization in stride and grow fat where lampposts have replaced trees."

These words about the common raccoon appeared in *National Geographic* magazine in 1956; since then urbanization in the United States, as elsewhere, has spread even further. Today, the raccoon is even more successful and widespread, extending its range northward into southern Canada.

Although the raccoon has always been found in a wide variety of natural habitats, its favorite spot has consistently been wooded and brushy areas. It is particularly common near water—lakes, ponds, slow-flowing rivers, and streams. The most widespread of any animal in this family, it ranges from the southern edges of Canada south through most

Carol Farneti/Planet Earth Pictures

The kinkajou (right) looks a lot like the olingo and lives in similar habitats.

Hans Reinhard/Tony Stone Worldwide

of the United States into Central America. It is generally absent from the Rocky Mountains and parts of Nevada and Utah.

The common raccoon has also been introduced into parts of Europe and Asia, where it is extending its range with typical ease. Here, too, it has learned to live alongside humans—as a scavenger of waste and a plunderer of crops and livestock.

SOUTHERN RELATIVES

The various other species of raccoon, range from the southern United States down to the northern and central countries of South America. The crab-eating raccoon is found from Costa Rica south to northern Argentina, while at least three of the other species are confined to islands. The Tres Marías raccoon is an inhabitant of María Madre Island off the west coast of Mexico; the Cozumel Island raccoon, as its name suggests, inhabits Cozumel Island, which lies to the east of the Yucatán Peninsula in Mexico; and the Barbados raccoon is found on the island of the same name in the West Indies.

In northern regions, raccoons (left) combat the cold of winter by growing longer, denser coats.

ISTRIBUTION

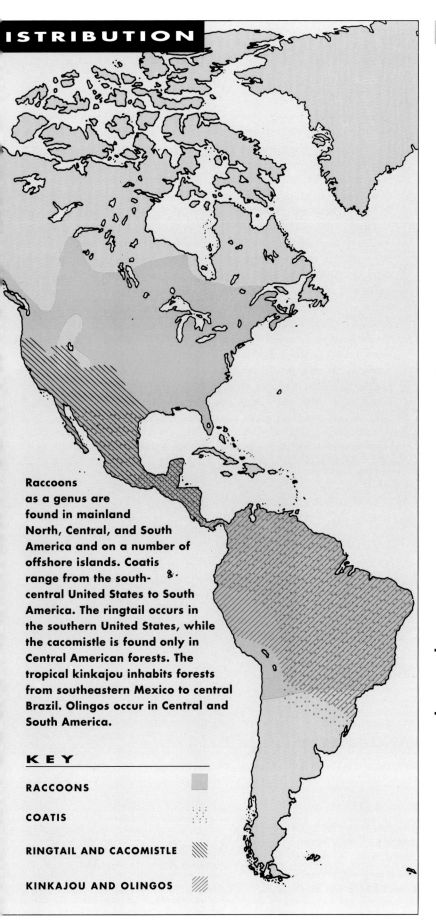

Raccoons as a genus are found in mainland North, Central, and South America and on a number of offshore islands. Coatis range from the south-central United States to South America. The ringtail occurs in the southern United States, while the cacomistle is found only in Central American forests. The tropical kinkajou inhabits forests from southeastern Mexico to central Brazil. Olingos occur in Central and South America.

KEY

RACCOONS

COATIS

RINGTAIL AND CACOMISTLE

KINKAJOU AND OLINGOS

(in)SIGHT

ISLAND RACCOONS

Other than the common and crab-eating raccoons, all raccoon species live on islands in the Caribbean and off Mexico. They differ from the common raccoon mainly in the colors and lengths of their coats.

Many of these island species are threatened by the introduction of the common raccoon. The common species is far more adaptable and, should humans ever introduce it to these island refuges, it would almost certainly cause the downfall of these rare island raccoons through competition for food and territory.

One species, *Procyon maynardi*, from New Providence island in the Bahamas, is actually thought to be the common raccoon, introduced there much earlier by humans.

The coati, with its arboreal habits, is another that favors wooded areas, although these may be anything from the lowland forests of the Tropics to temperate deciduous forests, or even those at high altitudes. Across its range, which comprises the southern states of the United States south through northern and central South America, it may also be found in rocky, wooded canyons.

The most common of the coatis, the ring-tailed coati, is found from southeast Arizona through southwest New Mexico and southern Texas. Within this range it is most abundant in the mountainous areas of the extreme south of Arizona. The white-nosed coati is found from southeastern Arizona through Mexico and central America

WHEN LIVING SPACE IS SCARCE IN AN AREA, RACCOONS WILL READILY MOVE INTO ABANDONED FOX BURROWS

south to western Colombia and Ecuador. The island coati shares Cozumel Island with its native raccoon, while the mountain coati, about which very little is known, lives in the Andean forests of western Venezuela, Colombia, and Ecuador.

The stronghold of the ringtail is America's southern states—southwestern Oregon, California, southern Nevada, much of Utah, western Colorado, and southern Kansas down through Arizona, New Mexico, Oklahoma, and Texas. It is found in a variety of habitats, but it is most common where the landscape is rocky, favoring canyons and areas where there are lots of big boulders. This perhaps reflects the fact that it spends less time in the trees than many of its relatives, although it is still a skillful climber. Like the raccoon, it is seldom found far away from water. The cacomistle has a much smaller distribution and is found only in forested areas of Central America.

The kinkajou is found only in tropical forests; its range extends from southeastern Mexico to central Brazil. It spends almost all its time among the branches, feeding and sleeping by day in a hollow trunk or, occasionally, lying out on a branch. The olingo is found from Central America down through Venezuela, Ecuador, Peru, and Brazil. It is also an inhabitant of tropical forests, but may be found at altitudes from sea level up to about 6,500 ft (2,000 m). Nocturnal in habit as well, it is thought to make a rough nest of dry leaves in a hollow for its daytime slumbers.

LOCOMOTION

The raccoon usually moves around its home range at a sort of slow amble, with its head held low, its back characteristically arched, and its tail dangling behind it. If need be it can move quite fast, however—up to about 15 mph (24 km/h)—in a lumbering gallop by which it takes short bounds, bringing its

hind feet down ahead of its forefeet. The coati, also a good swimmer, has a less pronouncedly arched back than the raccoon, so it appears to move a little less shamblingly on the ground, and it holds its tail almost vertically as it moves and forages. The kinkajou moves quickly in the tree branches, but it is generally a little more cautious as it travels over the ground from one tree to another. It tends to return to a particularly favorite tree each night. The olingo leaps from branch to branch with ease, making short work of gaps of 10 ft (3 m) or more. ∎

Alan & Sandy Carey/Oxford Scientific Films

FOCUS ON

WASHINGTON STATE

The most northwestern state in the United States, Washington has always proved excellent raccoon country. Although it is the smallest of the Pacific Coast states, it boasts three national parks—Mount Rainier, North Cascades, and Olympic—and nine national forests. It is known as the Evergreen State because of its richness of firs, hemlocks, pines, and other evergreen trees, and also because of its lush lowlands, which are typical of the western part of the state.

One of the most impressive areas is North Cascades, made a national park in the late 1960s. The Cascade mountains separate the western section of the state from the eastern section and are part of a long mountain range that stretches south from British Columbia into northern California. The range includes a number of volcanoes, including Mount St. Helens, which erupted in 1980. Many of the mountains have glaciers and permanent snowfields on their upper slopes, but lower down are the magnificent forests where the raccoons make their homes alongside beavers, martens, minks, muskrats, and western bobcats. American black bears, coyotes, cougars, and a subspecies of mule deer are all found in the Cascades, but it is thought that one-time residents grizzlies and wolves have long since disappeared.

TEMPERATURE AND RAINFALL

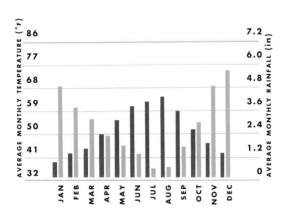

■ TEMPERATURE

■ RAINFALL

Western Washington State has a mild climate; the summers are pleasantly cool while the winters remain tolerable. But the winds from the Pacific Ocean are moist and bring a fair amount of rain to the west. The east has a considerably drier climate.

NEIGHBORS

The raccoon has a rich variety of neighbors, some of which it preys upon and others to which it is prey. With the decline of bears and wolves in many areas, the coyote is now its chief predator.

COYOTE

The best runners of the canids, coyotes have no problem in overtaking raccoons on the ground.

AMERICAN BLACK BEAR

The American black bear and common raccoon share many habitats—forested areas in particular.

Illustrations Peter Bull, Joanne Cowne, and Edwina Goldstone/Wildlife Art Agency

NORTH CASCADES NATIONAL PARK

Washington State borders Canada in the northwestern United States on the Pacific Coast. North Cascades National Park lies in the northwest of the state, between the cities of Seattle and Vancouver.

NORTH CASCADES

MUSTANG

he mustang usually lives on pen grassland—a habitat hat raccoons are slowly olonizing in some areas.

GOLDEN EAGLE

This majestic bird looks like a hawk but has a much larger wingspan. It preys on rabbits and rodents.

AMERICAN BULLFROG

This large frog takes its name from its bellowing call. Raccoons prey on several species of frogs.

RED-TAILED HAWK

One of North America's most impressive raptors, the red-tail has a soaring flight like that of an eagle.

CATTLE EGRET

This small heron is more often seen in Africa, but its range now includes the United States and even Canada.

RHINOCEROSES

Gerald Cubitt/Bruce Coleman Ltd.

A solitary Sumatran rhino (above) wades through a muddy swamp. Plenty of water and lush vegetation make this an ideal habitat for Asian rhinos.

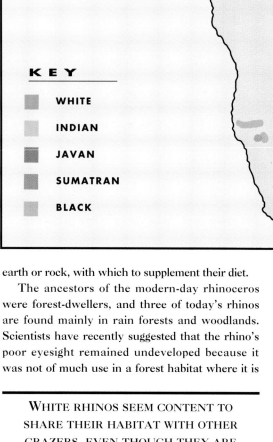

DISTRIBUTION

KEY

WHITE

INDIAN

JAVAN

SUMATRAN

BLACK

Where an animal chooses to live is determined by its needs. Rhinos must have access to enough vegetation to maintain their bulk and, since all species except the black rhino need to drink every day, they must also have access to water.

SECRET NATURE

Consequently, prime rhino habitat must have good rainfall or a river or spring nearby that flows year-round. If the soil is low in salts there should also be a salt lick, a natural exposure of mineral-rich earth or rock, with which to supplement their diet.

The ancestors of the modern-day rhinoceros were forest-dwellers, and three of today's rhinos are found mainly in rain forests and woodlands. Scientists have recently suggested that the rhino's poor eyesight remained undeveloped because it was not of much use in a forest habitat where it is

---

WHITE RHINOS SEEM CONTENT TO SHARE THEIR HABITAT WITH OTHER GRAZERS, EVEN THOUGH THEY ARE DIRECT COMPETITORS

---

difficult to see far in any direction. Two species, however, the white and the Indian, have evolved as grazers and so are found in open grassland, plains, or savanna habitats, providing there are clumps of trees or bushy areas to provide them with shade and cover.

The white rhino, as befits its reputation for gentleness, shows a great deal of tolerance toward the animals that share its habitat, even fellow grazers such as wildebeest, impala, and zebra, with which it competes for food. This is understandable

Hans Reinhard/Bruce Coleman Ltd.

A black rhino (right) browsing in the African grassland. Black rhinos are able to adapt to a wider range of habitats than white rhinos.

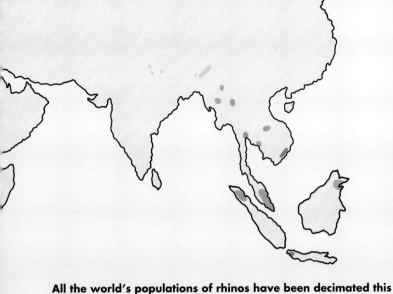

All the world's populations of rhinos have been decimated this century and almost all are isolated. Only Africa's white and black rhinos occupy a mutual habitat—in southern Africa. A population of about thirty northern white rhinos survives in Zaire, while Kenya, Namibia, Zimbabwe, and South Africa each have populations of a few hundred of the black species.

Of the Asian species, the Indian rhino is found in protected parks in northern India and Nepal; the Sumatran rhino inhabits rain forests from Malaysia to Myanmar (formerly Burma); and the Javan, rarest of all, survives in Indonesia's Udjung Kulon National Park and as a tiny population in Vietnam.

KEY FACTS

● Once the most widely distributed species of rhino, the Javan is now the rarest. At one time it extended over seven countries but is now found only in a small corner of Indonesia and in Vietnam.

● Despite their ability to go for up to a week without drinking, black rhinos will still travel up to 16 miles (25 km) every day in search of water.

● Some scientists believe that the dung heaps, or middens, that rhinos scatter around their territory may perform the role of a "mailbox." They allow rhinos in a particular area to keep up to date on the identity of their neighbors and their current reproductive state.

Javan rhinos (below) uproot saplings and spread seeds in their dung, thus helping to regenerate rain forests.

when early rains turn the normally brown, burnt savanna a lush green, rich in vegetation, but less so at the end of winter when drought can have a devastating impact on its food supply.

This tolerance extends to the presence of black rhinos, though such close proximity between the two species is comparatively rare. Black rhinos live in the forests, plains, and scrubland of southern and eastern Africa, browsing for twigs and leaves. They display a remarkable ability to survive in harsh environments such as the Namib Desert in Namibia, southwest Africa.

NO FEAR OF FIRE

Every year, fires spread across vast areas of the African plains. Though these fires serve an important purpose—they destroy the dying undergrowth that prevents new shoots from appearing—they also wreak havoc on local wildlife. The black rhino, however, appears to take it all in its stride, even feeding heartily on the charred remains of acacia scrub. At such times, the black rhino's ability to survive for days without water is crucial.

Indian rhinos, by contrast, are rarely found far from water. Though predominantly grazers, they

Dieter & Mary Plage/Bruce Coleman Ltd.

will supplement their diet of tall elephant grass with the fruits and shrubs that grow around densely thicketed swampland. This is perfect territory for wallowing. The *jheels*, muddy water holes found in northeast India and Nepal, provide one of the few places where the normally antisocial Indian rhinos will tolerate the presence of others—they are the public baths of the rhino world.

LITTLE IS KNOWN ABOUT THE LIFE OF
THE SUMATRAN AND JAVAN RHINOS
BECAUSE THEIR REMOTE AND DANGEROUS
TERRAIN IS RARELY EXPLORED

Asia's two other species of rhinos, the Javan and the Sumatran, are rarely seen and difficult to study. This is not just because they are rare creatures but also because of their jungle habitat and their secretive nature. Both these timid, elusive species travel alone along well-worn paths through dense rain forest, far from human settlement, browsing for

leaves and fruit and using their enormous weight to break down the young saplings from which they feed. Highly agile, despite their appearance, Sumatran rhinos are found on the steep slopes of mountainous jungle terrain. It is claimed that some have been sighted on the rims of volcanoes, though there appears to be little documented evidence of this. Javan rhinos, on the other hand, prefer to live in swampy lowland rain forests. ∎

FOCUS ON

SOUTHERN AFRICAN SCRUB

Between southern Africa's vast savanna and the Namib Desert lies the semiarid scrubland that is home to a small but now-expanding population of black rhinos. Though a relatively inhospitable environment for rhinos, it is one in which man, their chief enemy, is largely absent. The long summers are hot, with temperatures reaching over 86°F (30°C), though it can be bitterly cold at night. Rainfall is infrequent, often as low as 10 inches (250 mm) a year, and evaporates quickly under the intense sun.

For most of the year, the only vegetation consists of woody shrubs that reach about 6.5 feet (2 m) in height. Because these shrubs compete for the small amounts of moisture available, they tend to extend their roots over a wide area. Because food is scarce, the territories of individual rhinos are often large, and this helps to reduce competition between them.

Despite the lack of vegetation, a number of small herbivores such as gerbils manage to survive, as well as grazers like gazelles. These provide prey for carnivores such as leopards and the occasional lion. Creatures commonly associated with desert climates such as lizards and snakes are abundant.

SHARED INTERESTS

CATTLE EGRET   OXPECKER

Illustration Elisabeth Smith

Two birds are commonly associated with rhinos. The cattle egret feeds on insects disturbed by the rhino's feet and rides on its back, while the oxpecker feeds on the parasites that live on the rhino's skin. Both birds thus form mutually beneficial or symbiotic (sim-bee-OTT-ick) relationships with the rhino. The birds' prey includes (from the left) the fly Rhino-musca dutoiti (rie-no-MUSK-a doo-TOY-tee); the tick Dermacentor rhinocerinus (derm-a-KEN-tor rie-noss-er-EEN-uss); the flea Echidnophaga lavina (eck-id-no-FAY-ga lav-EE-na); and the worm Stephanofilaria poeli (steff-a-no-fill-AR-ree-a po-ELL-ee).

NEIGHBORS

All the creatures featured here share their habitat with the small population of black rhinos that inhabit the harsh semiarid scrubland bordering southern Africa's Namib Desert.

LAPPET-FACED VULTURE

Large scavenging vultures soar above the scrub searching for carrion, which they tear with their strong bills.

GENET

The catlike genet is a soli[tary] hunter and forager, noted [for] its climbing ability. It make[s its] home in hollowed-out tree[s]

Illustrations Elisabeth Smith

DESERT SCRUB
A great swath of scrub stretches from South Africa's southern Cape Coast through Namibia to Angola. It separates the grasslands and plains of southeast Africa from the Namib in the west and the Kalahari in Botswana and central South Africa.

SCRUB

MODERATELY DANGEROUS

LION
Opportunistic lions will try to ambush young or sick rhinos.

MODERATELY DANGEROUS

SPOTTED HYENA
Packs of hyenas harass rhino mothers and attack their calves.

Illustrations Elisabeth Smith

Clem Haagner/Ardea

COMMON DUIKER

small, shy antelope that eds nocturnally, the uiker or "diving buck" is rely observed in the wild.

SECRETARY BIRD

This ground-hunting bird builds huge nests in thorn trees.

ROBBER FLY

Common throughout sub-Saharan Africa, the robber fly feeds on other insects, which it catches in flight.

LEOPARD TORTOISE

The hard shell of the leopard tortoise presents an almost insoluble problem for any would-be predators.

OXPECKER

Similar in appearance to a starling, the oxpecker spends its time searching for para-sites on the rhino's skin.

SLOTHS

Sloths have precise habitat needs. They live only in dense forests that provide them with a constant supply of leaves, and the forest must be large enough to support a viable breeding population of sloths. Trees need to be large enough and close enough together to enable sloths to move around the forest at canopy height as and when necessary. In fact, the status of sloth species parallels the status of the neotropical deciduous forests and rain forests.

HABITAT PREFERENCES

Of the two-toed species, Linne's sloth is common and widespread in northern South America as far south as the Amazon Basin, whereas the generally smaller Hoffmann's sloth is less well known, although it has a wider range from Nicaragua to Peru and Central Brazil. The pale-throated three-toed sloth ranges from Central America to northern Argentina; it is the most common and familiar species. The brown-throated sloth has an enormous range, extending from Guatemala and Honduras to northern Argentina. The maned sloth is confined to eastern Brazil.

Despite widespread deforestation, forest cover still cloaks much of Central and South America, and sloths are still relatively common in many forest areas. The types of forest preferred vary among species: Studies in Venezuela have shown that pale-throated and brown-throated three-toed sloths occur mainly in evergreen forest, but also inhabit deciduous forest and scattered trees in woodland pasture

A female pale-throated sloth launches herself elegantly, if cautiously, toward some tasty foliage (right). Her youngster merely clings more tightly, sinking its tiny claws into her thick belly fur.

Luiz Claudio Marigo/Bruce Coleman Ltd.

DISTRIBUTION

All sloths are confined to the tropical forests of Central and South America. They cannot live in more open habitats because they rely on a dense tree canopy. They are not found in more temperate zones because they are unable to regulate their body temperature.

KEY

PALE-THROATED SLOTH

BROWN-THROATED SLOTH

MANED SLOTH

HOFFMANN'S SLOTH

LINNE'S SLOTH

areas. Although representatives of both two- and three-toed sloths coincide in tropical forests across much of their range, different species within the same genus occupy more or less exclusive geographical ranges. These closely related species differ little in body weight and have such similar lifestyles that it appears that they are unable to coexist.

Where two-toed and three-toed sloths occur within the same area of forest, the two-toed form is usually at least 25 percent heavier than its relative and the two species exploit the forest's resources in different ways. Body size does seem to affect the distribution and activity patterns of the two major types of sloths. Whereas the larger two-toed sloths can survive in tropical mountain slopes and range into cloud forest, the three-toed sloths are confined to lower elevations. This greater requirement for energy is thought to be the reason for the three-toed sloth's round-the-clock activities. In São Paulo Botanical Gardens, down south in the subtropical parts of its range, the pale-throated three-toed sloth can survive temperatures below freezing.

As might be expected, sloths do not often cover great distances within the forest; individuals may

stay put in the same tree for several nights. There is, however, some evidence of limited migration in the pale-throated three-toed sloth. In Guyana, a male of this species was recorded as having moved five miles (8 km) over a forty-eight-day period during the rainy season (May–June). If this rate of movement does not seem remarkable, it should perhaps be remembered that it is unusual for a sloth to move far at all—only one in ten pale-throated three-toed sloths move more than 125 ft (38 m) in a day.

ENEMIES

The slow sloth regularly provides a sought-after meal for predators. Three of its greatest enemies are the jaguar, the ocelot, and the world's largest species of eagle, the harpy. Although jaguars occur in savanna and semidesert areas, they are among the

A SIGNIFICANT NUMBER OF SLOTHS FALL TO FELINE PREDATORS, DESPITE THEIR SUPERB NATURAL CAMOUFLAGE

top predators within the tropical forests. They will eat peccaries, capybaras, and tapirs in addition to sloths, and are solitary, powerful hunters.

The ocelot is a much smaller species of cat, but like the jaguar it occurs in a wide range of habitats from semiarid deserts to tropical forests. It relies on its stunningly beautiful spotted coat to conceal it among the dappled, shady forest foliage while it

KEEPING WARM IN THE TROPICS

Like armadillos and anteaters, sloths have very low but variable body temperatures—in their case around 86–93.2°F (30–34°C) in waking hours. A sloth cools off during the early morning, on days of wet weather, or when otherwise inactive. This helps it to conserve energy—sloths turn food into energy less than half as fast as would be expected for a creature of their size. Their skeletal muscles are reduced, weighing only 25 percent of a typical animal's body weight, compared with 45 percent in most other mammal species. This lack of heat-producing muscle is part of the reason why sloths cannot control their body temperature.

When cool, a sloth cannot shiver to warm up, so it regulates its temperature by inhabiting trees with exposed crowns. In this way, it can warm up or cool down by moving into or out of sunlight. Out in the sunshine, a sloth's body temperature will rapidly rise to the ambient temperature within a couple of hours. At dawn, sloths can be seen hanging from the peaks of tree crowns, facing east, basking in the early rays of the sun. In some areas, locals refer to the three-toed sloth as the "sun sloth." This is due to its sunbathing activities, and also because this species exposes a brilliant orange-red patch of fine fur along its back when sunning itself.

ZEFA

stalks unwitting prey such as sleeping sloths. Both of these cat species suffer from persecution and the loss of their natural habitats.

The harpy eagle is a major predator on sloths. Three-toed sloths are particularly vulnerable to predation by this giant eagle early in the day when they are sitting on the sunlit side of the tree canopy sunning themselves. Sloth remains have also been found in the stomachs of an anaconda and a coati (a member of the raccoon family), although the coati probably scavenged the sloth as carrion. The remains of an immature sloth have been found in the stomach of a margay; in this instance, the cat's forehead had been badly slashed, possibly by the young sloth's mother.

ALGAE TO THE RESCUE

It is not surprising that sloths have so many enemies; to escape trouble, their top speed is a dismal 1.2 mph (1.9 km/h), and the 100-yard dash would take about twenty-two minutes. But sloths are not entirely defenseless: In addition to lashing out with tooth and claw, they can make use of the humid forest conditions to provide camouflage. Primitive algae thrive in such wet conditions, and the sloth's thick, matted body hair has evolved to nurture such algal growths. Two species of blue-green algae flourish in special

MPL Fogden/Bruce Coleman Ltd.

FOCUS ON

BARRO COLORADO ISLAND

The tiny Barro Colorado Island lies in the artificially created Gatun Sea, close to the northern coast of Panama. The Panama Canal, which splits the country from north to south, flows through the Gatun Sea. The island was created by the rising of the waters at the beginning of the century, resulting from the excavation of the Panama Canal. It has been protected as a biological research station since soon after its newfound isolation.

The island supports tropical forest, with many species found there that mirror those found on the Panamanian mainland. But this microhabitat lacks many of the predatory cats and eagles, so prey species such as sloths, peccaries, and coatis have thrived tremendously. The island is popular with bird-watchers, and several bird species are more easily observed on the island than elsewhere. These include the crested guan, great tinamou, white-whiskered puffbird, and barred woodcreeper.

As a sloth haven, Barro Colorado is ideal, but it is not a truly natural preserve area. It is too small to support viable breeding populations of, for example, solitary big cats, which typically occur at lower densities than their prey species. On small islands, such species eventually outstrip their food supply.

TEMPERATURE AND RAINFALL

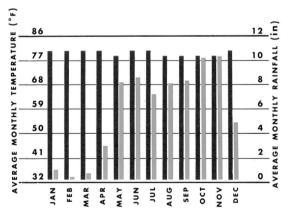

■ RAINFALL

■ TEMPERATURE

Panama's Caribbean (northeast) coast is far wetter than the Pacific (southwest) coast, because the northeasterly trade winds shed their rain as they reach land. This climatic pattern is consistent even in the narrowest parts of Panama.

grooves running along the hairs. The growth of these primitive plants on the sloth gives the fur a greenish tinge, which is particularly noticeable during the wet season—the time of year when the algae grow most profusely. In addition to adding a greenish hue to the sloth's fur, this algae provides a source of food for three species of small pyralid moths which also live within the sloth's shaggy coat. Huddled up and suspended from a branch, the moldering green sloth resembles a bunch of old leaves and is invisible to its would-be predators. ■

NEIGHBORS

The jaguar-free Barro Colorado is ideal for ground-nesting birds such as the tinamou and guan, although the locally abundant coatis and peccaries tend to rob them of their eggs.

GREAT TINAMOU

This elusive gamebird is far more often heard than seen. It prefers humid lowland forests.

CRESTED GUAN

The guan's overall range and numbers are declining due to deforestation and hunting pressure.

BARRO COLORADO

The island covers an area of about 5.8 sq mi (15 sq km) and lies northwest of the Panama Canal in the Gatun Sea. Panama itself forms a narrow isthmus between Costa Rica in Central America and Colombia in South America; the Gatun Sea lies roughly halfway along the Panama mainland.

PANAMA

Panama Canal

Pacific Ocean

■ BARRO COLORADO ISLAND

COLLARED PECCARY

This small, abundant, and social pig lives in a wide range of habitats, from dry deserts to tropical forests.

PUFFBIRD

Puffbirds have prominent "mustache" tufts. They feed on large insects, frogs, and small lizards in the forests.

BOA CONSTRICTOR

Boas grow to 11 ft (3.4 m) long and can kill mammals as large as young peccaries and deer.

MORPHO BUTTERFLY

These bright blue butterflies drift over the forest canopy, the males flying high to attract the females.

WOODCREEPER

Using its curved bill, the barred woodcreeper probes crevices in tree bark for its insect prey.

SPERM WHALES

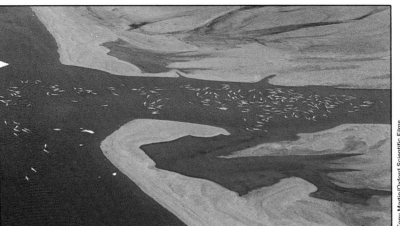

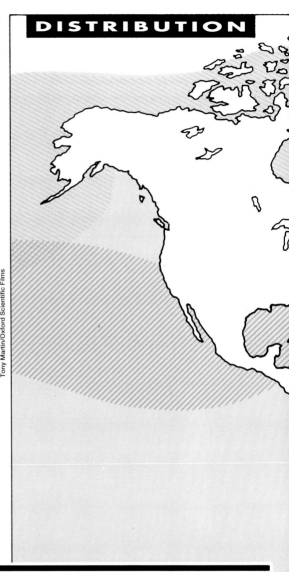

B elow the surface, oceans are as varied as the land. Currents are like winds, pushing water from place to place. Temperatures vary, getting cooler from equator to pole and from surface to seabed, and also being altered by currents. The seabed has flat plains, high mountains, jagged cliffs, and deep ravines.

This means that there are many different marine habitats. Like land creatures, each type of whale is adapted to one or more of these, but their distribution pattern is complicated by the fact that many species migrate during the year.

Great sperm whales are usually found far from land, or near oceanic islands where the sea floor plunges steeply into a deep trench. Females and youngsters tend to stay in warmer waters around

Belugas (above) arriving at an estuary after a migration of about 186 mi (300 km). It is in these warmer coastal waters that young from the previous year's mating are born.

IT WAS ONCE THOUGHT THAT THE NARWHAL USED ITS LONG TUSK TO MAKE A BREATHING HOLE IN THE ICE

---

the equator and temperate regions, where the surface temperature is 60°F (15°C) or above. Adult males may venture to the cold poles in summer.

The pygmy sperm and dwarf sperm whales prefer the warmer temperate and tropical waters all around the globe. They tend to stay closer to land, over regions of continental shelf, where the depths are less than 820 ft (250 m).

Narwhals have been seen all around the Arctic Circle, but they are less common in the waters around eastern Asia, Alaska, and western Canada. They swim near the coast or along the edge of the pack ice and ice floes. Belugas also live in cold northern waters. They tend to stay in shallower waters even closer to the coast or the edge of the ice.

THE MOST NORTHERLY WHALE

Narwhals live in colder, more northerly waters than any other whale. They even venture into patches of clear water among the pack ice, swimming below the floating, frozen-in lumps and floes. If the small area of open water freezes over and they cannot reach a patch of ice-free sea to surface and breathe, they will drown. Narwhals tend to congregate and surface regularly—the resulting splashing of water helps to keep it from freezing. Their extra-strong skin and blubber insulate them from the intense cold.

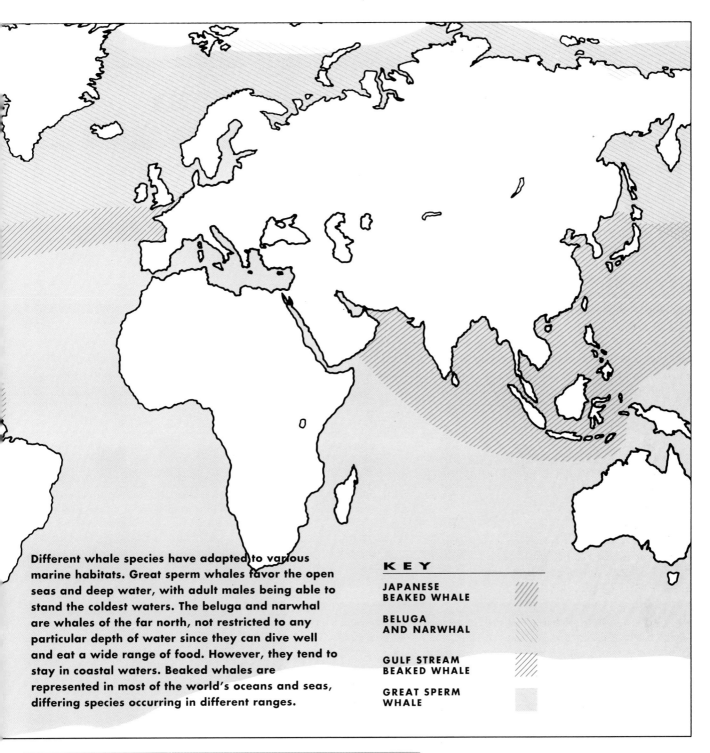

Different whale species have adapted to various marine habitats. Great sperm whales favor the open seas and deep water, with adult males being able to stand the coldest waters. The beluga and narwhal are whales of the far north, not restricted to any particular depth of water since they can dive well and eat a wide range of food. However, they tend to stay in coastal waters. Beaked whales are represented in most of the world's oceans and seas, differing species occurring in different ranges.

KEY

JAPANESE
BEAKED WHALE

BELUGA
AND NARWHAL

GULF STREAM
BEAKED WHALE

GREAT SPERM
WHALE

K E Y   F A C T S

● Most catchings and sightings of northern bottlenose whales have been in water deeper than 3,300 ft (1,000 m) and between 28°F to 63°F (-2°C to 17°C).

● Sighted off southern South America, southern Africa, and the southern third of Australia, the southern bottlenose rarely strays into water less than 820 ft (250 m) deep.

● Patches of clear water among the pack ice are called *savssats* in Inuit. It is here that the beluga loves to swim, often swimming underneath the ice floes.

Northern bottlenose whales range across the North Atlantic, occasionally coming as far south as the New England states or Portugal in Europe.

The southern bottlenose whale has a similar habitat in the Southern Hemisphere, although it extends across the South Pacific as well as the South Atlantic.

Cuvier's beaked whale is one of the most wide-ranging of all whales. It has been caught and observed in tropical and temperate seas all around the world. In contrast, Gervais' beaked whale is restricted to the western Atlantic Ocean, with sightings and strandings from New York down to the Caribbean. A few strays have reached West Africa and Ascension Island in the South Atlantic. ■

TASMANIAN DEVILS

The Tasmanian devil favors coastal scrublands and sclerophyll forests with rocky outcrops, found mainly in the northern half of Tasmania. Sclerophyll forest consists mainly of trees with leathery leaves to reduce water loss because of low rainfall or rocky, fast-draining soils. The forest trees and rocky outcrops provide fallen logs, or cracks and caves, where the devil can rest by day.

In the past few decades, the devil has spread into other habitats, partly due to the availability of food. Sick or dying livestock, especially sheep, are an easy meal for a carrion-feeder, as are wallabies and other animals that have been killed on roads. In addition, various grubs, beetles, and other plant pests have spread as a result of agriculture, and the devil is not above eating these morsels as small but tasty midnight snacks.

As a result, the devil has taken to living in bushy scrub, wasteland, farmland, parkland, and even the outer suburbs of towns. It sometimes uses dens under old outbuildings. It is now widespread across most of Tasmania, except for parts of the south. However, the hilly, rocky, wooded country of the interior is still its main stronghold.

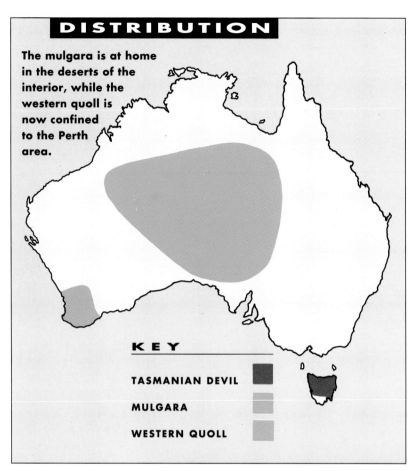

DISTRIBUTION

The mulgara is at home in the deserts of the interior, while the western quoll is now confined to the Perth area.

KEY

TASMANIAN DEVIL

MULGARA

WESTERN QUOLL

in SIGHT

ANT/NHPA

AUSTRALIA'S SOLE BURROWER

Although a few of Australia's mammals will readily take to a hole in the ground, one alone is truly adapted for a burrowing lifestyle. The marsupial mole, *Notoryctes typhlops*, is a living drill bit. It has a toughened forehead and rigid vertebrae to help it thrust through the soil, and its shortened limbs are armed with huge, flat claws. It even lacks functional eyes and ears. It lives in the central deserts where, unusually for a burrower, it does not make permanent tunnels but allows the sand to collapse behind it as it progresses.

Hans & Judy Beste/Ardea

Tasmania may look insignificant on a map when compared with mainland Australia, but with an area of 26,250 sq mi (68,000 sq km), it is a little larger than West Virginia—with a comparatively tiny population. And compared with countries such as Great Britain, large areas of Tasmania are still very rural and unspoiled. They make fine wilderness areas.

FOREST NEIGHBORS

The Tasmanian devil shares some of its habitats with the much more secretive eastern native cat (*Dasyurus viverrinus*). This stoatlike, white-spotted dasyure was once common around southeastern Australia but has disappeared from most parts of the mainland. This has occurred despite its ability to adapt to sclerophyll forest, heathland, scrub, and farmland. The disappearance may be due to a disease epidemic at the turn of the century, coupled with competition from introduced cats and foxes.

The devil's range is also home to larger animals such as kangaroos and wallabies, the widespread brush-tailed possum, the common wombat, the brown bandicoot, and other marsupials. In addition, the hilly, rocky forests support various bats, owls, and hawks and other birds of prey, snakes such as the copperhead, and lizards such as the fence skink. The locally famous Tasmanian cave spider inhabits damp, sheltered cracks and corners, from caves to

Kathie Atkinson/Oxford Scientific Films

Two young common planigales (above) at play. Tiny but fierce, they will pick on prey as big as themselves.

The fat-tailed dunnart (left) is usually solitary, but in cold conditions it will huddle with others to keep warm.

old logs or road drains. Almost all of these neighbors may be eaten by the devil when they die.

The northern native cat, or satanellus (*Satanellus hallucatus*), has also adapted well to human habitation. It is the smallest of the four quoll species and prefers the warmth of the tropics. It is fairly widespread along the northern coastal districts, from Western Australia across the Northern Territories to Cape York Peninsula and down Queensland to Townsville. Within this range it can occupy most habitats, from dry, rocky countryside with sparse vegetation to thicker woodland, and even around farms and outlying buildings.

KEY FACTS

● **The Tasmanian devil is one of the few marsupial carnivores to hold its own since Europeans arrived in Australia.**

● **The devil has few natural enemies or competitors. This is partly because dingoes and introduced foxes have not spread from the Australian mainland across to Tasmania, and partly because the thylacine is now believed to be extinct.**

● **Some dasyures have been generally unaffected by the European settlements, chiefly because they inhabit the dry interior, which is unsuitable for pasture or crops.**

● **Another group of dasyures, such as the sandstone, cinnamon, and Atherton antechinuses, have an extremely limited range—in a few cases, down to less than ten square miles.**

The habitats of certain other dasyures are also well known, but few are spreading their range. Most have become restricted since the European settlement of Australia began in the 19th century. One example is the western quoll, or native cat (*Dasyurus geoffroyi*). When the settlers arrived, it could be found in almost any place with scattered woodland and sclerophyll forest. This meant around most of the continent, from Esperance in the southwest in a clockwise direction all the way to Adelaide. The quoll was thought to be absent only from the southern coasts along the Great Australian Bight and from the dry interior.

Today, the western quoll is rare or absent from most of its former range. It is limited chiefly to the heavily forested southwest corner of Western Australia, from Perth across to Ravensthorpe. It hunts both in trees and on the ground, sneaking up silently on birds as they roost at night, as well as taking small mammals and reptiles such as lizards. It also consumes smaller prey, from insect grubs and larvae, such as caterpillars, to earthworms.

OUT IN THE OUTBACK

Fortunately, some dasyures have suffered little from the European invasion. This is because they are adapted to the harsh, dry habitat of Australia's

FOCUS ON

CHEYNE BEACH

The coastal stretch of Cheyne Beach, near Albany, Western Australia, is the stronghold of the dibbler or freckled marsupial mouse. This tiny dasyure eats insects, worms, and other small invertebrates, and also nectar and pollen. When disturbed, it has been observed to dash and hide in leaf litter, where it also hunts for food.

The main flowers of Cheyne Beach are species of banksia with spiked or bottlebrush blooms. There are also thick swards of grass and scattered trees. Two of the very rare recorded captures of the dibbler were on flowers of *Banksia attenuata*.

Since the discovery in 1967 of dibblers in the area, further searches have found only a few specimens. The indications are that the dibbler occupies a tiny area in the extreme southwestern tip of Western Australia—one of the most restricted ranges of any marsupial.

There are now nature preserves to protect this extremely threatened marsupial around Cheyne Beach and Jerdacuttup. Since much of the habitat is, however, close to human settlements, marauding cats and foxes also present a threat.

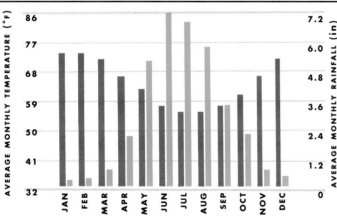

TEMPERATURE AND RAINFALL

| | TEMPERATURE |
| | RAINFALL |

Perth, lying on the western coast, escapes the blistering heat of Australia's interior, but it is still hot in summer (U.S. wintertime) and does not freeze in winter. There is almost no rain at all in high summer, while the winter is relatively moist.

"red center"—a huge expanse of hot, dusty land that is of little use for grazing or plowing.

The rat-sized mulgara can survive in areas where the annual rainfall is 4 in (10 cm). It extracts all the moisture it needs from its diet of mice, birds, and beetles, and it hides in its cool burrow during the hottest hours of the day. Even in these most arid habitats, which stretch from Pilbara in Western Australia across to southwestern Queensland, the mulgara is still relatively common among the stones and scattered bunches of spinifex grass. ∎

NEIGHBORS

Unlike neighboring New Zealand, Australia is rich in endemic (native) species. The grassy cover of Cheyne Beach is an ideal habitat for small marsupials.

BANDICOOT

The southern brown bandicoot nests on the ground in southern scrub, heath, and forest areas.

BOOBOOK OWL

This small hawk owl of Australia also lives in New Zealand and New Guinea.

CHEYNE BEACH AND THE ALBANY AREA

Cheyne Beach, near Albany, is some 220 mi (350 km) southeast of Perth. It lies on the southernmost point of Western Australia, although it is still several degrees latitude north of Tasmania.

ANT/D. Whitford/NHPA

BROWN GOSHAWK

premely
ile, the
shawk preys on almost
ything it can find.

COPPERHEAD SNAKE

The copperhead is one of Tasmania's two venomous snakes, although it is most common in Victoria.

GRAY BUTCHERBIRD

The sweet song of this thick-billed bird belies its grisly habit of impaling its insect prey on thorns.

KANGAROO

These familiar marsupials occupy most of Australia, including both Tasmania and the Albany area.

COMMON WOMBAT

Absent from most of the continent, this burrowing grazer is widespread throughout Tasmania.

TIGERS

her on the hunt, she must be able to find food close to her den so that she can suckle them at regular intervals. When the cubs are a little older, she can travel farther afield, but she must be able to find enough food to feed both herself and her growing brood.

A male tiger's range is usually three or four times bigger than a female's and overlaps the territories of several females so that he can father cubs. Tigers are renowned for their wandering, and each territory will have several dens or sheltered resting places in it. The tiger uses whichever one is most convenient at the time.

Bengal tigers live in all types of forests, including the wet, evergreen, and semievergreen forests of Assam and eastern Bengal; the mangrove forests of the Ganges Delta; the moist deciduous forests of Nepal; and the thorn forests of the Western Ghats.

(Left) The Siberian tiger's coat is lighter than that of other tigers, which suits its local habitat.

Typical tiger country has three main features: It will always have good cover, allowing the tiger to stalk its prey without being seen; it will always be close to water; and it will always have plenty of prey animals on which the tiger can feed. Within such country, tigers mark out and operate within individual territories.

The importance of the territory is particularly relevant to the female. If she is familiar with an area, she can be reasonably certain of killing prey with some regularity, allowing her to raise young. When her cubs are very young and cannot follow

SWIMMING TIGERS

Unlike other cats, which tend to avoid water, tigers actively seek it out. During the extreme heat of the day, they are often found cooling off in pools. Tigers are excellent swimmers, capable of swimming up to four miles (six kilometers), and can even carry their dead prey across water.

It has happened that sleeping fishermen have been killed by tigers. The unfortunate victims had anchored their open boats some distance from the shore, but a boat has to be far out to be beyond a tiger's range.

DISTRIBUTION

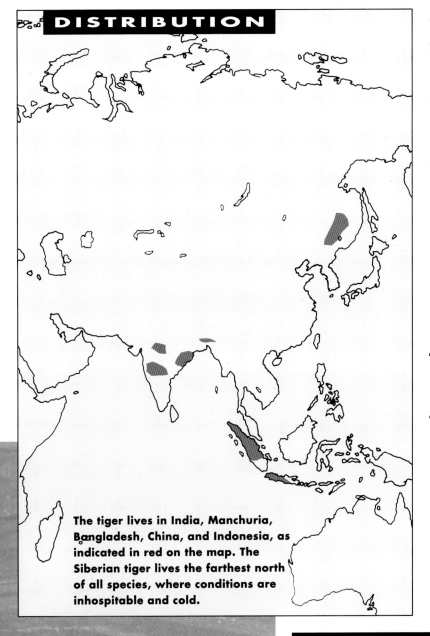

The tiger lives in India, Manchuria, Bangladesh, China, and Indonesia, as indicated in red on the map. The Siberian tiger lives the farthest north of all species, where conditions are inhospitable and cold.

ZEFA

They are also equally at home in heavy grass jungles, bamboo thickets, swamps, and scrubland, which has plenty of cover. Their priorities are water and enough cover to allow them to hunt effectively.

In Burma the tiger is often found in thick forests, while the Indonesian tigers favor dark, humid rain forests. Siberian tigers roam the Amur Basin, preferring the mountain forests, which are not inhabited by humans. Here temperatures can fall to as low as -31°F (-35°C), and there is much snow covering the ground. At this time of year, the Siberian tiger develops an insulating layer of fat on its belly and flanks.

Unlike lions and leopards, tigers do not habitually climb trees; however, females and cubs have displayed considerable climbing abilities when escaping from wild dogs called dholes. Dholes hunt in packs of about thirty, and although the dogs are much smaller than tigers, packs have been seen attacking them.

THE SIBERIAN TIGER OFTEN HAS
TO TRAVEL GREAT DISTANCES
TO FIND FOOD

Tigers are much stronger than dholes. They are capable of smashing a dhole's skull with just a single swipe from their enormous forepaws. But dholes hunt in packs, nipping the cat's flanks and hindquarters and diverting its attention. Such battles are usually ferocious and noisy. The tiger will inflict heavy casualties on the pack, sometimes killing as many as ten or twelve dogs, before being killed itself. A pack of dholes will also chase a fully grown tiger away from its fresh kill.

Unlike most cats, the tiger loves water, and

KEY FACTS

● When tigers enter the water they often go in backward so that they can keep a watchful eye on their surroundings.

● A tiger's roar can be heard up to 1.5 mi (2.4 km) away.

● A tiger kills the equivalent of 30 buffalo a year. The Siberian tiger needs between 19 and 22 lb (9 and 10 kg) of meat a day.

● It is estimated that more than half of all tiger cubs die before they reach maturity.

● A tiger's nighttime vision is six times better than a human's.

in hot weather it is often seen splashing around in streams and rivers. It is an excellent swimmer capable of long distances. It will even chase prey across a pool, catch it, and swim back to shore with the animal in its mouth. This demonstrates the tiger's remarkable strength: A single tiger can pull a male water buffalo weighing about 2,000 lb (908 kg) to a quiet spot in which to feast. It would take thirteen humans to move such a weight.

Tigers are opportunist hunters. This means they will attack and eat almost any vertebrate animal. Their diet consists mainly of deer such as sambar and chital, wild pigs, birds, monkeys, and even fish, frogs, and lizards. A wounded, elderly, or sick tiger will attack easy targets such as cattle and livestock, and in some instances it has even been known to attack humans.

COMMUNICATION

Tigers have a variety of methods of communication within their territories. They regularly spray bushes and trees with a mixture of urine and anal gland secretions and scratch tree trunks. Both of these marks alert other tigers to their presence.

Tigers also have a wide range of vocal calls, and their roars can travel far. Calling is used to invite other tigers to mate. Sometimes female tigers call

FOCUS ON

THE SUNDARBANS TIGER RESERVE

The Sundarbans Tiger Reserve stretches from West Bengal east to Bangladesh. The world's largest mangrove swamp, it has the largest tiger population of any tiger reserve in India. The maze of narrow channels and the lush vegetation provide plenty of cover; proximity to water and a bountiful supply of prey animals ensure that hunting is good.

Sundarbans is an area of low islets and estuarine swampland situated in the Ganges Delta. It covers an area of some 998 square miles (2,585 square kilometers). The land seldom rises much above sea level. Cyclones and tidal waves regularly occur. Like all predators, tigers play an important role. By killing deer and other prey animals, they help keep the numbers of these animals under control. Most of their prey are herbivores (plant-eaters), and, without some control, they would quickly eat all the vegetation, leaving the area unable to sustain any life.

Sundarbans is home to many other animals, including the estuarine crocodile and the olive ridley sea turtle, both of which are endangered species. Human access across the whole area is restricted, allowing the animals maximum freedom from human molestation.

TEMPERATURE AND RAINFALL

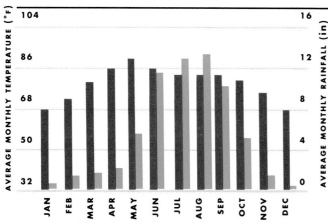

Temperatures in the Sundarbans range from 68 to 104°F (20 to 40°C), and there is heavy rainfall during the monsoon months. The area is very flat and is prone to flooding during the rainy season.

their cubs to share a kill but, frequently, roaring, growling, and snarling noises are used to warn other tigers off.

When tigers meet they curl their lips in the *flehmen* reaction. This is most commonly used when a male and female tiger meet. Their tails also tell whether or not a tiger is receptive to another tiger. An excited tiger will lash its tail quickly from side to side. A nervous or tense tiger will keep its tail low, slowly twitching it. ∎

NEIGHBORS

These animals all live in the same area as the Bengal tiger. Although they are all predators, they depend on the rich plant growth for their survival.

VULTURE

The tiger hides its catch from bearded and other vultures, which look for easy pickings.

WATER MONITOR

A large, agile lizard that hun its prey by day, the water monitor becomes inactive i periods of drought.

THE SUNDARBANS

The Sundarbans region is situated to the north of the Bay of Bengal. A small part lies in northeast India, but the majority belongs to Bangladesh. The Ganges River flows through the region into the Bay. The region is low lying and prone to flooding.

Tony Stone Worldwide

RUSSELL'S VIPER

...e venom squeezed from ...ands on either side of the ...er's head swiftly ...ralyzes its prey.

WHIP SCORPION

Unlike many scorpions, the nocturnal Asian whip scorpion does not have a sting in its tail.

MUGGER CROCODILE

Distinguished by its short snout and powerful jaws, this crocodile eats both large and small mammals.

FLYING FROG

A tree frog that glides rather than flies, it uses its webbed feet like little parachutes.

WOLF SPIDER

The wolf spider does not spin webs to catch its prey; instead it stalks a likely meal, then pounces on it.

TREE SQUIRRELS

Between them, tree squirrels and flying squirrels have a distribution that spans most of five continents; they are absent only from southernmost South America, Australasia, and the oceanic islands. In the more arid habitats of tropical and temperate zones, their place is taken by ground squirrels.

Most squirrel species are highly dependent on woodland and forest habitats of various types. Across the world, they occur in dense, coniferous forest; mixed and deciduous woodland; open, heathy woods and dry woodland savanna; seasonal monsoon forests; and tropical rain forests. The fullness of the canopy and the lushness of the foliage differ considerably among these habitats, but they are all places where trees predominate, providing the food and shelter the animals require.

Some squirrel species are rather particular about the type of habitat they require. The Russian flying squirrel, for example, prefers conifer forests with tall trees, usually of spruce or pine. It keeps to the treetops so much that, given its nocturnal habits, it is seldom seen even in areas where it is common. The four species of neotropical dwarf squirrels prefer hill forests up to cloud level, in which palm trees are abundant. Palm fruits and nuts are their favorite foods.

THE AMERICAN RED SQUIRREL IS ALSO CALLED THE PINE SQUIRREL BECAUSE OF ITS FONDNESS FOR PINE WOODS

In some cases where closely related squirrel species overlap in range, it is noteworthy that they do not overlap in habitat. Among the Asiatic striped palm squirrels of India, there are species that prefer tropical forest and jungle, while others inhabit open palm woodland and scrubland. Two species of sun squirrels occur in West Africa—one is limited to rain forest, the other dwells in woodland savanna. Sometimes the differences are quite subtle: In the eastern broad-leaved woodlands of North America, for example, gray squirrels tend to inhabit the denser parts, while fox squirrels prefer the more open areas.

Squirrels also have a reputation for being adaptable and opportunist. Many are adept at finding what they need in a variety of habitat types. The red squirrel is often regarded as an animal of coniferous forests, but it can be equally at home in mixed and broad-leaved woodland. Some squirrels readily colonize man-made habitats, such as forest

ZEFA

DISTRIBUTION

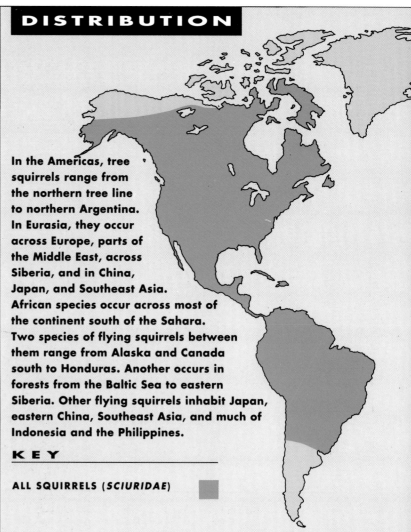

In the Americas, tree squirrels range from the northern tree line to northern Argentina. In Eurasia, they occur across Europe, parts of the Middle East, across Siberia, and in China, Japan, and Southeast Asia. African species occur across most of the continent south of the Sahara. Two species of flying squirrels between them range from Alaska and Canada south to Honduras. Another occurs in forests from the Baltic Sea to eastern Siberia. Other flying squirrels inhabit Japan, eastern China, Southeast Asia, and much of Indonesia and the Philippines.

KEY

ALL SQUIRRELS (SCIURIDAE)

Chasing is a key element of social behavior among tree squirrels. Individuals readily pursue one another around trunks, often in territorial disputes or pre-mating scuffles (left). These scrambles, which are a delight to watch, are accompanied by loud chatters and barks.

KEY FACTS

● **The front incisor teeth of squirrels grow continuously to compensate for the wearing down caused by gnawing. The cheek teeth used for chewing are, by contrast, rooted.**

● **The little-known woolly flying squirrel of Kashmir is an unusual creature. It apparently lives in cold, rocky, open terrain at very high altitudes, where it probably feeds largely on mosses and lichens.**

● **One of the arrow-tailed flying squirrels, a group of squirrels that live in Southeast Asia, is said to nest sometimes in hollowed-out coconut shells still suspended in palm trees.**

● **A giant squirrel can make leaps between branches of 20 feet (6 m) or more, but this pales against the longest recorded glide of a giant flying squirrel, which stands at over 1,450 feet (450 meters).**

● **Occasionally young squirrels are forced to disperse large distances once they have left the nest. One juvenile fox squirrel migrated 40 miles (64 km) from its natal area.**

clearings, plantations, and areas of thick cultivation. The gray squirrel, when it was introduced into Britain from North America, spread rapidly not only through lowland wooded habitats, but it also very successfully colonized leafy English suburbs and city parks. Indeed, gray squirrels in London's Hyde Park and Regent's Park are so at ease in their urban surroundings that they will take food from people's hands. Some species among the beautiful squirrels of Asia have also moved into cultivated areas and suburbs.

In tropical and subtropical regions, forests covering the lower slopes of mountains provide lush habitats that are markedly cooler than the lowland forests. Several kinds of squirrels have become specialized for these forests, which for much of the time are shrouded in clouds. The five species of red-cheeked squirrels, genus *Dremomys*, inhabit montane forests in Asia; and the giant flying squirrels generally live in forests above 3,000 ft (900 m) in altitude, with some Himalayan species ranging as high as 13,200 ft (4,000 m). Given the rocky terrain on which many of the trees grow, it is not suprising that giant flying squirrels have been observed perching on vegetated cliffs.

Other squirrels have a closer association with rocks. The complex-toothed flying squirrel of China actually nests in cliff crevices and cavities, while the groove-toothed squirrel of Borneo forages mainly on the ground and often takes refuge among rocks. The largely ground-dwelling Berdmore's palm squirrel of Southeast Asia is one of the few tree squirrels that does not actually need trees: In parts of its range it lives among rocky shrubs.

Giant flying squirrels are known to make brief springtime migrations to lower altitudes to feed on early fresh growth of vegetation. In more northerly habitats, the season that brings about the most change in behavior is winter. Unlike many mammals of northern climes, squirrels do not hibernate, but they react to the cold weather by spending much more time in the nest or drey.

WARM AND DRY IN THE DREY

Perched on a fork of a branch or even on an old crow's nest, the drey is a hollow ball or dome of sticks, bark, and leaves lined with softer material such as dried grass, moss, and feathers. A squirrel will typically build several alternative nests for resting and refuge from predators, although one is usually a favorite. Females build maternity dreys in the breeding season, where their young spend the first weeks of life.

In midwinter, a red squirrel may leave its cozy drey to forage for only two hours per day. A thick winter coat grown after the autumn molt provides insulation, along with extra fat reserves that also

FOCUS ON

THE SCOTCH PINEWOOD

The ancient pinewoods of Scotland are among the remaining strongholds of the red squirrel in Britain. Having retreated from its former woodland haunts across most of the island, the red squirrel finds welcome refuge in these majestic wildwoods. Yet the natural pinewoods too have undergone a drastic decline. A few centuries ago they blanketed most of the Highlands, forming the vast Caledonian Forest. But land clearance and logging have reduced the forest to scattered remnants in remote valleys.

The natural pinewoods are dominated by Scotch pine—Britain's only native pine tree. A mature Scotch pine, with its fissured, rusty-red bark and unruly, flattened crown, may rise 100 ft (30 m) or more into the air. In some of the woods, the pines crowd close together, creating a shady, closed forest; elsewhere, the woods are more open and roomy. Scattered among the pines may be silver birches; and beneath the taller trees, rowan, aspen, yew, and juniper claim their spaces. In the clearings lie carpets of purple heather, bilberry, and bracken. The Scotch pines provide food and shelter for the red squirrel. The animal builds its drey within the evergreen crown of the tree, and pine seeds are its principal source of nourishment.

TEMPERATURE AND RAINFALL

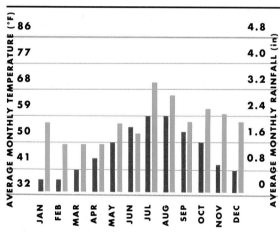

- TEMPERATURE
- RAINFALL

In the mild, moist summer, the pinewood is alive with floral color, birdsong, and the hum of insects. In the winter, gales blow and snow lies thick, but the red squirrel continues to forage in all but the worst weather.

help keep the animal going when food is hard to come by. In very cold or stormy weather, tree squirrels will remain in the shelter of the nest for up to several days until hunger forces them to emerge and look for buried food stores that they had set aside in the autumn. In particularly hard autumns, red squirrels have been known to make mass migrations to richer feeding grounds. A few tree squirrels may share the same drey to combine their warmth, and as many as twenty flying squirrels have been found huddling in the same winter nest. ∎

NEIGHBORS

The clearings and shaded glades of the pinewood offer shelter and food to mammals, insects, and birds, many of which depend exclusively upon the rich harvest of cones and needles.

RED DEER

In high summer, newborn spotted fawns lie low and still in the heather while the adult red deer browse.

CAPERCAILLIE

This huge gamebird forages among the heather for berries, pine needles, shoots, insects, and spiders.

SCOTCH PINEWOODS

Relics of the ancient Caledonian Forest survive in pockets of Scotland, particularly in the west and in the valleys of the Dee and Spey in the east. Their total area of some 20,000 acres (8,000 hectares) is far exceeded by the area of land under commercial pine plantations.

■ PINEWOOD

ENEMIES

EXTREMELY DANGEROUS

PINE MARTEN
This mustelid pursues red squirrels, racing and leaping along branches with almost as much agility as its prey.

MODERATELY DANGEROUS

LONG-EARED OWL
This owl is robust enough to snatch squirrels from the trees at dusk, tracking them mainly by sound.

M. Danegger/NHPA

PINE BEAUTY MOTH

...e striped green-and-...hite caterpillars of the ...ne beauty moth feed on ...ne needles.

CROSSBILL

The crossbill's twisted beak is ideal for clipping out the seeds from the scales of pinecones.

WOOD ANT

Wood ants construct piles of pine needles over their subterranean nests on the pinewood forest floor.

SISKIN

The agile siskin is typical of the Scotch pinewoods, where it lives year-round. This finch feeds on pine seeds.

EYED LADYBUG

Larger than most ladybugs, this species and its larvae hunt devotedly for pine-needle aphids.

TRUE SEALS

The true seals are commonly associated with the freezing conditions of the Arctic and Antarctic, yet several species thrive in warm waters far from the floating pack ice of the polar seas. The common seal is found as far south as Baja California in Mexico, and the Hawaiian monk seal breeds on the subtropical shores of the Leeward Islands near Hawaii, basking on beaches of coral sand and chasing colorful fish through coral reef lagoons. A similar species of monk seal was once widespread throughout the Mediterranean, and scattered populations still survive in the few areas that have escaped development for tourism. These monk seals probably developed from stock that evolved in warm waters, and therefore have no cold-water ancestors, yet they are similar in all major respects to species that regularly endure months of subzero temperatures. The layer of blubber beneath the skin of the Hawaiian monk seal is roughly the same thickness as that of many ice-breeding species, indicating that the true seals were already well equipped to survive low temperatures long before they colonized the coldest seas on earth.

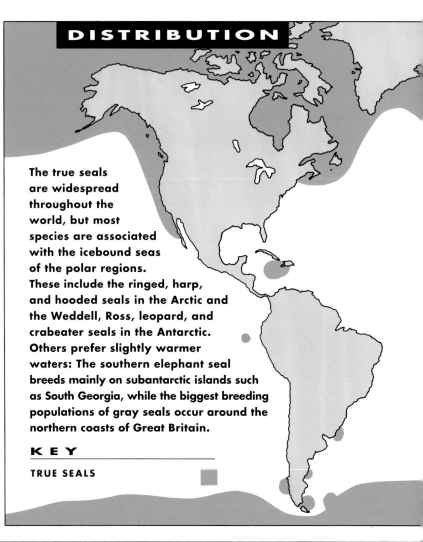

DISTRIBUTION

The true seals are widespread throughout the world, but most species are associated with the icebound seas of the polar regions. These include the ringed, harp, and hooded seals in the Arctic and the Weddell, Ross, leopard, and crabeater seals in the Antarctic. Others prefer slightly warmer waters: The southern elephant seal breeds mainly on subantarctic islands such as South Georgia, while the biggest breeding populations of gray seals occur around the northern coasts of Great Britain.

KEY

TRUE SEALS

Jonathan Scott/Planet Earth Pictures

FOCUS ON ANTARCTIC CRABEATERS

The crabeater seal is the most widespread and numerous of the Antarctic seals—indeed, with a total population of up to 40 million, it is probably the most abundant large mammal in the world. Crabeaters feed on shrimplike crustaceans, called krill, hunting by night when the krill rise from the ocean depths to feed on the plankton near the surface. By day the seals generally haul out onto the ice, where they are safe from predatory leopard seals and killer whales. Groups of crabeaters frequently bask on drifting rafts of ice, often in company with other seals and penguins, for the floes make convenient, secure floating bases with ready access to deep water. In this way a crabeater seal may spend its whole life at sea and never set a flipper on solid ground.

The excellent insulation of a true seal—any true seal—is in fact an adaptation for living in the water. Even in the tropics, ocean water is considerably colder than a seal's core temperature of 98.6°F (37°C), and the heat-conducting properties of water are so good that the animal would suffer an unacceptable loss of heat and energy if it lacked the necessary insulation. Having acquired it, however, the seals were ideally equipped to radiate north and south into colder seas and exploit some of the richest of all marine habitats.

Rich resources are the lure that draws all kinds of animals to the apparently inhospitable waters of the Arctic and Antarctic. By comparison with the land at high latitudes, the salt seawater is a sheltered environment: Until it actually freezes, the sea is far warmer than the land in winter, and there is always water under the sea ice offering a safe haven for all kinds of organisms. The polar oceans are also particularly rich in minerals scoured up from the bottom by wind-driven ocean currents, and because of their low temperature they hold a lot of dissolved carbon dioxide and oxygen. As a

IN ANTARCTICA THE WEDDELL SEAL OVERWINTERS UNDER THE ICE SHEET, SINCE THE INSULATING BLANKET OF ICE KEEPS THE SEA RELATIVELY WARM

result they are immensely fertile, providing ideal growing conditions for the floating microscopic algae called phytoplankton. These algae attract a host of tiny floating animals such as copepods and the great swarms of krill that flourish in the southern ocean; the whole teeming mass provides a feast for crustaceans, squid, and fish. These in turn attract larger animals such as seabirds, whales, and, of course, seals.

There are drawbacks, though, even for animals that do not apparently feel the cold. In winter, large areas of the sea freeze over, sometimes forcing seals to migrate to places where they still have access to the water and prey. The harp seal, for example, migrates south from its High Arctic feeding grounds to areas of broken, drifting pack ice. There are three distinct populations overwintering respectively in the warmer waters around Newfoundland, the Greenland Sea north of Jan Mayen Island, and the White Sea in northwestern Russia. The seals breed in their winter refuges and disperse to the richer waters in the north as the northern sea ice breaks up; the Newfoundland population migrates some 2,170 miles (3,500 km) to spend the summer in Baffin Bay to the west of Greenland. The larger hooded seal undertakes similar migrations, although it does not travel as far. ■

ANTARCTICA

Centered on the South Pole, Antarctica is the coldest place on Earth, surrounded by the world's stormiest seas and a belt of pack ice. There is no native human population or any animals that depend completely on land. Birds and seals that spend any time on land depend entirely on the sea for food.

WILD PIGS

Joe van Os/The Image Bank

The warthog (above) is an inhabitant of the African savanna grasslands and woodlands. It usually forages and drinks in small groups. It eats mainly grass and plucks the tips of the grass off with its lips. It is active during the day.

The wild pigs occupy a wide variety of habitats across Europe, Asia, and Africa north and south of the Sahara Desert. In Europe they are found mainly in broad-leaved woodlands dominated by oak trees and in Asia in tropical forests and mangroves. Forest and savanna grasslands are the preferred habitats of most African species, although the giant forest hog also frequents the transitional zone between forest and grassland. In East and central Africa giant hogs are found in small numbers in the highlands and montane (mountain) forests.

The thorn forest of the Chaco in South America covers a total of some 243,000 sq miles (630,000 sq km). The driest part of the Chaco is in the west and is home to the Chacoan peccary. Here, the mean annual temperature exceeds 75°F (24°C), with rainfall of between 8 in (200 mm) a year in the

Survival Anglia

The three species of peccary live in Central and South America. Their habitats range from dry and wet forest regions to woody grasslands and dense thickets. They are found at various altitudes. They are active during the day when they feed on roots, seeds, and fruits.

DISTRIBUTION

KEY

- WILD BOAR
- WARTHOG
- COLLARED PECCARY
- BABIRUSA
- GIANT FOREST HOG
- BUSHPIG

The wild boar lives in Europe, North Africa, Asia (including the southeast islands of Indonesia), Japan, and Taiwan. Feral populations are found in North and South America and Australasia.

The giant forest hog makes its home in east, west, and central regions of Africa. Also found in Africa, south of the Sahara, are the warthog and the bushpig, the latter also being found on the island of Madagascar.

The babirusa is confined to the Indonesian islands of Sulawesi, Togian, Sula, and Buru.

Peccaries are found from the southwestern United States to northern Argentina.

KEY FACTS

- As a family the wild pigs have no special adaptations that restrict them to a particular habitat. This has been a major factor in their widespread distribution.

- Apart from their need to be near water, the major limitation on the spread of wild pigs is probably deep, snow-covered areas, which prohibit them from searching for food.

- The straight tail of the wild boar is used for swatting flying insects or twitched when it is cross. It uses its snout to root for food.

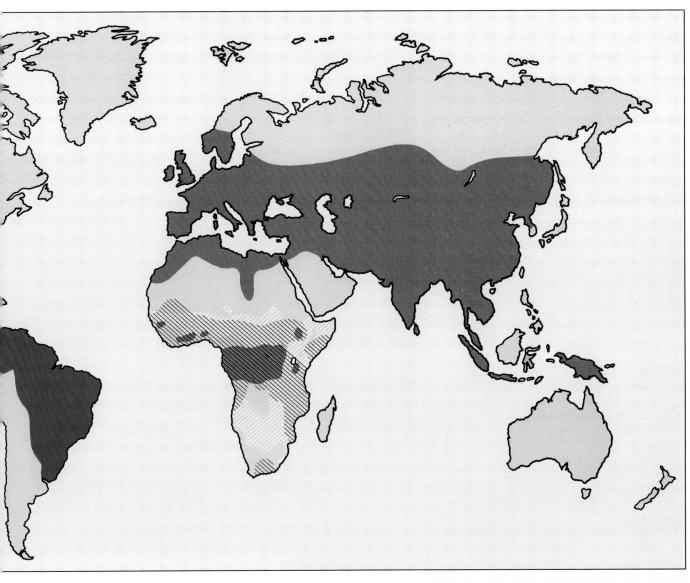

western parts to 35.5 in (900 mm) in the east. The dry season lasts for five months.

Vegetation in the thorn forests consists largely of emergent trees and a dense underlayer of brush consisting mainly of acacia. Bromeliads and cacti grow on the ground. Cacti are the main food of the Chacoan peccary, but it also feeds on acacia fruit, bromeliads, and low-growing herbs from which it gets most of the moisture it needs. In the wetter, more easterly regions the vegetation of the dry areas is replaced with grassland dotted with palms.

Jaguar, puma, and ocelot occur in the Chaco and often prey on the peccary, which forages in small herds of up to ten animals. The peccary is very brave when confronting the enemy and is at its most vulnerable when it strays from the herd.

The bushpig, or red river hog, is found in Africa south of the Sahara and also in Madagascar. It inhabits both grasslands and woodlands (right).

Nigel Dennis/NHPA

183

Tropical forest species include the white-lipped and collared peccaries of South and Central America, although some also occur in oak grasslands and on the chaparral (thorny scrub, originally of evergreen oaks). The babirusa, bearded pig, and Celebes wild pig inhabit similar forests in Asia while the giant forest hog and bushpig are sometimes found in the forests in Africa.

In tropical forests everywhere the sunlight is strong and the mean monthly temperature is greater than 68°F (20°C). Almost constant sun combined with varying amounts of rain determine the type of vegetation in tropical forests. Where rainfall is moderate—often less than 20 in (50 cm) a year—trees are limited in type and density. Acacia, or thorn trees, are typical. These trees are deciduous, losing their leaves in the dry season in order to conserve water. Animal life is limited to those creatures that can survive on smaller animals or dried vegetation and need little or no water.

In those areas where rainfall is more abundant, but occurs mainly at definite periods in the year, the vegetation is more luxuriant. This is the monsoon forest, characteristic of parts of southern India, the

FOCUS ON

THE BLACK FOREST

A mountainous area in southwest Germany, this region is one of the last refuges in western Europe of the wild boar. This area encompasses 2,320 sq miles (6,009 sq km); its highest peak is Feldberg, which lies at 4,897 ft (1,493 m) above sea level. The region is divided in two by the deep Kinzig Valley. On the lower slopes are some of the remnants of the broad-leaved forest that once covered much of Germany, the typical temperate woods of oak and beech. Here the climate is moderate with a plentiful rainfall and the seasons are well marked. Summers are warm and winters cold.

The animals that inhabit the woods cope with cold winter conditions in different ways. They either hibernate, living on food stored in the body during the summer, migrate to warmer countries farther south, or adapt to living in a harsh environment where food in winter is scarce.

The wild boar is one of the latter, surviving because it has an extremely varied diet and a coat that becomes thicker as winter approaches.

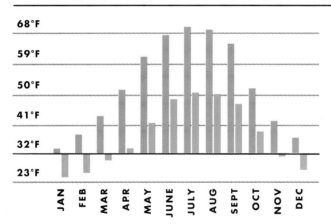

BLACK FOREST CLIMATE

- ▉ MAXIMUM AVERAGE TEMPERATURE
- ▉ MINIMUM AVERAGE TEMPERATURE

The Black Forest is carpeted in snow during the winter months. At the higher altitudes alpine plants abound in spring but the forest really comes to life in the summer and supports vineyards, rich pastures for cattle, and a profusion of wildflowers.

foothills of the Himalayas, and mainland Southeast Asia. Trees are deciduous but more varied. In the Indian monsoon forest the trees are bare of leaves in summer and in leaf in winter.

With the arrival of the monsoon the water holes, or jheels, fill to overflowing. Many of these depressions are fairly large and form small lakes. In the dry season they shrink to small pools fringed with muddy beaches. In both dry and wet seasons the jheels are the favored haunts of wild boars, providing them with water and the much-needed mud for wallowing. The wild boars are joined at these watering places by exotic birds such as the lesser whistling teal, demoiselle crane, purple heron, and painted storks. ■

NEIGHBORS

The mixed woodlands of the Black Forest attract a host of animals and birds. Rare butterflies flutter across the gentle grass slopes found at lower altitudes and there are many wildflowers.

RED DEER

Essentially a woodland animal, the red deer is common in the forest, living in protected sites.

EUROPEAN HEDGEHOG

Ideal habitat for the hedgehog, which can be seen shuffling on its nighttime hunting forays.

THE BLACK FOREST

The Black Forest is bordered by France to the east and Switzerland to the south and shares features with both. The Rhine River also partially borders it. The area takes its name from the many dark, tree-covered summits, a mixture of coniferous trees and broad-leaved woodland.

Hans Reinhard/Oxford Scientific Films

RHINOCEROS BEETLE

...o called because of the "horn" on its head, the ...eetle uses the horn to lift ...nd carry rival males away.

WILDCAT

Resembling the domestic tabby, the wildcat is heavier. It is confined to wooded and inaccessible mountainsides.

CAPERCAILLIE

The capercaillie is the largest member of the grouse family. It eats the buds and shoots of pines.

EUROPEAN BADGER

A typical woodland animal, the nocturnal badger lives in the higher regions of the Black Forest.

WOOD ANT

Close to the bottom of the food chain, wood ants are preyed upon by great spotted woodpeckers.

ZEBRAS

A heat haze settles over the sprawling grasslands of Africa's Serengeti. Enormous herds of mixed animals—wildebeest, gazelles, and zebras—begin to amass, fidgeting restlessly and snorting into the still air. Eventually the herd, which may number up to half a million animals, rolls into motion. The zebras alternate their role, first traveling at the head and flanks of the huge group, then acting as the pathfinders. The vast migration of grazers, headed for the Masai Mara Reserve in Kenya, more than 124 miles (200 kilometers) away, has begun.

Among the equids, zebras as a whole occupy one of the world's richest grass-producing habitats; the wild horse and ass species, by contrast, occur naturally in arid steppes and even desert borders. In spite of its apparent lushness, however, most zebra country is subject to seasonal shortages of grazing because of the annual dry season. This necessitates seasonal migrations of varying distances.

DRYLAND DAZZLERS

The most widespread of zebras now is the plains zebra, still found from southern Ethiopia and Sudan south through to central Angola and eastern South Africa. Possibly the secret of its success, compared to the other two species, is that it is the most adaptable of grazers and will flourish equally in savanna, light woodland, and open scrubland. The savanna may comprise a short growth of grass and no trees, or it may feature tall grassland and scattered woodland—the plains zebra is happy with either. It may even be found in rocky, hilly country and on mountain slopes up to elevations of 14,435 ft (4,400 m). The one essential condition for the plains zebra, however, is the availability of fresh water, for it needs to drink regularly. Clearly it feels at home near water, for this zebra has been observed swimming in rivers in the wild.

The plains zebra will occasionally overlap with Grevy's zebra in the northernmost part of its range. Grevy's zebra is greatly reduced in numbers from former times and is almost entirely confined to northern Kenya—possibly extending into southeastern Ethiopia and maybe Somalia, although it may actually be extinct there. Its ideal ecological niche is subdesert, falling between areas favored by the water-dependent plains zebra and the significantly arid region farther north that is home to the African wild ass.

As its name suggests, the mountain zebra is truly adapted to upland conditions, although, strangely, the plains zebra is occasionally found at higher elevations in parts of its range. Subdesert plains, rocky slopes, and often barren plateaus in the mountainous areas of southwestern Angola, Namibia, and western South Africa are home to the mountain

The lush, forested banks of the Aguarico River in Ecuador are home to the secretive Brazilian tapir (below).

Michael Fogden/Oxford Scientific Films

KEY

TAPIRS

GREVY'S ZEBRA

MOUNTAIN ZEBRA

PLAINS ZEBRA

Richard Coomber/Planet Earth Pictures

DISTRIBUTION

All three zebra species are confined to Africa. The plains zebra has a wide distribution from Ethiopia and Sudan south to Angola in southern Africa, where it overlaps with the mountain zebra. Grevy's zebra lives in Ethiopia, Somalia, and northern Kenya. The three New World tapirs are found collectively from Mexico and Central America south to Colombia, Ecuador, Paraguay, Peru, Brazil, and Venezuela. The Malayan tapir occurs from Burma and Thailand south to Malaya and the island of Sumatra.

A herd of plains zebra seek out water on the open grasslands of Serengeti National Park (left).

zebra and it is much more agile and surefooted than the other species on steep slopes. Once widespread along the dry mountain ranges that run parallel to the coast from southern Angola to the Transvaal, the mountain zebra—particularly the Cape subspecies—is sadly reduced in numbers. It is found up to heights of 6,560 ft (2,000 m), but will frequently descend to lower elevations after rainfall, extending into the desert and coastal dunes, to slake its thirst at replenished water holes.

Although less water-dependent than the plains zebra, mountain zebras nevertheless need to drink at least once, sometimes twice a day in the hot dry season. Both the mountain and Grevy's zebra have been seen using their front hooves to dig for subsurface water in dry streambeds. Having exposed a supply in a small pit, they will fiercely defend it from other grazing animals, even from members of their own herd. If necessary, Grevy's and mountain zebras can exist on fairly brackish water.

FOREST AND SWAMP

The Malayan tapir is a denizen of the dense primary rain forests, both lowland and highland, of southern Burma and Thailand, Malaysia, and Sumatra. It may also occur in Laos. On the island of Sumatra it is only found to the south of Lake Toba in the northern part. This huge lake appears to mark a boundary for several rain-forest species, which are found only to the south of this point.

AFTER THE DOMESTIC HORSE, THE PLAINS ZEBRA IS THE MOST SUCCESSFUL EQUID IN TERMS OF DISTRIBUTION

At one time, tapirs were considerably more widespread in Southeast Asia; in prehistoric times they were found on the other Sunda Islands, Java and Borneo. A giant form was also found in China. Tapirs have disappeared from some of these areas since the evolution of man and it is thought he may have overhunted it even in those earlier times.

The Malayan tapir has a liking for low-lying swampy areas and is at least partly aquatic in habit; it will remain submerged in water for hours on end. Its short legs make easy work of steep, rocky inclines. Active mainly in the hours of darkness, it travels around a limited area using the same paths night after night, reducing them to swampy ruts.

The Brazilian tapir has the largest range in South America, extending from east of the Colombian Andes and Venezuela south to northern

Argentina and southern Brazil. Its swimming prowess is frequently called into account, for its range is laced with rivers, but it is also found in the dry deciduous forest of the Chaco Plains of Argentina. It, too, moves along habitual paths, often entering and leaving rivers by the same path each time.

Baird's tapir, the largest of the three New World species, is the only species to be found in Central America, extending south from Mexico to Colombia and Ecuador, west of the Andes. At one time, tapirs were widespread through North America and were present in the Florida Peninsula until about 11,000 years ago—roughly the same time that equids disappeared from northern America. Tapirs probably migrated into South America from North America, in search of a more amenable environment.

Baird's tapir prefers mainly lowland swampy or hilly forests. Like the Malayan tapir, it is primarily nocturnal. Agile like all tapirs, it negotiates very steep cliffs and awkward terrain, including limestone cliffs, with ease and speed, once more repeatedly using the same tracks.

The mountain tapir has the smallest distribution of the New World species and is an inhabitant of the high elevations of the Andes Mountains in Colombia and Ecuador. Never found lower than altitudes of 6,560 ft (2,000 m), it is equally at home

FOCUS ON

TROPICAL FORESTS OF BURMA, THAILAND, AND MALAYSIA

Nearly three-fifths of Burma is covered by forest, while more than half of the land surface of Thailand and the Malay Peninsula is also covered with trees.

In Burma, the eastern mountain system separates Burma from Thailand, Laos, and China; the western mountain belt is a region of thick forests along the border between Burma and India, and the fertile central belt is irrigated by the Irrawaddy River. In the north of Thailand lie mountains covered with thick evergreen forests; to the south lies the central plain, where rice is grown. The southern peninsula consists mainly of tropical forest.

The forests in these areas have some of the richest animal and plant life of anywhere in the world. In Burma there are elephants, tigers, leopards, gibbons, monkeys, gaurs and bantengs, and the very rare Asian two-horned rhino. There are more than a thousand bird species and many reptiles, including vipers, crocodiles, turtles, and a variety of lizards. Thailand's forests have many of the same animals as well as a proliferation of wild boars and poisonous snakes such as banded kraits and cobras.

Planet Earth Pictures

TEMPERATURE AND RAINFALL

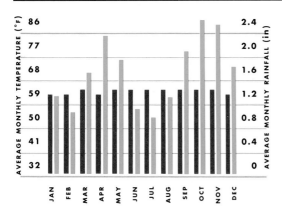

■ **TEMPERATURE**

▨ **RAINFALL**

These areas have a subtropical and/or tropical climate. Thailand is typical with three seasons: a hot dry spring, a hot wet summer, and a mild winter. From July to December is the monsoon season; in Burma this runs from May to October.

as high as 14,765 ft (4,500 m), above the tree line. It may also be seen grazing at the evergreen grasslands below the snow line.

Possessing the same agility and hill-climbing ability that typifies all tapirs, the mountain tapir is further equipped for the colder climes of its environment in being more compact, which enables it to conserve body heat more efficiently. It also has a dense coat of hair, which comprises a thick underfur and a long-haired outercoat, protecting it from the freezing nighttime temperatures. ■

NEIGHBORS

The warm, moist tropical forests are blessed with a huge diversity of flora and fauna: One-half of all living species reside in the equatorial belt of rain forests that once encircled the globe.

LEOPARD

Abundantly equipped with feline hunting skills, the leopard is one of the tapir's principal enemies.

DHOLE

The dhole also preys on the Malayan tapir. A tireless hunter, it pursues its quarry either alone or in packs.

Neighbor illustrations Richard Tibbits